THE NORTHWEST PASSAGE: ARCTIC STRAITS

INTERNATIONAL STRAITS OF THE WORLD

Series Editor: Gerard J. Mangone,
Center for the Study of
Marine Policy
University of Delaware, U.S.A.

Also in this series:

1. Butler W.E.: Northeast Arctic Passage. 1978.
   ISBN 90-286-0498-7

2. Leifer M.: Malacca, Singapore and Indonesia. 1978.
   ISBN 90-286-0778-1

3. Ramazani R.K.: The Persian Gulf and the Strait of Hormuz. 1979.
   ISBN 90-286-0069-8

4. Truver S.C.: The Strait of Gibraltar and the Mediterranean. 1980.
   ISBN 90-286-0709-9

5. Lapidoth-Eschelbacher R.: The Red Sea and the Gulf of Aden. 1982.
   ISBN 90-247-2501-1

6. Alexandersson G.: The Baltic Straits. 1982.
   ISBN 90-247-2595-X

INTERNATIONAL STRAITS OF THE WORLD

THE NORTHWEST PASSAGE: ARCTIC STRAITS

Donat Pharand, S.J.D., F.R.S.C.,
Professor of Law, University of Ottawa

in association with

Leonard H. Legault, Q.C.,
Legal Adviser, Department of External Affairs, Ottawa

1984 **MARTINUS NIJHOFF PUBLISHERS**
a member of the KLUWER ACADEMIC PUBLISHERS GROUP
DORDRECHT / BOSTON / LANCASTER

Distributors

for the United States and Canada: Kluwer Academic Publishers, 190 Old Derby Street, Hingham, MA 02043, USA
for the UK and Ireland: Kluwer Academic Publishers, MTP Press Limited, Falcon House, Queen Square, Lancaster LA1 1RN, England
for all other countries: Kluwer Academic Publishers Group, Distribution Center, P.O. Box 322, 3300 AH Dordrecht, The Netherlands

Library of Congress Cataloging in Publication Data

Pharand, Donat.
The Northwest Passage.

(International straits of the world ; 7)
1.Northwest Passage. I. Legault, Leonard. II. Title.
III. Series: International straits of the world, v. 7.
G640.P46 1984 909'.096327 84-8190
ISBN 90-247-2979-3

ISBN 90-247-2979-3

PRINTED IN THE NETHERLANDS

TABLE OF CONTENTS

Foreword by Gerard J. Mangone xiii

List of Figures xvii

List of Tables xviii

Preface xix

Chapter 1

DESCRIPTION OF THE NORTHWEST PASSAGE 1

- Eastern Approaches 2
- Western Approaches 4
- Routes of the Northwest Passage 6
  - Route 1, through the Prince of Wales Strait 6
  - Route 2, through the M'Clure Strait 11
  - Route 3, through Peel Sound and the Victoria Strait 12
  - Route 3A, through Prince Regent Inlet 17
  - Route 5, through the Fury and Hecla Strait 18
  - Route 5A, through the Fury and Hecla Strait and Prince Regent Inlet 20
- Conclusion 20

Chapter 2

THE NORTHWEST PASSAGE BEFORE 1880 – BRITISH PERIOD 22

- Up to Franklin's Expedition (1576–1847) 22
  - Martin Frobisher (1576, 1577, 1578) 22
  - John Davis (1585, 1586, 1587) 23

Henry Hudson (1610–11) 23
T. Button (1612), W. Gibbons (1614), R. Bylot (1615) 23
R. Bylot and W. Baffin (1616) 23
Jens Munk (1619–20) 23
Luke Foxe and Thomas James (1631) 24
C. Middleton (1741) 24
William Moor and Francis Smith (1746) 24
James Cook and Charles Clarke (1776–80) 24
Charles Duncan and George Taylor (1791–92) 25
George Vancouver and William R. Broughton (1791–95) 25
Sir John Ross (1818) 25
W.E. Parry (1819–25) 25
Sir John Ross (1829–33) 27
Sir John Franklin (1845–1847) 27
Search for Franklin's Expedition (1847–1859) 28
Sir James Clark Ross (1848–49) 28
James Saunders (1849–50) 29
Horatio T. Austin (1850–51) 29
William Penny (1850–51) 30
Sir John Ross (1850–51) 30
C.C. Forsyth (1850) 30
Edwin J. De Haven (1850–51) 30
William Kennedy (1851–52) 31
E.A. Inglefield (1852, 1854) 31
Robert M'Clure (1850–54) 31
Sir Richard Collinson (1850–55) 32
Sir Edward Belcher (1852–54) 33
Henry Kellett (1852–54) 34
W.J.S. Pullen (1852–54) 34
Dr. John Rae (1853–54) 35
Dr. E.K. Kane (1853–55) 35
Sir F. Leopold M'Clintock (1857–59) 36
After the Search for Franklin's Expedition 36
The Northwest Passage and British Whalers (1751–1880) 37

Chapter 3

THE NORTHWEST PASSAGE AFTER 1880 – CANADIAN PERIOD 38
First Sailing of the Northwest Passage (1903–06) 38

Canadian Expeditions and Patrols 39
A.P. Low (1903–04) 39
J.E. Bernier (1904–05) 41
J.E. Bernier (1906–07) 41
J.E. Bernier (1908–09) 42
J.E. Bernier (1910–11) 43
Vilhjalmer Stefansson (1913–18) 43
Eastern Arctic Patrol (1922–1944) 43
Patrols of the Royal Canadian Mounted Police (1929, 1940–44) 44
A.H. Joy (1929) 44
Henry Larsen (1940–42, 1944) 45
Navigation in the Northwest Passage Since 1945 45
Navigation from 1945 to 1969 46
Navigation from 1969 to 1982 47
Summary Tables of Navigation in the Northwest Passage 49
Full Transits of the Northwest Passage (1903–1983) 49
Partial Transits of the Northwest Passage (1977–1982) 49
Current Canadian Activities in the Northwest Passage 54
Coast Guard Activities 54
Hydrographic Service Activities 55
Naval Activities 56
Conclusion 57

Chapter 4

COMMERCIAL DEVELOPMENT OF THE NORTHWEST PASSAGE 59

Resource Potential in Adjacent Areas 59
Alaska North Slope/Beaufort Sea 60
MacKenzie Delta/Beaufort Sea 62
Canadian Arctic Islands: Oil and Gas 64
Canadian Arctic Islands: Hard Minerals 66
Resource Development Technology 68

Chapter 5

MARINE TRANSPORT AND SUPPORT SYSTEMS IN THE NORTHWEST PASSAGE 71

Pipeline Systems 71
Alaska Highway Pipeline (Gas) 71
Dempster Lateral Line (Gas) 73
Polar Gas "Y" Pipeline (Gas) 73
Beaufort Sea-Edmonton Pipeline (Oil) 74
Tanker Systems 74
Canadian Proposals 75
Dome's Icebreaking Tanker (Oil) 75
Arctic Pilot Project Tankers (Gas) 76
TransCanada Pipelines Project (Gas) 76
American Proposals 78
U.S. Maritime Administration (Oil) 78
Seatrain Lines (Oil) 78
Globtik Tankers (Oil) 78
Globtik Tankers (Gas) 79
General Dynamics Submarine Tankers (Gas) 79
Other Proposals 80
Choice of Transportation Mode 80
Marine Traffic and Support Systems 82
Projected Traffic 82
Projected Support Systems 83
Icebreaking 84
Weather and Ice Forecasting 85
Search and Rescue 85
Pollution Prevention and Control 86
Conclusion 87

Chapter 6

THE LEGAL STATUS OF INTERNATIONAL STRAITS 88

Definition and Classification of International Straits 89
Definition of International Straits 89
Geographic Criterion 90
Functional Criterion 91
Classification of International Straits 95

Chapter 7

THE LEGAL STATUS OF THE NORTHWEST PASSAGE 99

The Northwest Passage: An International Strait? 99
Geographical Criterion 99
Functional Criterion 101
Right of Passage in the Northwest Passage 102
Innocent Passage 102
Passage of Warships 104
Canada's Right of Protection in the Northwest Passage 105
General Right of Protection 106
Special Right of Protection 107

Chapter 8

THE FUTURE LEGAL STATUS OF THE NORTHWEST PASSAGE 110

The Northwest Passage: An International Strait? 110
Sufficient International Shipping 110
Canadian Measures to Deny International Character 111
Sovereignty Through Legislation 111
Technological Sovereignty 112
User Agreements 113
The Northwest Passage: An International Regime? 114
Transit Passage 114
Passage of Warships 115
Canada's Protective Rights over the Northwest Passage 118
General Right of Protection 118
Special Right of Protection 119
Conclusion 120

Chapter 9

COMMERCIAL DEVELOPMENT AND ENVIRONMENTAL POLICY 122

Ecologically Sensitive Areas 122
Impacts of Year-Round Shipping 125
Impacts of Routine Shipping Operations 125

Tanker Tracks and Ice Regimes 125
Ice Platform and Tanker Contacts 126
Tanker and Flight Noise 126
Operational Waste Discharge 127
Risk and Impacts of Shipping Accidents 127
Oil Tanker Accidents 127
Gas Tanker Accidents 131
Appraisal and Policy Implications 132

Chapter 10

COMMERCIAL DEVELOPMENT AND INUIT POLICY 134

Canada's Inuit Population 134
Inuit Culture 134
Inuit Economy 136
Impacts of Year-Round Shipping 139
Socio-Economic Impacts 139
Impacts on Rights to Offshore Areas 141
Appraisal and Policy Implications 143

Chapter 11

CANADA'S NATIONAL SECURITY IN THE ARCTIC 144

Strategic Importance of the Arctic 144
Submarine Activities in the Arctic 147
The Protection of Canada's Sovereignty 147
Appraisal and Policy Implications 151
Surveillance of the Northwest Passage 151
Ice-Breaking Capability for the Northwest Passage 153
Cooperation with Other Arctic States 157
Conclusion 158

SUMMARY AND POLICY IMPLICATIONS FOR CANADA 160

Description 160
Historical Development 160
Future Development 160
Legal Status 160
Policy Implications 161

Chapter Notes 162

Selected Bibliography 186

Indexes 193

FOREWORD

This is the seventh book in the series of studies organized and edited at the Center for the Study of Marine Policy at the University of Delaware on international straits of the world.

From 1974 to 1982 the nations of the world labored to produce a comprehensive international convention governing the law of the sea, involving many questions of territorial sea limits, an exclusive economic zone adjacent to coastal states, jurisdiction over the continental shelf, and the exploitation of mineral resources in the deep seabed beyond national jurisdiction. One of the salient issues was the legal regime for straits used for international navigation, an issue that at one time seemed likely to divide the law of the sea conference into irreconcilable positions.

At that time the Center for the Study of Marine Policy embarked upon a world-wide examination of the straits used or likely to be used for international navigation, describing their physical attributes, their regional economic and political setting, and their legal status, with an evaluation of the prospects for economic development and peaceful cooperation in the area. This study of the Northwest Passage comes after the 1982 UN Convention on the Law of the Sea has been signed by many states and ratified by a dozen or so. While the convention is not yet in force, many of its articles are a codification of widespread state practice.

The creation of a new right of transit passage through straits used for international navigation either may gain legal force through state practice and the ultimate ratification of the 1982 convention or the articles in the convention may give rise to conflict between maritime states that have not ratified the convention and strait states.

In any case, no definition of an international strait was provided in the 1982 convention. The convention did nothing to clarify the uncertainty about "straits which are used for international navigation", as described in the 1958 Geneva Convention on the Territorial Sea and the Contiguous Zone, either with respect to their physical geography or their use for navigation.

The Center was most fortunate in persuading Professor Donat Pharand of the University of Ottawa to undertake a comprehensive study of the Northwest Passage in its series on international straits of the world.

No passage has had more of an influence upon western European history since the discovery of America by Christopher Columbus in 1492 and the two voyages in 1535 and 1541 by Jacques Cartier, who died believing that he had found in the St. Lawrence River the route that would lead him to Asia. In this book Professor Pharand describes in detail five major and two subsidiary routes to navigate from the Atlantic Ocean via the Labrador Sea, Davis Strait, or Baffin Bay to the Pacific Ocean via the Beaufort Sea and the Arctic Ocean.

Moreover, he traces in detail all the attempts at passage or actual passages from the sailings of John Davis in 1585 down to recent transits in 1982, a period studded with the names of Cook, Vancouver, Ross, Parry, Franklin, Bernier, and especially Amundsen, who made the first sailing of the full length of the Northwest Passage in 1905.

Since the major part of the inquiry in this work concerns the legal status of the Northwest Passage with respect to Canada and other states of the world that may have economic and strategic interests in the passage, Professor Pharand thoroughly investigates the commercial development of the region through which the waterways pass. He analyzes the resource potential in oil and gas in the Alaska North Slope, the McKenzie Delta, and the Canadian Arctic Islands, all of which depend upon existing or planned technology for marine transport and support systems.

After reviewing generally the status of international straits by custom and positive convention under international law, Professor Pharand diligently addresses the current legal status of the Northwest Passage and possible future issues. He pays special attention to Canadian measures and Canadian policy as he deals with the adequacy of international shipping in the passage, the concept of transit passage, the navigation of warships, and the protective rights of Canada.

Much of the interpretation of the legal status of the Northwest Passage in the future, indeed, the very need to fix its legal status, will depend upon commercial development and economic policy in this region.

Professor Pharand returns to this theme, expanding his analysis to include the ecological significance of development, and he describes Canadian policy with regard to the Inuit. Finally, he examines Canada's national security in the Arctic as related to the Northwest Passage, including submarine activities, and he makes certain recommendations for better surveillance and improved icebreaking capabilities by the Canadian government.

Donat Pharand received his LL.B. and LL.M. degrees from Dalhousie Law School, and thereafter received diplomas from the Hague Academy and the University of Paris and his doctoral degree from the University of Michigan. He is Professor of International Law and Organization at the University of Ottawa and has taught at many academic institutions, including McGill, New South Wales, Louvain, Thessalonica, Toulouse, Nantes, and the University of

Michigan. He is an eminent authority on the legal status of Arctic waters and the waters of the Canadian Archipelago, author of *The Law of the Sea of the Arctic* among other distinguished works. The Center was extremely pleased that Leonard Legault, Legal Adviser to the Department of External Affairs of Canada, could join in counsel and association with Professor Pharand in the writing of this book.

The Center for the Study of Marine Policy launched this series of studies of international straits of the world with the encouragement and support of the Rockefeller Foundation, and I wish to express my deep appreciation to that Foundation for its counsel and tangible assistance.

At the same time I have had the benefit of observations and comments, with constructive suggestions, from a distinguished advisory council including T.T.B. Koh, Permanent Representative of Singapore to the United Nations, Maxwell Cohen, formerly on the International Joint Commission (Canada – U.S.A.), Ali Moertopo, Center for Strategic and International Studies, Indonesia, Takeo Iguchi, Consul-General of Japan for New England, and Lewis Alexander, former Geographer of the Department of State.

All statements, judgments, or opinions within this study are the sole responsibility of the author and not to be attributed in any way to the Rockefeller Foundation, the Center for the Study of Marine Policy at the University of Delaware, or to any member of the International Advisory Council.

Gerard J. Mangone

Center for the Study of Marine Policy
University of Delaware
1 May 1984

LIST OF FIGURES

1. Winter Ice Conditions in the Canadian Arctic, Late February 3
2. Main Routes of the Northwest Passage insert
3. West Barrow Strait and Prince of Wales Strait 8
4. Search for the Northwest Passage: 1576 to 1847 insert
5. Search for Franklin's Expedition: 1847 to 1859 insert
6. Two Canadian Expeditions in the Northwest Passage: 1908–09 and 1940–44 40
7. Major Petroleum Areas of Alaska North Slope/Beaufort Sea 61
8. Major Petroleum Areas of Mackenzie Delta/Beaufort Sea 63
9. Major Petroleum Areas of Canadian Arctic Islands 65
10. Mine Sites in the Canadian Arctic 67
11. Exploration and Production Systems for the Beaufort Sea 69
12. Possible Oil and Gas Pipelines from the Arctic 72
13. Route No. 1 of the Northwest Passage (via Prince of Wales Strait) 77
14. International Straits in 1982 Law of the Sea Convention 97
15. Ecologically Significant Areas of Canadian Arctic 123
16. Extent of Sea-Ice Use by the Inuit 135
17. Shipping Safety Control Zones 156

LIST OF TABLES

1. Full Transits of the Northwest Passage (1903–1983) 50
2. Partial Transits of the Northwest Passage (1977–1982) 53
3. Most Demanding Forecast of Transits of Northwest Passage (1986–1995) 83
4. Approximate Minimum Annual Canadian Harvest of Marine Mammals in Parry Channel, Baffin Bay, and Davis Strait 138
5. Approximate Minimum Annual Canadian Harvest of Marine Mammals in the Beaufort Sea and Amundsen Gulf Areas 138
6. Known Submarine Operations in the Arctic (1931–1981) 148
7. List of Ship Categories for Shipping Safety Control Zones 154

PREFACE

Scientists have claimed that the world climate is cooling, but there has been a definite warming-up of public interest in the Arctic. This is particularly so in the Arctic states in relation to the vast hydrocarbon resources in the region. All have done some preliminary exploration, and the United States and Canada, determined to attain energy self-sufficiency as soon as possible, have intensified their drilling activities in recent years.

In 1980 Canada adopted a National Energy Program, with a view to gaining control of its own energy future through security of supply and ultimate independence from the world oil market. In June 1982 Ottawa announced its planning strategy for a phased approach to northern hydrocarbon development. Under this strategy, the government will encourage initial production on a small scale demonstration basis, commensurate with proven commercial reserves, and will support incremental expansion as need and capability are demonstrated. In 1982 Canada also adopted an Arctic Marine Services Policy to ensure that when year-round navigation begins in the Northwest Passage for the transportation of hydrocarbons, the necessary services will be available. In 1983 the Department of Transport was preparing an Arctic marine shipping policy for both domestic and international shipping.

With the assistance of the federal government through special depletion allowances (now replaced by a system of incentive grants), Dome Petroleum, Esso Resources Canada, and Gulf Canada Resources have been pursuing their exploration activities vigorously in the Beaufort Sea. In 1982 these developers submitted an environmental impact statement to the government, and this statement, along with submissions from concerned individuals and organizations, forms part of the compulsory environmental assessment process. In addition, a comprehensive drilling program has been ongoing in the Canadian Arctic Islands for many years. The principal operator has been Panarctic Oils, a joint venture between private enterprise and the federal government.

The estimates of total recoverable oil and gas reserves in the Canadian Arctic vary somewhat from one source to another, but these reserves are unquestionably very considerable and well worth developing in spite of the special difficulties posed by the hostile environment. Although the urgency for the development of these reserves has declined because of the lowering in the price and demand for oil during the last year, the long-term need for these resources still exists and the Canadian government appears to remain committed to developing them in accordance with the planning strategy. In February 1984, the Minister of Indian and Northern Affairs announced the conclusion of 16 exploration agreements with oil and gas companies, bringing to more than 4.3 billion the total investment pledged to oil and gas exploration in the North during the next three to six-year period. The government is also pursuing its preparations to have the necessary regulations and services in place when production and transportation begin, which is now expected to be in the early 1990s instead of the late 1980s.

Both pipelines and tankers are envisaged as transportation modes. However, numerous studies on this question would seem to indicate that tankers through the Northwest Passage will constitute the predominant mode. This prospective use of the Northwest Passage raises a number of problems relating to the protection of the marine environment and the Inuit, as well as the legal status of the Northwest Passage itself. The present study addresses those problems and includes: (1) a description of the Northwest Passage, (2) its historical development, (3) the future commercial development, (4) the legal status of the Northwest Passage and (5) the policy implications of the future development of the Northwest Passage.

The study is basically one in international law, but in order to set an appropriate background for the legal analysis and the appraisal of consequent policy implications, it is necessary to begin by a thorough examination of the physical, historical, and commercial aspects of the topic. A word of caution is appropriate and perhaps, even necessary about the nature of the book. Although it is one in a series entitled *International Straits of the World*, it does not necessarily follow that the Northwest Passage should be considered as an "international strait" from the point of view of international law. This is a major issue addressed by this study.

The book has had the benefit of the collaboration of an imposing number of dedicated individuals, most of whom with a special interest and expertise in the Arctic. The first and foremost collaborator was Leonard Legault, Q.C., Legal Adviser to the Department of External Affairs of Canada and long-time student of the international law problems relating to the Arctic in general and to the Northwest Passage in particular. Mr. Legault was associated with the preparation of this study from the beginning. Indeed, it was originally intended that the study should be a joint undertaking in the fullest sense of the term. Unfortunately, Mr. Legault's other commitments interfered. Nevertheless, I have benefitted from his comments and suggestions on all parts of the book, particularly the last two dealing with the legal status of the Northwest Passage and the policy implications of its future development. It is for this reason that his name has been associated with the author's on the cover and title page.

A group of people to whom I am particularly endebted are the five members of my Review Committee. All of them possessed a special expertise on Arctic questions and they were kind enough to read and comment on the manuscript. These are François Bregha, Chief Policy Analyst, with the Department of Energy, Mines and Resources; Cyril Champ, Staff Assistant to the Dominion Hydrographer; Captain T.C. Pullen, R.C.N. (ret.), long-time Arctic navigator and consultant to industry and governments; Graham Rowley, Research Professor in Canadian Studies at Carleton University; and Dr. Gordon W. Smith, foremost legal historian on the Arctic regions.

A second group of people to whom I gladly acknowledge my gratitude are those who acted as research assistants: Gerald Graham and Sarita Verma, during the early months of research, and Adam Roberts, during a good deal of the actual drafting, particularly the last part on policy implications for the marine environment and the Inuit.

A special endebtedness is very gratefully acknowledged to the Canadian Hydrographic Service for its assistance in the preparation of most of the figures, in particular to S.B. MacPhee, its Director General, and Richard Cashen as well as the staff of the Marine Cartography Branch.

I am also endebted to the Dean of the Civil Law Section of the Faculty of Law, University of Ottawa, Raymond Landry, and to that Faculty's Director of Graduate Studies and Research, Jean-Paul Lacasse, for their strong encouragement and support in making some research assistance available.

Finally, since no book can be written without a secretary, I am most grateful to Lise Fraser, who managed to find time, even when she did not have any, to do the typing of the manuscript.

In spite of all the valuable assistance and advice I have received, errors will be found; hopefully, none of them will be so severe as to be unforgiveable. In any event, those errors are attributable to me and nobody else. Fortunately, the general editor of the series, Professor Gerard J. Mangone, did not hesitate to use his editing pen throughout the manuscript and has thus improved considerably the form and style of the book. I am most grateful to him.

Ottawa, Canada
29 February 1984

Donat Pharand

POST SCRIPTUM

By the summer of 1984 the expectations of northern hydrocarbon development differed considerably from what they were in 1981–1982. The world oil price in 1984 was 15% lower than it was in 1980 and, according to current forecasts, that price will not increase in real terms (above the inflation rate) until the early 1990s. In addition, the results of drilling activities in the Beaufort Sea had been disappointing in that commercial discoveries were not made on the Canadian side. In these circumstances, tanker traffic in the Northwest Passage will probably not occur in any important way until the latter part of the 1990s. This change in perspective should be kept in mind by the reader.

Ottawa, Canada
15 July 1984

Donat Pharand

Chapter 1

DESCRIPTION OF THE NORTHWEST PASSAGE

The Sailing Directions of Arctic Canada states that "the Northwest Passage spans the North American Arctic from Davis Strait and Baffin Bay in the east to Bering Strait in the west". This is certainly how the Passage was understood by the early explorers and probably represents the most accurate definition.

In recent times, however, starting with the 1969 voyage of the *Manhattan*, there has been a general tendency to limit the Northwest Passage to the constricted waters within the Canadian Arctic Archipelago between Baffin Bay and the Beaufort Sea. Although this restricted definition is historically incomplete, it will be adopted, for to do otherwise would require a description and study of the legal regime of at least two series of bodies of water, in addition to those within the Archipelago. One group, in the east, includes the Labrador Sea, Davis Strait, Baffin Bay, Kane Basin, Kennedy Channel, Hall Basin, Robeson Channel and Lincoln Sea which collectively join the Atlantic Ocean with the Arctic Ocean. The other group, in the west, includes the Bering Sea, the Bering Strait, the Chukchi Sea, and the Beaufort Sea which collectively link the Pacific Ocean with the Arctic Ocean. Such a venture is beyond the scope of this study of the Northwest Passage.

Throughout this description of the Northwest Passage, three factors will be emphasized: geography, bathymetry and ice. These are the most important natural elements to be taken into account for navigational purposes. Additional factors include climate, winds, currents and tides, and occasional reference will be made to them.

The importance of Arctic bathymetry cannot be overstressed, considering the 20-meter draft requirement of the icebreaking tankers envisaged for the transportation of hydrocarbons from the Beaufort Sea and similar high-latitude Arctic areas. Unfortunately, most of the waters of the Canadian Arctic Archipelago have not been surveyed to modern standards, that is, with a closely spaced pattern of sounding lines permitting an accurate description of submarine topography. However, the waters of the primary deep draft route of the Northwest Passage have either been completely surveyed or will be in the near future. Specifically, Lancaster Sound, the Barrow Strait, the Prince of Wales Strait, the Amundsen Gulf, and the southeastern portion of the Beaufort Sea have been surveyed to modern standards. Viscount Melville Sound has been covered by spot soundings, particularly along the northern shore where there is a corridor of dense 500-meter spot soundings. The other deep draft routes envisaged are either in the process of being completed or awaiting their turn.

Over-the-ice hydrographic surveys are difficult and call for special techniques, so that many more years will be necessary to complete an adequate survey of all Canadian Arctic waters. However, the Canadian Hydrographic Service has presently a very active program underway in the Arctic and priority is being given to deep draft routes.

The bodies of water on either side of the Canadian Arctic Archipelago, which reach the Pacific Ocean in the west and the Atlantic Ocean on the east, can be called approaches to the Northwest Passage and will be described briefly.

EASTERN APPROACHES: LABRADOR SEA, DAVIS STRAIT, AND BAFFIN BAY

A huge area, comprised of the Davis Strait and Baffin Bay, constitutes the main approach to the eastern portal of the Northwest Passage. The ice regime in the Davis Strait and Baffin Bay is controlled basically by three factors: a warm current flowing north along the Baffin coast and a major polynya, or open water area, at the northern extremity of Baffin Bay.[1]

The warm current flowing north along the Greenland coast delays ice formation in the eastern part of the Davis Strait and causes an earlier break-up in the spring, whereas the cold current flowing south along the Baffin Island coast has exactly the opposite effect there, as shown in Figure 1. The polynya in Smith Sound, also called the ''North Water'', which is an area of open or almost open water most of the year, extends southward in the spring and assists in clearing the northern half of Baffin Bay, which then joins the open water already formed along the coast of Greenland. Consequently, the recommended route to enter Lancaster Sound, at the eastern end of the Northwest Passage, is to favor the west coast of Greenland up to about 74° north latitude, thence westward across Baffin Bay entering Lancaster Sound on its northern side. This is the route which the proponents of the Arctic Pilot Project originally planned to adopt for the transportation of liquefied natural gas.

A special feature of the eastern approaches to the Northwest Passage is the presence of icebergs, calved mostly from the glacier tongues off west and north Greenland, with a few also from glaciers on Ellesmere and Devon Islands. These icebergs drift southward eventually with the cold Canadian current mainly and are found in greater numbers along the Canadian coast than on the Greenland side. Some rise to 200 to 300 feet above the sea level, although show-

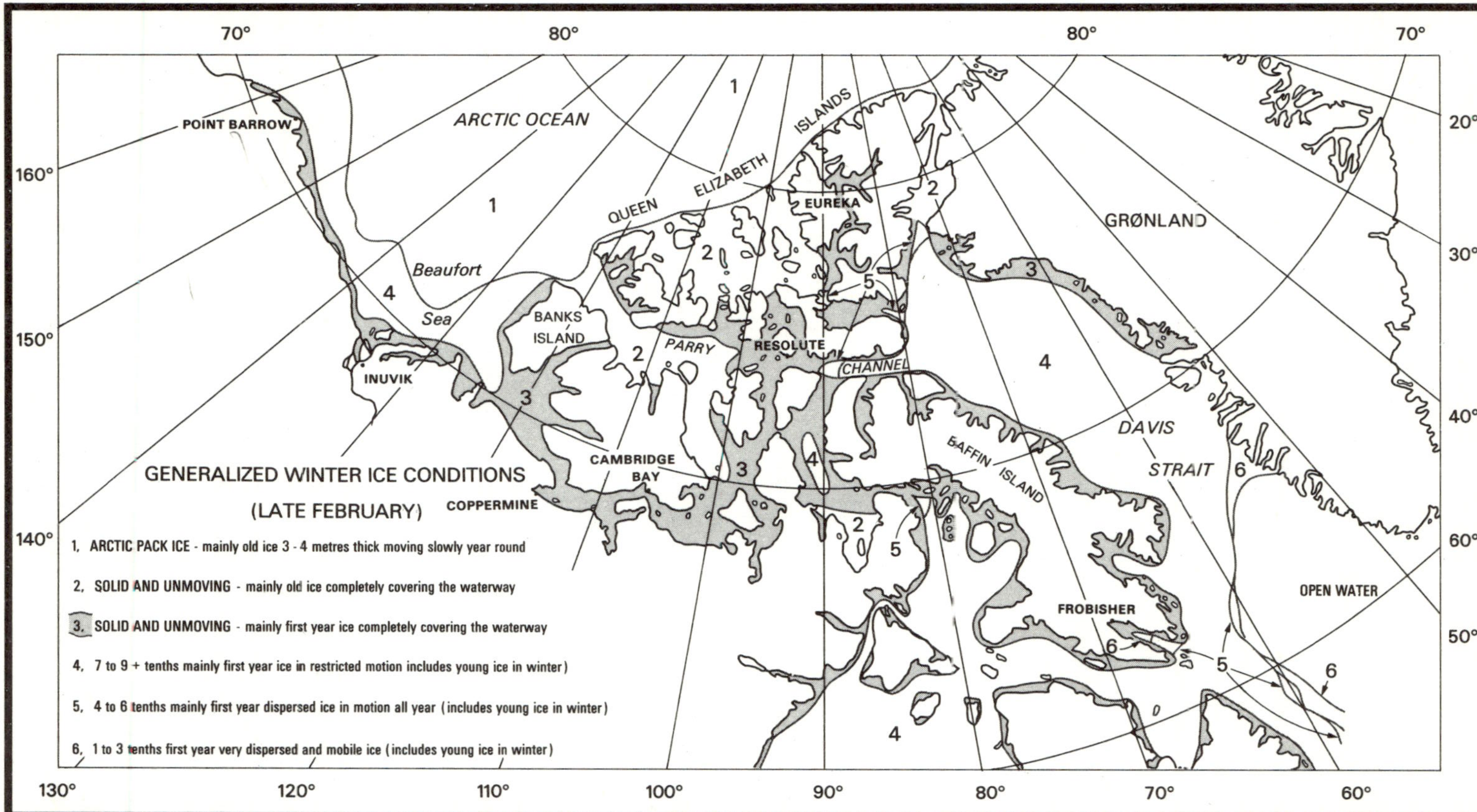

Fig. 1: WINTER ICE CONDITIONS IN THE CANADIAN ARCTIC, LATE FEBRUARY
Prepared for the author by the Canadian Hydrographic Service, Dept. of Fisheries and Oceans, Ottawa.

ing only about 1/9th of their mass, and can constitute a considerable hazard to navigation. This is one of the reasons why the Dome Petroleum Company has envisaged using the Fury and Hecla Strait as an alternative route and thus by-passing Baffin Bay and the Davis Strait.

Freeze-up in North Baffin Bay begins in mid-September and spreads southward down the Baffin Island coast during October, growing into an unmoving ice cover in the whole of Baffin Bay and along the Baffin Island coast in the Davis Strait. Sea ice also extends to the Labrador Sea during the winter and its thickness varies considerably, the thickness of the typical floe averaging more than one meter. Spring break-up in Northern Baffin Bay is greatly facilitated by the "North Water", which expands southward, usually opening the entrance to Lancaster Sound by the end of June.

WESTERN APPROACHES: BERING STRAIT, CHUKCHI SEA, AND BEAUFORT SEA

The Bering Strait and the Chukchi Sea generally offer more favorable ice conditions than does the Beaufort Sea because they lie south of the normal range of the permanent polar ice pack. It is also due in part to the warmer waters of the Pacific Ocean flowing through the Bering Strait, even if this strait is a relatively shallow one. Consequently, there is a recurring winter lead at the edge of the landfast ice along the northwest coast of Alaska between Point Hope and Point Barrow, offering open water normally from late May to early November. However, there are a number of pressure ridges in the Bering Strait and the Chukchi Sea, particularly in the latter. According to the U.S. Coast Guard, which carried out trafficability tests from 1979 to 1982, the ice fields in this area are highly irregular and "vessels transitting these ice-laden waters must be designed to negotiate the most severe environmental conditions likely to be encountered, e.g. maximum level ice thicknesses and pressure ridges."[2]

Ice in the Beaufort Sea forms an integral part of one of the two major ice circulation patterns in the Arctic Ocean. One is known as the transpolar drift, which carries ice from the general area of the East Siberian Sea, passing across the North Pole and continuing into the Greenland Sea between Greenland and the Svalboard Archipelago. The other major circulation movement follows an anti-cyclonic or clockwise movement on the Canadian side of the North Pole. This second ice movement, averaging a couple of miles a day the year round, travels along the western side of the Canadian Arctic Archipelago, across the M'Clure Strait, toward Barter Island at the boundary of Alaska and the Yukon, thence along the Alaskan coast past Point Barrow, carrying polar or multi-year ice averaging about three meters in thickness.

Although the limits of the polar pack do not generally reach the coast of

Banks Island and the continental coast of Canada and Alaska, the coast itself does not always offer open water. In winter, there is a belt of fast ice along the coast, extending several miles offshore to approximately the 20-meter depth contour. This ice does not generally break up until the end of July.

Between the fast ice and the polar ice, there is a transition zone of first-year ice which may vary from 50 to 100 miles wide, forming early in October and breaking up at the end of June.[3] This middle zone or active shear zone generally widens upon approaching the Amundsen Gulf where a polynya is usually formed off Cape Bathurst during March and April and which accelerates the ice disintegration process.[4] Of course, there is seldom a clear demarcation between this zone of first-year ice and the polar pack to the north. Indeed, a number of polar pack floes, some of which are heavily hummocked, are often mixed with the first-year ice and sometimes grounded in as much as 20 meters of water. Ice conditions may vary from year to year and a number of passages have been made from Point Barrow to the Amundsen Gulf without seeing any ice from late July to the first week of September. For instance, in its 1969 voyage the S/T *Manhattan* experienced virtually open water from the Amundsen Gulf to Point Barrow from 16 to 21 September.

Aside from the large multi-year ice floes mentioned above, which can constitute a serious obstacle to navigation because of the difficulty of long range identification, the Beaufort Sea presents a hazardous region with submarine features off the Tuktoyaktuk Peninsula much like the well-known pingos (conical shaped mounds with a central core of ice) on the Tuktoyaktuk Peninsula and probably formed in a similar way. They vary from 15 to 45 meters in height and range from about 500 to 1,000 meters in diameter at their base, and they pose a threat to navigation for deep draft vessels. By 1971 some 178 such features had been located in the Beaufort Sea, north of the Tuktoyaktuk Peninsula.[5] The Hydrographic Service completed a 10-mile shipping corridor across the pingo area in 1983 and more than twenty pingos were located. The least depth found was 19.8 meters, which could make this the ruling depth for deep-draft shipping using the Northwest Passage unless it can go north of the pingos.

Freeze-up in the Beaufort Sea generally occurs at the beginning of October, but may not take place until early November if the polar pack is well offshore. There may not be open water until that time, however, and the *Manhattan* encountered heavy ice north of Mackenzie Bay on her return from Point Barrow in the latter part of September, 1969.

ROUTES OF THE NORTHWEST PASSAGE

The Northwest Passage consists of five basic routes, plus at least two variations of two of those routes, as shown in Figure 2.* All the routes are potentially feasible for navigation but each presents varying degrees of navigational difficulties, mainly because of the presence of ice for most of the year. The choice of route will depend largely on the size of the ship, its icebreaking capability or that of the accompanying icebreaker, if any, and the local ice conditions, as well as the adequacy of hydrographic surveys.[6]

Of the five basic routes, only two are presently known to be suitable for deep draft navigation. They are Routes 1 and 2, which may be referred to as the northern routes. Routes 3 (and its variation 3A) and 4, which may be considered as the southern routes since they follow the continental coast of Canada for more than half the distance, are not suitable for deep draft navigation. As for Route 5, it presently leads only to Routes 3 and 4. However, if it proves possible to avoid certain shoal areas in the Fury and Hecla Strait, its variation Route 5A could lead to Routes 1 and 2 for use by deep draft ships.

A description of the five basic routes from east to west follows to facilitate understanding and comparison.

Route 1, through Prince of Wales Strait

Route 1 is presently the most feasible one for icebreaking tankers and has been chosen by the Dome Petroleum Company as its primary route. It lies through five bodies of water: Lancaster Sound, the Barrow Strait, Viscount Melville Sound, the Prince of Wales Strait, and the Amundsen Gulf.

Lancaster Sound. With an entrance width of 51 miles, between Cape Hay on Bylot Island to the south, and Cape Sherard on the southeast coast of Devon Island to the north, Lancaster Sound is a steep-sided strait, extending westward 160 miles to Prince Leopold Island at the northeast tip of Somerset Island. Because of winds, tides, and currents constantly moving the ice, there is no true freeze-up in winter in that the ice does not normally consolidate completely. The most favorable period for navigation is between mid-July and the end of October, during which Lancaster Sound is normally open. Quite frequently, however, the westward-moving current along the south coast of Devon Island carries icebergs into the Sound, icebergs which otherwise would continue their route southward across its entrance.[7] Vessels are advised to enter the Sound on its northern side, because of the heavy sea ice which usually lies off the north-

* See insert.

ern coasts of Baffin and Bylot Islands to the south. Modern surveys have now been carried out through this deep sound and its bathymetry presents no difficulty.

Barrow Strait. The eastern approach to the Barrow Strait is 28 miles wide between Prince Leopold Island to the south and Cape Hurd on Devon Island to the north. It extends westward 170 miles to its junction with Viscount Melville Sound, where it widens to 66 miles in the vicinity of Cape Cockburn, the southwest extremity of Bathurst Island.

Proceeding from east to west, the Barrow Strait averages about 30 miles in width and is free of islands for about half of its length, as shown in Figure 3. The strait then begins to broaden and, southwest of Resolute, lies a relatively large island, Griffith, on the north side of the strait. To the northwest of Griffith are two small islands, Somerville and Browne. These three islands along the southwest coast of Cornwallis Island form Resolute Passage which, at its narrowest, is 6.5 miles wide. At its western end the Barrow Strait offers a string of five islands lying across the strait in a zigzag fashion. Beginning on the south side they are Russell, Hamilton, Young, Lowther and Garrett Islands. Although the Barrow Strait itself is 70 miles wide at this point, the widest inter-island passage is 15.5 miles. The latter is Kettle Passage between Lowther Island lying in mid-strait and Young Island to the south-west. To the north of Lowther Island the two passages are both about 13 miles wide, one being Hayes Channel between Young and Garrett, and the other is Intrepid Passage between Garrett and Moore close to the Bathurst Island coast. To the south of Young Island the widths are 8 miles for the passage between Young and Hamilton and 11 miles for that between Hamilton and Russell.

All these passages and channels have sufficient water depths for large deep draft ships, but there are shoals off most of the islands. As stated in the Sailing Directions for Arctic Canada, "depths become shoalier in the area of the islands south of Intrepid Passage, with a shoal depth of 22 meters (12 fathoms) lying 1.2 miles north of Garrett Island. Off the east side of Lowther and Young Islands, shoal depths may be found at a distance of 5 miles, and off the west side of Hamilton Island, soundings of 29 meters (16 fathoms) are to be found 9 miles westward. Depths in mid-channel between the islands appear to indicate that they are clear of dangers. However, it is advisable to give these islands a wide berth."[8] In addition to the above, the 1982 edition of Canada's chart for the western portion of Barrow Strait indicates a shoal of 24 meters near the middle of Kettle Passage. It is therefore evident that although the Barrow Strait is generally deep, its western portion must be navigated with caution becaue of the mid-strait islands and shoals. Indeed, the Barrow Strait was rightly termed "the bottleneck" by Captain G.P. Steele, commander of the submarine U S S *Seadragon*, at the time of its transit in 1962.[9]

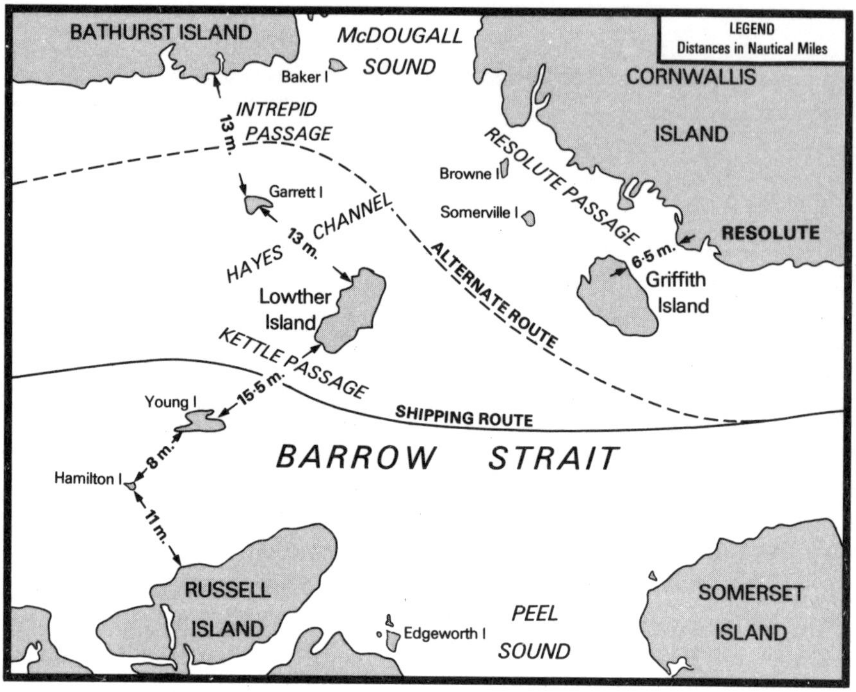

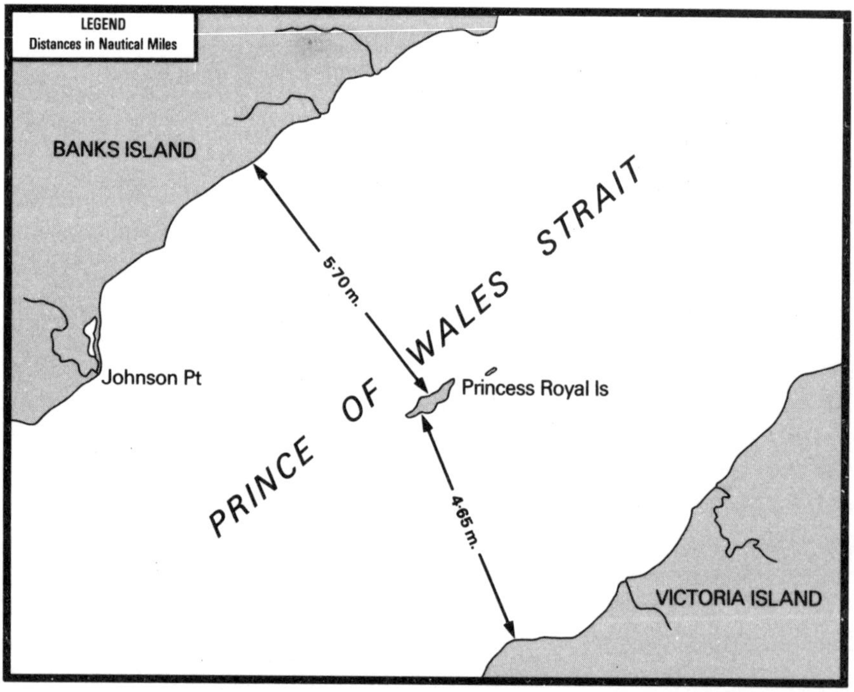

Fig. 3: WEST BARROW STRAIT AND PRINCE OF WALES STRAIT
Prepared for the author by the Canadian Hydrographic Service, Dept. of Fisheries and Oceans, Ottawa.

As for the ice conditions, the eastern part of the Barrow Strait does not normally freeze up until the end of November and does not consolidate until the end of December. It begins to break up in July at the eastern end and this process continues until about the middle of August in the western half of the strait. Indeed, west of Resolute, the ice conditions become more severe as one approaches Viscount Melville Sound and a considerable amount of ice sometimes remains throughout the summer. Navigation from the east is usually feasible as far as Resolute Bay by the end of July and to the western end of the strait by the end of August. Navigation conditions are generally more favorable on the north shore of the strait through Resolute Passage and Intrepid Passage. But, if a ship is proceeding west into Viscount Melville Sound, the shorter route lies in mid-strait, that is, Kettle Passage. This is the passage normally followed in a transit of the Northwest Passage and, indeed, was the one taken by the S/T *Manhattan* in 1969.

The ice edge between the unconsolidated ice regime of Lancaster Sound already described and the consolidated ice regime of the Barrow Strait in winter usually appears across the Barrow Strait near Leopold Island, which is the boundary between those two bodies of water. The ice edge provides an important habitat for many species of animals, such as the ringed seal, the polar bear, arctic fox, some whales, and many birds, while the consolidated ice in the central and western parts of the Barrow Strait provides a convenient bridge for caribou during the winter.

Viscount Melville Sound. The Viscount Melville Sound is an immense body of water between Victoria Island in the south and Melville Island in the north. It has an entrance of 66 miles from Cape Berkeley on Prince of Wales Island to Cape Cockburn at the southwest extremity of Bathurst Island on the north side. It extends in a westerly direction about 220 miles up to its junction with the M'Clure Strait where the width of the Sound between Banks Island and Melville Island is 74 miles. The average width of the Sound is about 80 miles and it is uncluttered by islands.

A solid ice cover, prevailing throughout the winter, is predominantly multiyear ice much of which has come down from the Arctic Ocean through the M'Clure Strait, does not fracture until about the end of July. Break-up progresses from east to west during the month of August and open water leads appear along the north side of the sound by early September. Although this is the side offering the best route for navigation, heavy ice is often discharged from the channels on either side of Byam Martin Island to the north posing a considerable obstacle to navigation. Freeze-up normally begins by the middle of September and consolidation of the ice cover across the sound usually occurs by the end of October. In summary, Viscount Melville Sound has consistently a higher concentration of polar ice and less open water than any of the five bodies of water making up Route 1. A reconnaissance spot-sounding survey completed in 1982 showed depths ranging from 200 to 500 meters.

Prince of Wales Strait. Because of the severe ice conditions prevailing in the M'Clure Strait, the Prince of Wales Strait will normally be used instead for the transportation of oil and gas from the Beaufort Sea. This is the primary route that has been proposed by the Dome Petroleum Company, although it has considered the M'Clure Strait as a possible secondary route. The Prince of Wales Strait separates Banks Island from Victoria Island and links Viscount Melville Sound (and the M'Clure Strait) to the north with Amundsen Gulf to the south. The Prince of Wales Strait is some 145 miles long and has an average width of about 10 miles, with a minimum width of 6.5 miles, as shown in Figure 3. This minimum width narrows to less than six miles, however, because of the Princess Royal Islands, located nearly half way down the strait approximately 65 miles from its northern entrance. Because of an extensive shoal area in the channel on the northwest side of the small islands with a least depth of 4.2 meters, vessels use the channel to the southeast of the islands where there is deep water with some shoal areas in mid-channel over which there is a least depth of 32 meters.[10] The strait has now been surveyed to modern standards and the maximum draft which can be carried is about 60 meters. Just southwest of the 32-meter shoal the channel is reduced to a width of one mile.

The ice cover of the Prince of Wales Strait is generally made up of first-year ice, since the prevailing winds in the M'Clure Strait and Viscount Melville Sound tend to carry the polar ice past the north entrance of the strait, effectively clearing a multi-year ice plug. Break-up develops at the south end of the strait from Amundsen Gulf in late July and spreads northward through the strait by mid-August, with an appreciable delay in the northern part of the strait. Maximum open water occurs in early September and occasionally complete clearing may occur. Freeze-up begins in the latter part of September and a complete consolidation of the ice cover is established by early November.

Amundsen Gulf. Amundsen Gulf, named for the Norwegian explorer Roald Amundsen, is a large elongated body of water lying in an east-west direction, separating the mainland coast of northern Canada from Banks and Victoria Islands. The gulf links the Prince of Wales Strait with the Beaufort Sea, thus completing the western end of the Northwest Passage when using Route 1. The entrance of Amundsen Gulf has a width of 92 miles, following a line from Cape Bathurst on the mainland coast to Cape Kellett at the southwest extremity of Banks Island. It is a very irregularly shaped gulf approximately 200 miles in length with two large bays on its south side, and the Prince of Wales Strait, as well as a bay and a couple of large inlets, to the north. The eastern extremity of the gulf, 56 miles wide, opens into the Dolphin and Union Strait.

In winter Amundsen Gulf is usually covered with unmoving first-year ice, with an odd polar ice floe which has come either through the Prince of Wales Strait or the Beaufort Sea itself. Exceptionally, however, the ice can remain virtually mobile throughout the winter. This is due to the presence of a polynya around Cape Bathurst at the entrance of the gulf, which normally forms during the month of May and expands outside and inside the gulf. Consequently, break-up is usually completed by July, with clearing occurring in early August. Freeze-up normally commences at the beginning of October and spreads over the gulf by the end of the month. Amundsen Gulf has been surveyed to modern standards with depths varying between 90 and 350 meters.

Route 2, through M'Clure Strait

This route, envisaged by the Dome Petroleum Company as an alternative shipping corridor, is the same as Route 1 except at its western end. Having traversed Lancaster Sound, the Barrow Strait, and Viscount Melville Sound, Route 2 reaches the Beaufort Sea by continuing through the M'Clure Strait north of Banks Island. Those four straits and sounds are collectively called the Parry Channel after Lieutenant W.E. Parry, Royal Navy, who, in 1819, commanded the first expedition to navigate the Northwest Passage as far west as the entrance to the M'Clure Strait. As for the M'Clure Strait itself, it was named after Commander Robert M'Clure, Royal Navy, who, in 1853, became the first to cross (albeit on foot) the unsailed part of the strait. He did so from west to east, after leaving his ship, HMS *Investigator*, beset in ice at Mercy Bay, on the north side of Banks Island, and heading a sled party across Viscount Melville Sound to reach Winter Harbour, on the southeast coast of Melville Island.

The eastern entrance of the M'Clure Strait is 74 miles wide, following a line from Russell Point on the northeast extremity of Banks Island to Cape Providence on Melville Island. This huge strait, separating Banks Island to the south from Prince Patrick Island and Melville Island to the north, extends approximately 165 miles to the Beaufort Sea. The width of its western entrance measures 108 miles along a line from Cape Prince Alfred on the northwest tip of Banks Island to Griffiths Point, the southwest extremity of Prince Patrick Island. The bathymetry of the strait is not completely known, but what depth information is available indicates it is deep throughout with mid-strait depths of 500 meters.

Until July, the strait normally is covered by consolidated ice, most of which is multi-year ice from the Arctic Ocean. Narrow shore leads then develop along the north shore of Banks Island and the south shore of Prince Patrick Island. Major leads may also develop at any time, even during winter, along the northwest coast of Banks Island. Break-up progresses from west to east and, by the second week of August, a fracturing of the ice has normally taken place. The strait, nevertheless, usually remains choked with polar ice throughout the summer. Freeze-up usually begins around the middle of September and the ice consolidates by the end of October and early November. Indeed, in years of heavy ice, the ice-cover may consolidate by late September.

The M'Clure Strait has seldom been completely navigated by surface ships because of the presence of old multi-year ice. The American tanker S/T *Manhattan*, followed by the Canadian icebreaker *John A. Macdonald*, attempted its navigation in 1969 but was unsuccessful. The ship eventually retreated and used the Prince of Wales Strait instead. The strait, however, has been traversed by submarines at least twice, once in 1960 by USS *Seadragon*, and again in 1962 by USS *Skate*.

Route 3, through Peel Sound and Victoria Strait

The third route follows Routes 1 and 2 westward for about a quarter of the way, turns southward as far as the northern continental coast of Canada, and then continues westward along the coast for the rest of the route. Proceeding from east to west, a ship would have to cross the following eleven bodies of water: Lancaster Sound, the Barrow Strait, Peel Sound, the Franklin Strait, Larsen Sound, the Victoria Strait, Queen Maud Gulf, the Dease Strait, Coronation Gulf, the Dolphin and Union Straits, and Amundsen Gulf. The first two narrows of this route, Lancaster Sound and the Barrow Strait, as well as the last body of water (Amundsen Gulf), were described in Route 1. A description of the remaining eight follows.

Peel Sound. Peel Sound separates Prince of Wales Island from Somerset Island. The sound runs from the Barrow Strait to the Bellot Strait, separating Somerset Island from Boothia Peninsula, where it joins the Franklin Strait to the south. Its width is 15 miles or more and in mid-channel is free of islands. The bathymetry of the sound does not present any obstacles to navigation, mid-sound depths ranging between 200 and 450 meters.

A solid sheet of fast ice blankets the sound during winter, with a thickness of approximately two meters. Although the ice cover is mainly first-year ice, there can be small inflow of older ice from Barrow Strait. Break-up normally begins during the first week of August and is completed by the first week of September. Freeze-up usually begins during the third week of September and there is a consolidation of the ice cover by the end of October.

Franklin Strait. The Franklin Strait separates the southeast coast of Prince of Wales Island from the northern part of Boothia Peninsula to the east. The strait runs from the Bellot Strait to the southern tip of Prince of Wales Island

and has an average width of about 20 miles. The middle of the strait is free of obstructions and mid-strait depths range from about 70 meters in the south to some 400 meters in the north. These conditions are virtually identical to those just described for Peel Sound.

Larsen Sound. Larsen Sound is a large body of water lying between Victoria Island to the west and Boothia Peninsula to the east, with King William Island to the south and Prince of Wales Island to the north. It opens onto four straits: the Victoria Strait and the James Ross Strait to the south, and the M'Clintock Channel and the Franklin Strait to the north. It is a completely open body of water, except for Gateshead Island on the west side, and soundings show depths mostly between 90 and 180 meters.

Break-up normally begins during the last week of July and the sound is clear of ice by the end of August. Freeze-up usually begins at the end of September with a solid ice cover forming at the end of October. It was here that Larsen's *St. Roch* over-wintered in Pasley Bay, on the west coast of Boothia Peninsula, from 3 September 1941 to 4 August 1942, during her eastward crossing of the Northwest Passage.

Victoria Strait. The Victoria Strait lies between Victoria Island to the west and King William Island to the east. It links Larsen Sound and the M'Clintock Channel to the north with Queen Maud Gulf to the south. It is a wide strait free of islands for the most part but with the relatively large Royal Geographical Society Islands at the southern extremity upon entering Queen Maud Gulf. Although an adequate survey has not been completed, charted soundings already indicate several patches of 10-meter depth only.

The strait is covered with rough ice most of the year, some of which is polar ice that has drifted down the M'Clintock Channell[11] from Viscount Melville Sound. Significant break-up does not begin until the end of July and freeze-up develops during the latter part of September. The Victoria Strait was used for the first time in 1967 by the icebreaker *John A. Macdonald* when she went to assist shipping in the western Arctic. In 1975 it was transited twice by the same ship and twice again in 1976 by two other icebreakers, the *Louis St. Laurent* and the *J.E. Bernier.*

Queen Maud Gulf. Starting at its eastern entrance with an opening eight miles wide, Queen Maud Gulf quickly expands into a very large body of water extending some 170 miles to the west as far as the Dease Strait, where the entrance is also only eight miles wide. The gulf stretches along the continental coast to the south and faces the southeast corner of Victoria Island and the southwest coast of King William Island to the north. Navigation in the gulf soon becomes rather difficult because of the presence of numerous islands, reefs, and shoals. The Sailing Directions specify that the channels at that point are among the most difficult to navigate in the western Arctic.[12] It is a fact, however, that the U.S. Coast Guard ship *Storis* did negotiate the difficult Requisite Channel in 1957. Although this channel is obstructed by numerous isolated shoals, the *Storis* managed to find a passage with a least depth of 12.5 meters. Another difficult channel is Storis Passage which connects Requisite Channel with the Simpson Strait. There are several detached shoal patches in this passage, some of which have only 5.5 meters of water over them.

The ice conditions in Queen Maud Gulf are described as being the most difficult on this coastal route, east of Cape Parry on the south shore of Amundsen Gulf. The reason is probably the influx of cold water, coming from Viscount Melville Sound through M'Clintock Channel and the Victoria Strait, which brings with it a considerable portion of old ice. Break-up begins during the last week of July but does not conclude until the middle of August; even then, old ice still comes down from Victoria Strait. Freeze-up begins in the first week of October and turns the Gulf into a solid layer of fast ice by the end of the month, increasing steadily in thickness through the winter.

Dease Strait. The Dease Strait lies in a general east-west direction separating Victoria Island from the Kent Peninsula. It is about 100 miles long, has an eastern entrance of 12 miles and a western opening of 38 miles into Coronation Gulf. The strait is free of islands except four or five small ones at its eastern end, west of Cambridge Bay. The bathymetry does not appear to give rise to any special navigational difficulties, except in the vicinity of Simpson Rock where the depth is only 3.4 meters, and vessels are recommended to use the buoyed channel.

The Dease Strait is covered by a solid sheet of unmoving first-year ice during the winter. It begins to fracture in the third week of July and leaves the strait completely clear by the first week of August. Freeze-up begins in late September and, by the third week of October, the strait is usually frozen solid except for a strip of unconsolidated ice in mid-channel at the entrance to Queen Maud Gulf which does not consolidate until early December.

Coronation Gulf. Coronation Gulf lies also in an east-west direction and is over 100 miles long. Its eastern entrance from the Dease Strait is 38 miles wide and it closes with an opening 15 miles into the Dolphin and Union Strait. The gulf has two main chains of islands of various sizes throughout its length, one along the south shore and the other in the northern half of the gulf. Fortunately, the gulf is virtually free of islands along the south shore of Victoria Island and the topography of that area does not seem to present special navigational difficulties. Soundings, however, have been sparse.

The gulf is covered with a solid sheet of unmoving ice during the winter. It begins to break up during the first week of July and normally clears completely by the end of that month. As a rule, freeze-up begins during the second week of October and is completed by the third week. Consolidation of the ice cover, however, is not complete until December.

Dolphin and Union Strait. The eastern entrance of the Dolphin and Union Strait is 15 miles wide; the strait measures 90 miles in length, terminating with a 56-mile opening into Amundsen Gulf. There are several low islands and a number of reefs and shoals at the eastern end of the strait. The Sailing Directions recommend a specific route which should be followed closely and specify that the least known depth within .5 mile of the recommended route is 13.2 meters. The Directions further recommend that passage through the east part of the strait be made only by day in good visibility.[13]

The Dolphin and Union Strait is covered with a solid sheet of unmoving first-year ice during the winter and break-up normally begins during the first half of July. Freeze-up occurs about the middle of October.

Route 3A, through Peel Sound and James Ross Strait

Route 3A is only a variation of Route 3, in that it passes on the east side of King William Island instead of the west side. This was the route followed by Roald Amundsen in 1903-06 when he became the first man to complete the Northwest Passage in his 47-ton herring boat, *Gjoa*. It is slightly longer than Route 3 and presents considerable navigational difficulties. The maximum draft of vessels using this route has been five meters. The additional bodies of water traversed by this variation of Route 3 are the following five: the James Ross Strait, St. Roch Basin, the Rae Strait, Rasmussen Basin, and the Simpson Strait.

James Ross Strait. The James Ross Strait lies in a north-south direction, completing the separation of King William Island from Boothia Peninsula, and linking Larsen Sound with St. Roch Basin. The islands lying on the west side, including the Tennent Islands, leave a 30-mile wide passage. There are several mid-channel shoals, however, at the south end of the strait, one extensive shoal area being at a depth of only 3.7 meters. The strait is therefore suitable only for small vessels and yachts.

Ice conditions vary considerably, but break-up normally begins by the end of July and clears up by September. Freeze-up usually begins during the last week of September with a complete ice cover forming during the last week of October.

St. Roch Basin. St. Roch Basin lies between King William Island to the west and Boothia Peninsula to the east. It is entered by the James Ross Strait and leads to the Rae Strait to the south. St. Roch Basin is free of islands except to the northwest end. At that end there is a large island, Matty Island, almost divided in two by an inlet, with numerous islets and shoals to the south, as well as one island to the east. The passage on the east side of those islands following the west coast of Boothia Peninsula, has a number of shoals, particularly upon approaching Spence Bay, where there is considerable shoaling. Special directions are given for ships bound for Spence Bay. It does not appear suitable for deep draft ships.

Break-up in St. Roch Basin generally begins toward the end of July and freeze-up starts about the end of September or early October.

Rae Strait. The Rae Strait is a very short strait separating two small peninsulas: Gibson Peninsula of King William Island to the west and Adelaide Peninsula of the larger Boothia Peninsula to the east. Rae Strait, which is 13 miles wide, links St. Roch Basin to Rasmussen Gulf.

Reconnaissance soundings show an uneven bottom with depths varying from 9 to 77 meters and an extensive shoal area in mid-channel of 5.5 to 18.3 meters. The Rae Strait would seem hardly suitable for deep draft navigation.

Rasmussen Basin. Rasmussen Basin, about 60 miles in length, lies along the continental coast, southeast of King William Island. It opens onto the Rae Strait at the north at its eastern end and on the Simpson Strait to the west where the entrance is 13 miles wide. Except for a few islands in the approaches of Gjoa Haven on the southeast coast of King William Island, where Amundsen spent the winter of 1904 and 1905, the basin is clear and would appear to offer no special navigational difficulties. Depth soundings, however, have been very limited.

Because of the restricted entrances to the Basin and the presence of large islands north of the Rae Strait, there is little ice movement. A solid, even layer of fast ice covers the basin in winter with a maximum thickness of approximately 1.8 to 2.2 meters. Freeze-up usually begins during the first week of October and is completed by the middle of the month. Break-up develops in the last half of July and the basin is normally clear of ice by the middle of August.

Simpson Strait. The Simpson Strait is a narrow passage separating Adelaide Peninsula on the continent from King William Island to the north.[14] This 45-mile strait begins with an eastern entrance with a width of about seven miles, narrowing to about two miles and then terminating on Queen Maud Gulf where it widens again to about eight miles. The strait is obstructed by a number of islands and, indeed, the least width of two miles is further reduced by the presence of small islands and shoals to a navigable channel of about 0.15 mile in places. The channel is marked by beacons and beacon ranges and has a least charted depth of 7.3 meters. The Sailing Directions recommend a particular track, through Storis Passage, and mariners are strongly advised to use the recommended track. The strait is obviously suitable for small ships only.

There is practically no intrusion of ice in this narrow strait studded with islets and shoals and, in winter, it is covered with an even layer of fast ice in the range of 1.8 to 2.0 meters in thickness. Freeze-up normally begins in the first week of October, with the ice cover being completed by the last week of the month. Break-up develops in late July and, by the second week of August, the strait is normally clear of ice.

Route 4, through Prince Regent Inlet

Route 4 is basically the same as Route 3. It was the one followed by Henry Larsen with the *St. Roch* in 1940-42 in his easterly crossing. The only difference is that Route 4 follows the east side of Somerset Island through Prince Regent Inlet instead of the west side. At the southern tip of Somerset Island, a westbound ship must navigate the short Bellot Strait to reach the Franklin Strait in Route 3.

Prince Regent Inlet. Prince Regent Inlet separates Somerset Island to the west from the northern part of Brodeur Peninsula to the east. The inlet runs south from Lancaster Sound and joins with the Gulf of Boothia at the latitude of the Bellot Strait. The northern part of the inlet is about 40 miles wide and its southern part about 65 miles. The inlet is completely free of islands, there are no obstacles to navigation, and the water is deep throughout.

Break-up of the ice generally begins in late June and progresses slowly southward, aided by a south flowing current from Lancaster Sound which follows the east coast of Somerset Island. The southward retreat of the ice normally reaches the latitude of the Bellot Strait by the middle of August. Freeze-up, which begins at the south end of Boothia Peninsula by early September, reaches Prince Regent Inlet in early October when it is also underway in Lancaster Sound. The occasional iceberg that finds its way into Lancaster Sound sometimes enters Prince Regent Inlet.

Bellot Strait. The Bellot Strait is a very narrow, fiord-like passage between cliffy elevations of some 300 meters. The water throughout the strait is generally deep but there is a dangerous and extensive shoal area in the vicinity of Magpie Rock where the depth is only about 18 meters. The rock is described in the Sailing Directions as being "a formidable danger". The Sailing Directions specify that "the Rock is awash at low water but due to the strong currents never uncovers. It extends over an area of about 500 square feet (45 m^2) then drops sharply on all sides to deep water. Magpie Rock is marked by violent tide rips and eddies except at the very brief slack water periods''.[15] Two beacon ranges have been established to lead ships through the narrow channel north of Magpie Rock and specific directions are given on how to approach the Bellot Strait from the east and from the west. The Sailing Directions emphasize that passage through the strait should not be undertaken in reduced visibility as the range beacons might not be seen. The minimum depth on the range line is 22 meters.

Route 5, through Fury and Hecla Strait

Route 5 is an alternative to using Lancaster Sound to reach Route 4 at the Bellot Strait. It follows the south and west sides of Baffin Island and runs through the Fury and Hecla Strait. The bodies of water traversed by the eastern part of this route are the Hudson Strait, Foxe Channel, Foxe Basin, the Fury and Hecla Strait, and the Gulf of Boothia.

Hudson Strait. The well-known Hudson Strait, which is over 400 miles long and about 60 miles wide, lies between the Ungava Peninsula and Baffin Island. It links the Davis Strait and Foxe Basin and also leads to the entrance of Hudson Bay. It has a few large islands at both entrances as well as on either side, but the middle of the strait is free of islands and has charted depths in general from 182 meters to 548 meters.

The ice in the Hudson Strait begins to break up at the end of June or early July. The strait is usually ice-free during August and September, except for some icebergs and growlers which enter the strait with the Baffin Bay pack and persist throughout the summer. Freeze-up begins in October and the strait becomes unnavigable by the middle of November.

Foxe Channel. Foxe Channel lies between Southampton Island to the southwest and Foxe Peninsula of Baffin Island to the northeast. It is a wide channel of about 80 miles and depths generally range between 50 and 400 meters. A shoal is reported in the middle of the channel, showing a depth of only 13 meters,[16] but there is ample room on both sides.

The ice in Foxe Channel begins to break up in late June or early July and the channel is usually free from the ice cover by August. Freeze-up begins during the latter part of October and is completed by early November.

Foxe Basin. Foxe Basin, north of Foxe Channel, is a large body of water bounded on the west by Melville Peninsula and on the northeast and southeast by Baffin Island. The north section of the basin in the approaches to the Fury and Hecla Strait is characterized by an irregular bottom and has several relatively large islands with a number of dangerous shoals. The Sailing Directions specify that "particular caution must be exercised when navigating there".[17] The greatest depths are found on the west side of the basin along Melville Peninsula, and although only a few soundings are available for the east side, it would appear that it is rather shallow.

The ice regime in Foxe Basin is essentially the same as in Foxe Channel. This regime is summarized in the Sailing Directions as follows: "The ice in Foxe Channel and Foxe Basin can be characterized by its extreme roughness, muddy appearance, large areas of land-fast ice and the fact that the pack is in motion".[18] The ice is predominantly first-year ice, but due to the influence of wind and tide, there is considerable hummocking and ridging with average heights of one to two meters and some as high as five meters. As many as 40 ridges per mile have been counted in northern Foxe Basin. Break-up begins in late June or early July, but significant decreases in the ice cover do not take place until late August. Freeze-up begins in the northern part of Foxe Basin and spreads southward to Foxe Channel during the last week of October and early November.

Fury and Hecla Strait. The Fury and Hecla Strait joins Foxe Basin with the Gulf of Boothia and lies in an east-west direction between the northwest part of Baffin Island to the north and Melville Peninsula to the south. The strait is about 105 miles in length and has a number of relatively large islands at its eastern entrance. The narrowest part of the strait, Labrador Narrows, is 0.5 mile wide south of a 3.9-meter patch. The shallowest known depths in Labrador Narrows vary from about 120 to 205 meters. West of Labrador Narrows the sounded channel, with depths reaching 253 meters, widens to two miles, but a 11.1-meter shoal one mile north east of Freuchen Point restricts its width between Liddon and Ormonde Islands to 1.2 miles.

The ice cover is made up of local ice and it is reported that because of the strength of the current, ice never forms in Labrador Narrows. However, occasionally the current will bring in nearby ice from the Gulf of Boothia. Break-up generally occurs in mid-July, with some ice remaining in August and September, and freeze-up usually develops at about mid-October. The Sailing Directions caution that "in normal years it is out of the question for a ship other than an icebreaker to attempt to reach Bellot Strait by way of Fury and Hecla Strait. This is not only because of the ice that may be in Fury and Hecla Strait, but because of the pack which lies to the west of that strait and south of Crown Prince Frederick Island in the Gulf of Boothia".[19]

So far, only a few ships have used the Fury and Hecla Strait. In September 1948 a U.S. Coast Guard icebreaker transited the strait from west to east and in September 1956 HMCS *Labrador* made the first east to west passage. That fall the *Labrador* actually completed three transits and found only scattered ice floes. In 1975 M.V. *Pandora II* and M.V. *Theta*, both under charter to the Canadian Department of Fisheries and Oceans, used this route in late September when eastbound.

Gulf of Boothia. The Gulf of Boothia is a continuation of Prince Regent Inlet to the north and lies between Boothia Peninsula on the west side and the Brodeur Peninsula on the east. It is free of islands in the middle, and Crown Prince Frederick Island in the distant approaches to the western entrance of Fury and Hecla Strait presents no navigational problem. The track for vessels navigating between the Strait and the Gulf lies well to the south and clear of the island.

The Gulf of Boothia is covered with consolidated ice in winter, a good proportion of which is made up of second and multi-year floes which have come down from Lancaster Sound. Break-up begins somewhat later than in Price Regent Inlet to the north and does not reach the latitude of the Fury and Hecla Strait before mid-September. Freeze-up begins in Committee Bay to the south of the Fury and Hecla Strait in early September but does not develop in the Gulf of Boothia until late September and early October. There may also be an occasional penetration by icebergs that have come down from Lancaster Sound.

Route 5A, through Fury and Hecla Strait and Prince Regent Inlet

A possible variation of Route 5 is to continue north past Bellot Strait into Prince Regent Inlet as far as Barrow Strait and thus join Routes 1 and 2. This is the variation which the Dome Petroleum Company envisaged as a secondary route for vessels to reach the site of its Beaufort Sea operations. However, the shoals found in 1981 make it uncertain that this route could be used for deep-draft vessels.

CONCLUSION

Of the five basic routes of the Northwest Passage, only two are presently suitable for navigation by deep draft ships of Arctic class 7 or better. Such vessels require up to a 20-meter draft, and in both Routes 1 and 2 the water depths are adequate. Route 1, through the Prince of Wales Strait, is the better of the two and the primary route that has been considered by the Dome Petroleum Company because the prevailing ice conditions are less severe. Route 2, through the M'Clure Strait, is usually clogged with polar ice and has seldom been completely navigated by a surface ship. Major leads, however, occasionally develop along the north shore of the strait, as well as along the west coast of Banks Island, and Dome has chosen the M'Clure Strait as a secondary route.

A third possible route for deep draft ships is Route 5A through Fury and Hecla Strait. However, in spite of the fact that it was thrice navigated by HMCS *Labrador* in 1956, the presence of shoals makes this strait a doubtful alternative to Lancaster Sound for deep draft ships.

Routes 3 and 4 are adequate only for small ships because of shoals and constrictions in a number of locations, and the maximum draft for vessels using Route 3A is only five meters.[20]

Chapter 2

THE NORTHWEST PASSAGE BEFORE 1880 – BRITISH PERIOD

In order to express a reasonably accurate opinion as to the legal status of the Northwest Passage, it is important to trace the discovery and the development of that sea route.[21] Since this study pertains only to the waters of the various routes of the Northwest Passage described in Chapter 1, and not to all of the waters of the Canadian Arctic Archipelago, this chapter and the next are confined to tracing the exploration and navigational activities involving the waters of these routes.

Efforts to find a sea route across the top of North America began with John Cabot in 1497 and lasted for nearly 400 years. One of these efforts, the expedition of Sir John Franklin, ended tragically in 1848, and the loss of the expedition led to some twelve years of intensive search. During this search, more than thirty ships wintered in the Canadian Archipelago and the great majority of the various bodies of water related to the Northwest Passage were discovered. Consequently Franklin's expedition may reasonably be used to divide a review of the British expeditions pertaining to the Northwest Passage during this period. The main expeditions are referred to by the year or years of duration and each expedition is identified by the name of its commander. Only those expeditions which contributed to the finding and development of the Northwest Passage are summarized here and shown in Figure 4.*

UP TO FRANKLIN'S EXPEDITION (1576–1847)

Martin Frobisher (1576, 1577, 1578)

Martin Frobisher led three expeditions in search of the Northwest Passage. The first one, sponsored by the Muscovy Company in 1576, led to the discovery of Frobisher Bay and the finding of a piece of stone which was reported to contain gold when returned to England. The 1577 voyage, sponsored by the Cathay Company and Queen Elizabeth I, was intended to mine gold in Frobisher Bay and to search for the Northwest Passage. Frobisher returned to Eng-

* See insert.

land with about 200 tons of ore, which proved to be valueless, and without finding the passage. The last voyage of 1578 was a mining expedition only and it returned to England with over 1,000 tons of worthless ore.

John Davis (1585, 1586, 1587)

In 1585, 1586, and 1587, John Davis made three voyages, sailing along the west coast of Greenland to a point roughly in line with the south coast of Lancaster Sound and then returning south along the south-east coast of Baffin Island and the east coast of Labrador, thereby circumnavigating the strait which today bears his name.

Henry Hudson (1610–11)

In 1610 Henry Hudson sailed along the southern shore of the Hudson Strait and the east coast of Hudson Bay, but his ship was frozen in ice during the winter of 1610–11. After mutiny broke out at the end of June 1611, Hudson and eight others were cast adrift in an open boat and were never heard of again.

T. Button (1612), W. Gibbons (1614), R. Bylot (1615)

Three successive expeditions, Button in 1612, Gibbons in 1614, and Bylot in 1615, all entered the Hudson Strait but were unsuccessful in finding the entrance to the Northwest Passage.

R. Bylot and W. Baffin (1616)

In 1616 Bylot and Baffin followed the west coast of Greenland as far as Smith Sound, turned southward following the coast of Ellesmere Island, crossed Jones Sound, followed the coast of Devon Island, crossed Lancaster Sound, and then continued southward along Bylot and Baffin Islands. Not having realized that Lancaster Sound was indeed a strait and not simply an inlet, Baffin concluded in his report that there was no hope of finding a passage north of Davis Strait. Consequently for nearly 200 years afterwards, explorers concentrated on finding a route through the Hudson Strait.

Jens Munk (1619–20)

Sponsored by the King of Denmark to search for the Northwest Passage by way of the Hudson Strait, Jens Munk reached the west coast of Hudson Bay and coasted south to Churchill River, where scurvy broke out and killed all but two of his 65-man crew. He managed to sail back to Norway the following summer with his two surviving men.

Luke Foxe and Thomas James (1631)

In 1631 two voyages in search of the Northwest Passage were made, one by Luke Foxe and the other by Thomas James, both circumnavigating Hudson Bay. James went as far south as James Bay, and Foxe as far north as the basin now named after him.

C. Middleton (1741)

Following all these unsuccessful voyages, interest in finding the Northwest Passage virtually disappeared and did not revive for over 100 years. In 1741 the British resumed their search for the Northwest Passage and sent two government ships, under Captain C. Middleton, to search again in Hudson Bay for an entrance to the Northwest Passage. After spending a difficult winter at Churchill, during which ten men died of scurvy, the expedition sailed northward along the west coast of Hudson Bay as far as Wager Bay on the west side of Southampton Island and returned without finding an entrance to the passage. However, since William Moor, who was second in command of the expedition, contended that Wager Bay was a strait and probably the entrance sought, the government offered a prize of £20,000 for the discovery of the Northwest Passage.

William Moor and Francis Smith (1746)

In 1746 Captain William Moor sailed for Hudson Bay with two ships, the second one under Captain Francis Smith, hoping to prove that Wager Bay was a strait leading to the Northwest Passage. The voyage being unsuccessful, since Wager Bay proved to be merely an inlet, few attempts were made at finding the Northwest Passage from the east coast during the following 75 years.

James Cook and Charles Clerke (1776–80)

Sent by the British Admiralty to search for a Northwest Passage on the west coast of America, James Cook and Charles Clerke rounded Cape of Good Hope, proceeded eastward as far as the American coast and then northward to the Alaska Peninsula. They then crossed the Bering Strait and rounded the coast of Alaska as far as Icy Cape in the fall of 1778 but were turned back by the ice of the Arctic Ocean. After returning south to Hawaii and despite Cook's death in an incident with the natives, Clerke made a second attempt in 1779 to find the passage but again failed to conquer the pack ice north of Alaska.

Charles Duncan and George Taylor (1791–92)

Sent by the Admiralty to search the coast of Hudson Bay north of Churchill for an entrance to the Northwest Passage, Charles Duncan and George Taylor sailed to Churchill where they were forced to winter. The next spring they reached Chesterfield Inlet on the northwest coast of Hudson Bay but, unable to find a passage from there, returned to England.

George Vancouver and William R. Broughton (1791–95)

Because there were deep inlets that had not been explored by Cook and Clerke, the Admiralty sent an expedition to explore those inlets in the hope of finding a low-latitude entrance to the Northwest Passage. George Vancouver and William R. Broughton surveyed the whole west coast of America as far as Cook Inlet, Alaska, during a period of four years and returned to England by way of Cape Horn.

Sir John Ross (1818)

In 1817 interest in the Northwest Passage was revived when the President of the Royal Society, Sir Joseph Banks, made representations to the government that there had been a warming up of the Arctic in recent years affecting ice conditions and that efforts should be resumed to solve the problem of the Northwest Passage. This being a period of relative inactivity, following the end of the Napoleonic wars in 1815, the government decided to send out two ships under command of John Ross in 1818. The expedition followed roughly the same route as had Bylot and Baffin in 1616, proceeding north along the west coast of Greenland, cutting across to the southeast coat of Ellesmere Island and then south across Jones Sound, and along the coast of Devon Island to Lancaster Sound. However, instead of proceeding into Lancaster Sound, Ross concluded that it was an inlet closed by what he called the "Croker Mountains" and returned to England. However, Lieutenant W.E. Parry, his second in command, openly disagreed with Ross upon their return to England and was given the command of two ships to explore Lancaster Sound and, if possible, pass through to the Bering Strait.

W.E. Parry (1819–20), (1821–23), (1824–25)

In 1819 Parry's expedition proceeded to Lancaster Sound with most of the officers and men who had formed the expedition the previous year with Ross. Parry entered Lancaster Sound at the beginning of August, traversed practically its full length as far west as Maxwell Bay, where heavy ice formed a barrier across the channel. He then returned south into Prince Regent Inlet in the hope of finding another passage to circumvent the ice but, not finding one, he turned back at Fitzgerald Bay on Brodeur Peninsula, retraced his steps to Lancaster Sound and resumed his voyage westward, the ice conditions having improved. He crossed Wellington Channel, west of Devon Island, discovered Cornwallis Island, traversed Barrow Strait completely, followed the north side of Viscount Melville Sound and was turned back by ice at the entrance of the M'Clure Strait, having reached almost the 113th meridian of longitude. The expedition took refuge at Winter Harbour on the south coast of Melville Island.

Parry had shown that Lancaster Sound was indeed the entrance to a great waterway, extending hundreds of miles westward and, at the same time, had qualified for the prize of £5,000 offered by the Board of Longitude to the first vessel crossing the 110th meridian in high northern altitudes.

The next summer, the expedition resumed its voyage but was stopped by heavy ice in the M'Clure Strait at 113° 47′ W. on August 16th and it was decided to turn back. Because of the ice barrier in the M'Clure Strait, Parry was now convinced that the only solution was to try to find a passage at a more southern latitude, starting from the Hudson Strait.

The success of Parry's first voyage having aroused great enthusiasm in England, he was sent by the Admiralty in 1821 to search for a passage along the west coast of Foxe Basin. Parry sailed through the south end of Foxe Basin (what is now Foxe Channel), then crossed the Frozen Strait north of Southampton Island and into Repulse Bay south of Melville Peninsula. Finding no passage through Repulse Bay, he sailed northward along the east coast of the peninsula, wintered at what is now called Winter Island, continued northward the next spring and found the entrance of the Fury and Hecla Strait. Having found this strait, Parry had discovered another entrance, in addition to Lancaster Sound, to the Northwest Passage. Ice conditions prevented him, however, from navigating the Fury and Hecla Strait but his overland journeys confirmed that the strait did lead westward. After spending another winter at Igloolik, he made a second attempt in the summer of 1823 to sail through the Fury and Hecla Strait but without success. Fearing scurvy, he returned to England.

Parry was sent once again by the British Admiralty to try to find a passage through Prince Regent Inlet, which he had discovered in his first voyage of 1819–20. He sailed from London in May 1824 but, because of bad weather and ice, did not reach Lancaster Sound until September. He crossed Lancaster Sound, entered Prince Regent Inlet and wintered at Port Bowen on the west coast of Brodeur Peninsula. In August 1825 one of his ships, the *Fury*, was driven ashore by ice on Somerset Island and was so badly damaged that it had to be abandoned. Parry continued south into Prince Regent Inlet with the remaining ship, *Hecla*, as far as Cresswell Bay. Not finding a westward entrance, Parry returned to England.

Sir John Ross (1829–33)

In 1829 Sir John Ross succeeded in mounting a private expedition and sailed for Prince Regent Inlet by way of Lancaster Sound in an effort to find a westward passage where Parry had failed. He reached Prince Regent Inlet, sailed past Bellot Strait without noticing it, and was stopped by ice in late September at Felix Harbour on Boothia Peninsula, where he ended up by spending three winters without finding a passage westward. In spite of several journeys along the west shore of Prince Regent Inlet, the expedition failed to discover the existence of Bellot Strait, which is sheltered by numerous islands in Brentford Bay hiding its entrance. In 1832 Ross decided to abandon his ship, the *Victory*, and he and his men spent their fourth winter at Fury Beach. The following summer they set out in *Fury*'s boats and reached Lancaster Sound where they were picked up by the whaler *Isabella* and taken back to England.

Sir John Franklin (1845–47)

In 1845, in spite of the realization that the Northwest Passage would have little commercial value but because of the prestige which would be attached to its successful navigation, the Admiralty decided to send another sea-borne expedition. The command was given to Sir John Franklin. Sir John had previously led two land expeditions, one in 1819–1822, and the other in 1825–1827, during which he had reached the mouth of Coppermine River on the south-west coast of Coronation Gulf and also discovered and chartered over 1,000 miles of coastline from Coronation Gulf westward.

Considering Parry's failure to navigate the M'Clure Strait because of the heavy ice barrier in 1819 and 1820, Franklin's instructions were to sail westward through Lancaster Sound and the Barrow Strait as far as Cape Walker, the eastern end of Russell Island, then steer southward into Peel Sound, and finally westward toward the Bering Strait. However, the instructions specified that, "should a permanent obstruction be found to the south-westward of Cape Walker, he is to consider the alternative of passing between Cornwallis Island and Devon if the strait between them (Wellington Channel) is open."[22] Franklin crossed the Atlantic with his two ships, the *Erebus* and *Terror*, sailed north along the west coast of Greenland, and was last seen by a whaling ship on 26 July, making for Lancaster Sound across Baffin Bay.

From the remains of the winter quarters found on Beechey Island and a fragmentary record left at Victory Point on the west coast of King William Island, it has never been possible to reconstruct the tragic events completely. Presumably Franklin could not at first move southward in Peel Sound or could not reach it at all because of ice; he would then have proceeded northward in Wellington Channel to about 77° latitude in the Penny Strait, between Bathurst Island and Grinnell Peninsula of Devon Island, and retreated southward along the east coast of Bathurst Island into the Barrow Strait. He would then have sailed eastward along the south coast of Cornwallis Island as far as the southwest tip of Devon Island, at Erebus Bay, spending the winter on Beechey Island at the entrance of the bay. There the expedition spent about ten months, and three men died before summer arrived.

It is presumed that Franklin's expedition sailed from Beechey Island in August or September 1846 and must have headed for Peel Sound. By 12 September the ship lay beset off the northwest coast of King William Island, at the entrance of the Victoria Strait. Franklin died in June 1847, the command of the ships being taken over by Captain Francis Crozier. In April 1848, Crozier abandoned the ships, with 105 officers and men then surviving, and they began a march southward toward Back River, located at the southern tip of Rasmussen Basin. From accounts given by Eskimos, it seems that they all died en route from starvation or scurvy. The last surviving members of the expedition, about 30 men or so, probably died at Starvation Cove on Adelaide Peninsula south of Simpson Strait.

Although Franklin did not succeed in navigating the Northwest Passage, his expedition was the first to sail from the Barrow Strait to King William Island and, by crossing the island and the Simpson Strait (albeit on foot) to the mainland, also effectively discovered what became one of the routes of the Northwest Passage, Route 3.

SEARCH FOR FRANKLIN'S EXPEDITION (1847–1859)

During this 12-year period in search for Franklin and his men, over seventy expeditions, as shown in Figure 5,* both government and private, were sent to the Canadian Arctic. The summary which follows will be limited to expeditions that discovered or further explored bodies of water which presently constitute the various routes of the Northwest Passage. Indeed, during this period all the routes were either discovered or developed.

Sir James Clark Ross (1848–49)

Three years having passed without any news from Franklin, the British government despatched three expeditions, one led by Sir James Clark Ross, who was making his seventh voyage to the Arctic and was to follow the route which had been recommended to Franklin in his official instructions. A second, under the command of Captain Henry Kellett, was to survey the Bering Strait approach-

* See insert.

es. A third expedition, an overland party under the command of Sir John Richardson, was to follow the Canadian coast eastward from the mouth of the Mackenzie River. Only the Ross expedition in the Northwest Passage is reviewed here. Ross sailed through Lancaster Sound into the Barrow Strait, but found the strait completely blocked with ice between Cornwallis Island and Somerset Island. He wintered, therefore, at Port Leopold on the northeast coast of Somerset Island. In the spring of 1849, he led sled parties along the north and west coasts of Somerset Island and down Peel Sound, nearly as far as the Bellot Strait. However, considering the state of the ice in Peel Sound, he did not think that Franklin's ships could have passed that way and turned back.

James Saunders (1849–50)

At the end of May 1849, Captain James Saunders sailed from London, commanding a store ship to provide supplies for Ross' expedition as well as Franklin's. Unfortunately he was caught in the pack in Baffin Bay, where he was confined for some two months, and he was eventually driven into Wolstenholme Sound on the northwest coast of Greenland, where he spent the winter. After being released from the ice on 1 August 1850, he resumed his trip, crossing Lancaster Sound as far as prince Regent Inlet. Unable to land his supplies at Port Leopold, he left a depot at Navy Board Inlet on the west side of Byot Island and returned to England.

Horatio T. Austin (1850–51)

A complete and well-equipped expedition to the Arctic was headed in 1850 by Captain Horatio T. Austin, comprising two sailing vessels, two screw steamers, and provisions for three years. The captain of one ship, the *Assistance*, Erasmus Ommanney, was the first to cross Lancaster Sound and arrived at Cape Riley on the southwest coast of Devon Island on 23 August. There, he found the first traces of the missing Franklin expedition, namely, remains of the 1845–46 winter quarters. No record had been left behind, but from the state of the camp and the articles found, it was concluded that Franklin's expedition had left in haste.

Prevented by ice from going northward in Wellington Channel, the Austin expedition proceeded westward in the Barrow Strait. The squadron became beset in the ice between Cornwallis and Griffiths Islands and had to spend the winter there. However, sled journeys were organized and they explored the north and west coasts of Price of Wales Island, as well as most of the small islands in the western part of Barrow Strait. The sled parties also explored the whole of the northern side of Viscount Melville Sound as far as Liddon Gulf on the south side of Melville Island, off the M'Clure Strait.

William Penny (1850–51)

The British Admiralty sent out another expedition to the Arctic in 1850, consisting of two ships and provisioned for three years, headed by William Penny. The expedition crossed Lancaster Sound and joined Austin's ships at Beechey Island, where it helped search the island and found the graves of some of Franklin's men. The expedition wintered in Assistance Bay, on the south side of Cornwallis Island, and in the spring and summer of 1851, carried out a search, partly by sled and partly by boat, along the shores of Wellington Channel as far north as Grinnell Peninsula. The search included the west coast of Devon Island and the south and north coasts of Cornwallis Island.

Sir John Ross (1850–51)

Sir John Ross, at the age of 73, came out of retirement and managed to convince the Hudson's Bay Company to sponsor an expedition consisting of two small ships. He left Scotland on 23 May 1850 and arrived at Beechey Island on 27 August, shortly after Ommanney had made his discovery. He wintered in Assistance Bay and the following summer made a further search of Beechey Island. Becoming short of provisions, he returned to Scotland in September, leaving one of his ships to be available to assist in the search.

C.C. Forsyth (1850)

Captain C.C. Forsyth, sponsored by Lady Franklin, set sail from Aberdeen on 5 June 1850 and arrived at Port Leopold at the end of August. He sailed south in Prince Regent Inlet as far as Fury Beach but was prevented by heavy ice from going further. Retreating north to Beechey Island, where he found the record left by Ommanney saying that he had located traces of Franklin's expedition at Cape Riley, Forsyth made one more attempt to enter Prince Regent Inlet and then sailed back for Great Britain with the news of Ommanney's discovery.

Edwin J. De Haven (1850–51)

In May 1850, the Brooklyn Navy Yard in the United States despatched an Arctic expedition, consisting of two ships, headed by Lieutenant Edwin J. De Haven, with the intention of sailing north in Wellington Channel. The expedition did reach the entrance of Wellington Channel, but the ships were frozen in and by 21 September had drifted to its northern part. Some time later in the fall they drifted back southward into Lancaster Sound and in the spring drifted eastward out of Lancaster Sound. The expedition finally sailed home in June 1851.

William Kennedy (1851–52)

In 1851 Lady Franklin sent out the *Prince Albert* for the second time, under the command of Captain William Kennedy and with Lieutenant Joseph Bellot of the French navy. Lady Franklin's instructions were to search the coast of Boothia Peninsula. The expedition proceeded across Lancaster Sound, down Prince Regent Inlet as far as Batty Bay, where it was forced by ice to spend the winter. In the spring of 1852, a sled party set out to explore the coast of Boothia Peninsula; it was during this journey that Lieutenant Bellot noticed a column of rising vapor at the head of Brentford Bay on the east coast and upon investigation discovered that the vapor came from open waters in a narrow strait (which now bears his name) separating Somerset Island from Boothia Peninsula. The party followed the strait to its western entrance and crossed the southern end of Peel Sound to Prince of Wales Island. They then travelled overland to Ommanney Bay and returned to the vessels at Batty Bay by way of Prince of Wales Island and the north coast of Somerset Island. The expedition sailed back to England in October 1852, having discovered Bellot Strait, one of the links of the Northwest Passage, but without any trace of the Franklin expedition.

E.A. Inglefield (1852, 1854)

In July 1852 E.A. Inglefield set out in a single ship to explore Smith and Jones Sounds. He sailed along the west coast of Greenland as far north as 78° 21′ north latitude in Smith Sound. He then returned southward along the east coast of Ellesmere Island, entered Jones Sound about a third of the way, turned back and proceeded southward along Devon Island and westward into Lancaster Sound as far as Beechey Island where he arrived on 7 September. He left the next day with mail for England.

In 1854 Captain Inglefield set out for Beechey Island with two ships for the purpose of landing stores and obtaining further information on the search for Franklin's expedition. He did accomplish his mission, although he lost his transport ship, the *Breadalbane*, on 21 August off Beechey Island when she gave way under pressure of the ice and sank within 15 minutes.

Robert M'Clure (1850–54)

Robert M'Clure commanded the *Investigator*, which was part of a two-ship expedition to the Arctic headed by Sir Richard Collinson, who commanded the *Enterprise*. They sailed together for the Bering Strait in 1850 but the ships became separated in the South Pacific after crossing the Strait of Magellan and, after that, each pursued the search for Franklin independently. M'Clure reached the Bering Strait without incident and proceeded eastward along the mainland coast to the vicinity of Cape Parry. He then crossed Amundsen Gulf, continued northward in the Prince of Wales Strait to approximately 30 miles from its northern opening into Viscount Melville Sound where he was stopped by ice. He wintered in Prince of Wales Strait and explored the north coast of Banks Island, as well as both shores of the Prince of Wales Strait.

In the summer of 1851, unable again to enter Viscount Melville Sound, M'Clure retraced his steps southward through the Prince of Wales Strait, rounded the south coast of Banks Island and then proceeded along its west coast. He advanced eastward along the north coast of Banks Island but, because of the heavy ice in the M'Clure Strait, had to set up winter quarters at Mercy Bay without completely navigating the full length of the strait. In April 1852, sled parties were sent out, one of which was led by M'Clure himself. His party completed the crossing of the strait in a northeasterly direction to Winter Harbour on the southeast coast of Melville Island. They left a record which was found by Captain Henry Kellett's sledge party (Belcher Expedition) in October 1852, which resulted in their rescue the following spring. In so crossing the strait which now bears his name, M'Clure had established the last link in one of the routes of the Northwest Passage. For this feat, in spite of protest on the part of some, M'Clure and his crew were awarded the Admiralty prize of £10,000.

Sir Richard Collinson (1850–55)

Sir Richard Collinson, commanding the *Enterprise*, reached the Bering Strait a week later than M'Clure. He found the coast of Alaska closed by ice and, after attempting unsuccessfully to penetrate norhtward into the Beaufort Sea, turned back and wintered at Hong Kong. In the summer of 1851, he navigated along the mainland coast and, like M'Clure, crossed Amundsen Gulf and entered the Prince of Wales Strait. Also, like M'Clure, he was prevented from reaching Viscount Melville Sound because of ice. He wintered in Walker Bay, at the southwest corner of Victoria Island, and sent out sled parties to search for both M'Clure and Franklin. Those parties failed to reach Winter Harbour and brought back no news of either M'Clure or Franklin.

The next summer, Collinson followed M'Clure's track around the southern tip of Banks Island and about half way along its west coast but, finding no trace of the *Investigator*, he turned back to continue his search for Franklin in the numerous inlets and straits south of Victoria Island. He crossed the bodies water now known as the Dolphin and Union Strait, Coronation Gulf, and the Dease Strait as far as Cambridge Bay on the southeast coast of Victoria Island. He spent the winter of 1852–53 at Cambridge Bay and, the next spring, continued his search along the south and east coasts of Victoria Island as far as M'Clintock Channel.

During Collinson's search of the east coast of Victoria Island, he came to about fifty miles west of the position where Franklin's ships had been abandoned. He actually found some wooden fragments and part of a ship's hatchway which he believed must have come from Franklin's ships. Unfortunately the high ridges of ice in M'Clintock Channel prevented him from crossing to the eastern shore where he might have discovered the fate of the Franklin expedition. He considered the idea of waiting for next spring to sail up Victoria Strait, which he correctly believed connected in some way with Peel Sound, but his supply of coal was low and he decided to return westward. He retraced his route through the Dolphin and Union Strait and wintered in Camden Bay on the north coast of Alaska. He reached England in the spring of 1855 by way of the Cape of Good Hope.

Sir Edward Belcher (1852–54)

Sir Edward Belcher's search expedition in 1852 was the largest sent to the Arctic. It consisted of five of His Majesty's ships: *Assistance, Resolute, Pioneer, Intrepid* and *North Star*, which set out on 21 April 1852. After reaching Beechey Island on 12 August and examining the relics of the Franklin expedition, Belcher decided to leave the depot ship, *North Star*, at Beechey Island under the command of W.J.S. Pullen and to proceed with the remaining ships of the expedition. The *Resolute* and *Intrepid*, headed by Captain Henry Kellett, were to sail west into Barrow Strait, and the other two ships, *Pioneer* and *Assistance*, under the command of Belcher himself, were to go north up Wellington Channel.

Belcher entered Wellington Channel, traversed Queens Channel, and entered the Penny Strait on the west coast of Grinnell Peninsula, where he wintered in Northumberland Sound. In the spring, sledging parties were sent out west and explored the north coast of Bathurst Island, crossed Byam Martin Channel, explored Sabine Peninsula and the southeast part of Melville Island. During the summer of 1853, Belcher retraced his steps in Wellington Channel, further exploring the area, but to no avail.

In the fall of 1853, the ships were forced over to the east side of the channel up to Baring Bay on Devon Island, where the ice did not break up until the first week of August 1854. The ice pressure was such that Belcher feared for the safety of his ship and decided to abandon it, as well as the ships of Kellett. He then proceeded with all the crews to Beechey Island, where they joined the remaining part of M'Clure's men from the *Investigator*, and they all boarded the *North Star* and began to sail for England. Fortunately Captain Inglefield had arrived back at Beechey Island with his two ships in time to relieve some of the crowding aboard the *North Star*, and all three ships returned to England together.

Henry Kellett (1852–54)

Captain Henry Kellett's orders were to proceed to Winter Harbour on Melville Island, deposit provisions for the crew of the *Investigator*, and despatch travelling parties during the spring to the north by Byam Martin Channel and to the west by Melville Island. It was found impossible to enter Winter Harbour and therefore the ships withdrew to Dealy Island at the entrance to Bridport Inlet, where they established quarters for the winter of 1852–53. During the fall, preparations were made for the sledging program for the next spring. The record left at Winter Harbour by M'Clure was found and the next spring a sledging party went to Mercy Bay across the strait where they found the last of M'Clure's crew, some 61 in all. They were unable to face a fourth winter and were brought to Dealey Island after abandoning the *Investigator* at Mercy Bay. Twelve of them were then taken to Beechey Island to board the *North Star*.

In the same spring of 1853, two main sledge parties were sent out to explore the area, one covering over 1,000 nautical miles and the other over 1,200 nautical miles, exploring all of the coast and sounds of Melville and Prince Patrick Islands. Considering his mission accomplished, although he had found no trace of Franklin, Kellett started his return trip eastward toward Beechey Island. Unfortunately he could only get as far as Cape Cockburn on the southwest tip of Bathurst Island.

While awaiting further instructions from Belcher, the expedition commander, Kellett sent out a party to search along the Prince of Wales Strait for Captain Collinson, who had sailed in the *Enterprise* for the Bering Strait in 1850. During this journey, the sledge party, led by G.F. Meecham, covered some 1,500 nautical miles in 71 days and, as well, discovered Collinson's records of his exploration during 1851–52. The instructions from Belcher having arrived, Kellett abandoned his ships at Cape Cockburn and with all his crew proceeded to Beechey Island. There they joined Belcher's crew and boarded the *North Star* under the command of Commander W.J.S. Pullen. The total sledging distance accomplished by Kellett's parties amounted to over 15,000 miles in two years, more than 2,000 of which where along new coastlines in areas adjacent to the Northwest Passage.

W.J.S. Pullen (1852–54)

As indicated when summarizing the Belcher expedition, *North Star* had remained at Beechey Island under the command of Commander W.J.S. Pullen, with instructions to establish depots along the east side of Wellington Channel. Pullen himself made a journey by boat from Erebus Bay to Maxwell Bay on the south coast of Devon Island. In the spring of 1854, Pullen explored Wellington Channel by dog team, crossing Queens Channel on his return journey to the *North Star.* Also, in March and April 1854, a sledge party paid a visit to Port Leopold on the south side of Barrow Strait.

Dr. John Rae (1853–54)

Dr. John Rae, who was in the employ of the Hudson's Bay Company, made some four overland journeys along the Arctic coast from 1847 to 1854. In April 1847, nearly two months before Franklin's death, Rae journeyed to within 150 miles east of Franklin's expedition without realizing how close he had come to finding the expedition. In 1853 he was sent by the Hudson's Bay Company to complete the coastal survey in the same general area, and it was then that he discovered that there was a strait between "King William Land" and Boothia Peninsula. The strait now named after him linked the Simpson Strait to the south of King William Island with the James Ross Strait to the north.

It was during this journey that Rae questioned natives, who told him of the fate of the Franklin expedition and from whom he obtained the crested silver and personal effects which unquestionably had belonged to members of the expedition. His report satisfied the British authorities as to the fate of the expedition and he received the reward of £10,000 as a result. The British authorities, however, did ask the Hudson's Bay Company to send a party to confirm Rae's finding. This was done by a small expedition in 1855, headed by James Anderson and James G. Steward, which found additional relics on Montreal Island off the southern tip of King William Island.

Dr. E.K. Kane (1853–55)

Dr. E.K. Kane led the second American expedition in the Arctic and chose the Smith Sound route to the north instead of Lancaster Sound in the belief that when the Franklin expedition went north in Wellington Channel, it had reached the Arctic Ocean, where it became imprisoned by ice. Some doubted this belief since the expedition continued after the news of Dr. Rae's discovery of the remains of the expedition. Be that as it may, Dr. Kane's expedition sailed northward along the Greenland coast, then up Smith Sound and Kennedy Channel as far as a basin which now bears his name at 70° 45′ north latitude. He then turned southward and followed the coast of Ellesmere Island, then back to the Greenland coast. All this was done during a period of two years, during which Kane encountered numerous difficulties, including sickness and death of some of his crew, leading to the abandonment of his ship *Advance* in Smith Sound. He ended up being rescued by a Danish ship in June 1855.

Sir F. Leopold M'Clintock (1857–59)

Lady Franklin, hesitating to accept completely Dr. Rae's report of the fate of her husband's expedition, even though confirmed by a special expedition of the Hudson's Bay Company, outfitted yet another vessel, the *Fox*, under the command of Captain F. Leopold M'Clintock. The expedition left Aberdeen on 1 July 1857, but became stuck in the ice in Baffin Bay and was not released until the end of April 1858. After having had his ship refitted in Greenland, he made his way to Lancaster Sound, entered the Barrow Strait, and began to enter Peel Sound. Forced back by ice, he returned east along the northern coast of Sommerset Island and then proceeded southward in Prince Regent Inlet. Failing to pass through the Bellot Strait, he wintered there and, in the spring of 1859, sent a sledging party to King William Island. It was south of Cape Felix, on the north tip of King William Island, that the only written record of the Franklin expedition was found. The expedition explored the coast of King William Island completely and did find other relics of Franklin's expedition along the route, thus definitely confirming Franklin's unfortunate fate.

AFTER THE SEARCH FOR FRANKLIN'S EXPEDITION (1859–1880)

The main routes of the Northwest Passage and the fate of Franklin's expedition having been discovered, British interest in the Northwest Passage came virtually to an end. Some fifteen years later, however, the Admiralty felt that it would be good for its prestige to have a ship navigate the Northwest Passage to the Pacific Ocean in one season. Consequently in 1875 the *Pandora* was sent out under the command of Sir Allen Young to "visit the western coast of Greenland, thence to proceed through Baffin's Sea, Lancaster Sound, and the Barrow Strait, towards the magnetic pole, and if practicable, to navigate through the Northwest Passage to the Pacific Ocean in one season".[23] Sir Allen sailed out of Plymouth on 28 June 1875, proceeded to the Greenland coast, called at some of the ports, and sailed for Lancaster Sound and into the Barrow Strait, reaching Beechey Island. The expedition then proceeded across Barrow Strait, down Peel Sound, and almost reached the latitude of Bellot Strait on 2 September, when the danger of besetment by ice was such that he decided to turn back and retrace his route through Lancaster Sound.

This expedition was the only one which took place between 1859 and 1880 with the object of navigating the Northwest Passage. Sir Allen Young had intended to make a second attempt in 1876 but changed his plans when he received a request from the Admiralty to rendez-vous with the Nares expedition, which was attempting to reach the North Pole by Smith Sound, and he limited himself to that mission.

THE NORTHWEST PASSAGE AND BRITISH WHALERS (1751–1880)

Before substitutes for whale oil and baleen were found around 1915, whaling in Arctic waters north of Canada was very common. The total number of Bowhead whales killed from 1719 to 1915 is estimated to have exceeded 38,000.[24] Three whaling grounds were exploited: the Davis Strait-Baffin Bay fishery, the Hudson Bay fishery[25] and the Beaufort Sea fishery.[26] The following review of whaling activities will be limited to the first whaling ground, which included the eastern approaches to the Northwest Passage and was eventually extended to the eastern straits of the passage itself. Whaling activities thus contributed to the development of navigation in the Northwest Passage.

The Davis Strait-Baffin Bay whaling ground is by far the oldest of the three fisheries and its exploitation by Dutch whalers goes back to at least around 1700. The Dutch dominated the fishery throughout the eighteenth century although there were also whaleships from Germany, the United States, and Great Britain. The Dutch and German whalers virtually ceased their activities by 1800 and were replaced by the British who dominated the fishery from 1814 to the end of whaling in that fishery in 1911. During this period, the British sent some 2,575 ships to those waters.[27] Their only competitors, the American whalers, sent 173 ships there during the same period.[28]

It appears that the British whalers began to follow the whale as far north as the Lancaster Sound area at about the same time as those waters were reached by the British expeditions in search for the Northwest Passage. Indeed, it is known that in 1817, the year before Sir John Ross' first Arctic voyage, two Scottish whalers were exploiting the rich whaling grounds off Lancaster Sound. And after Ross' voyage, British whaling definitely turned more to this area.[29]

Pond Inlet was the traditional rendezvous for whalers, but gradually they extended their activities into Navy Board Inlet, west of Bylot Island, and eventually for considerable distances into the Barrow Strait and Prince Regent Inlet. By 1874 whaling voyages to Prince Regent Inlet had become commonplace and one whaling ship is reported to have gone north in Wellington Channel, west of Devon Island. Other whaling ships sailed farther westward into the Barrow Strait when conditions permitted.[30]

Chapter 3

THE NORTHWEST PASSAGE AFTER 1880 – CANADIAN PERIOD

In 1880 Great Britain transferred to Canada all her British territories and possessions in North America not already included within the Dominion of Canada as well as all the islands adjacent to any such territories or possessions with the exception of the Colony of Newfoundland. This was meant to be a transfer to Canada of the Arctic islands that Great Britain had discovered and explored during the prior 300 years or so. The transfer was effected by Order-in-Council dated 31 July 1880, which specified that it was to take effect on September 1st of the same year. Canada, however, appeared to have no need to explore further or patrol the Arctic Islands and waters before some twenty-three years had elapsed, specifically in 1903.[31] This was also the year in which Amundsen set out to cross the Northwest Passage.

This chapter describes the first actual sailing of the Northwest Passage, outlines the Canadian patrols and expeditions in the Northwest Passage from 1903 to the end of 1945 and reviews the navigation which has taken place in the Northwest Passage since 1945. The chapter concludes with a summary of the current Canadian Coast Guard and naval activities in the Northwest Passage.

FIRST SAILING OF THE NORTHWEST PASSAGE (1903–06)

Although only British ships had sailed the Northwest Passage before the transfer of British territory to Canada in 1880, with the single exception of De Haven to Wellington Channel in 1850–51, the first actual sailing of the Northwest Passage after the transfer was not made by a Canadian ship. That honor went to the Norwegian explorer, Roald Amundsen, in the same way that the first sailing of the full length of the Northeast Passage was not made by a Russian navigator but rather by a Swedish explorer, Captain A.E. Nordenskiöld, in 1878–79.

Amundsen set out from Norway in May 1903 with his little 47-ton herring boat, *Gjoa*. He navigated to Greenland, followed its west coast as far north as Dalrymple Rock, crossed Baffin Bay, and entered Lancaster Sound on 20 August. He reached the well-known Beechey Island on 22 August, where he took a series of magnetic observations, and then sailed south in Peel Sound, the Franklin Strait, the James Ross Strait, and the Rae Strait. Upon entering the Simpson Strait, south of King William Island, he found a safe place to pass the winter and where he did in fact spend the following two winters. The place in question is now appropriately called Gjoa Haven.

In the spring of 1905, Amundsen made his way through the heavy ice of the Simpson Strait and proceeded west along the Canadian coast through Queen Maud Gulf, the Dease Strait, Coronation Gulf, and the Dolphin and Union Strait. In so navigating from James Ross Strait to Queen Maud Gulf, Amundsen had thus completed the last unsailed link in one of the routes of the Northwest Passage (Route 3A). He continued his route westward across Amundsen Gulf and along the Canadian coast as far as King Point on the Yukon coast, where he was forced by ice to spend the winter. In the summer of the following year, he completed his journey by arriving at Nome, Alaska, in August 1906.

CANADIAN EXPEDITIONS AND PATROLS (1903–1945)

Having felt the need to consolidate its title to the Arctic islands and its control over the water areas, including those of the Northwest Passage, the Canadian government sent a number of expeditions to the Arctic beginning in 1903, as shown in Figure 6. It established an Eastern Arctic Patrol in 1922 as well as posts of the Royal Canadian Mounted Police at various points along the east coast of the Canadian Arctic Archipelago from which extensive patrols were carried out by Mounted Police detachments. A brief review of the expeditions and patrols which contributed to the development of navigation in the Northwest Passage follows.

A.P. Low (1903–04)

Although previous Canadian expeditions had been made to the Arctic with the voyages of A.R. Gordon (1884 and 1886) and W. Wakeham (1897), those voyages had as their primary purpose the assertion of Canada's sovereignty in areas visited by some American whalers and did not extend north of Cumberland Sound. The expeditions, however, did establish stations for observing ice conditions in the Hudson Strait and thus helped develop navigation in part of the Fury and Hecla route of the Northwest Passage. In 1903 the government of Canada decided to send the *Neptune*, under the charge of A.P. Low, "to patrol the waters of Hudson Bay and those adjacent to the eastern Arctic islands."[32]

Expedition leader Low was accompanied by Captain S.W. Bartlett, Master of *The Neptune*, Major J.D. Moodie of the Northwest Mounted Police, and five other members of that force as well as a crew of twenty-nine and a scientific

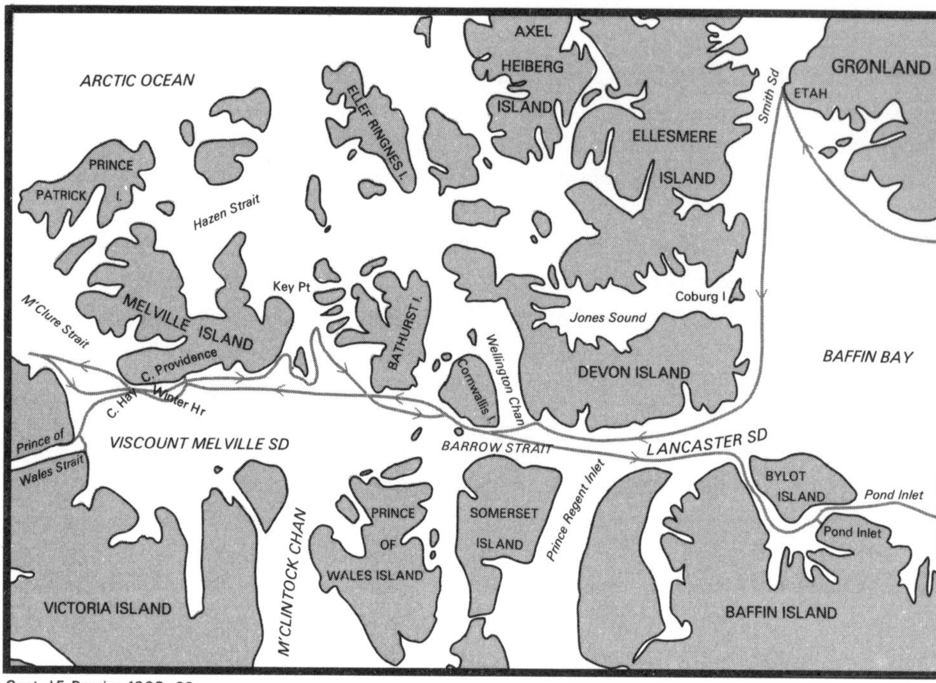

Capt. J.E. Bernier, 1908 - 09.

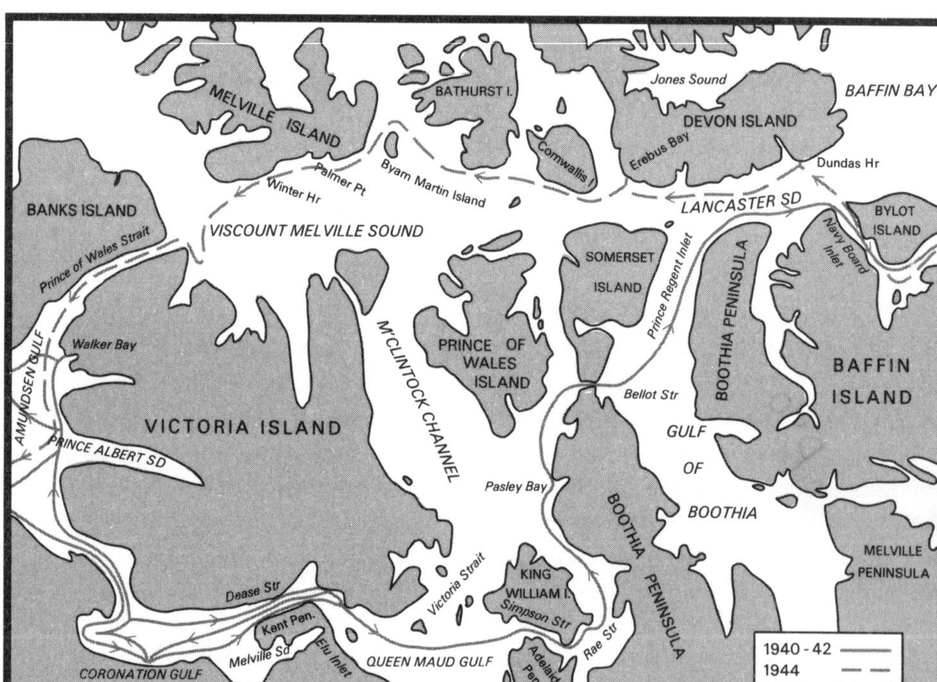

R.C.M.P. schooner St. Roch, 1940 - 44.

Fig. 6 : TWO OF CANADA'S EXPEDITIONS IN THE NORTHWEST PASSAGE : 1908 - 09 AND 1940 - 44

Prepared for the author by the Canadian Hydrographic Service, Dept. of Fisheries and Oceans, Ottawa.
from maps in A. Taylor, Geographical Discovery and Exploration in the Queen Elizabeth Islands (1955), at pp 115 and 130

staff of five. The Order-in-Council appointed Low as Fishery Officer for Canada, with authority to exercise the powers of a justice of the peace for all purposes of the fisheries laws and regulations. Major Moodie was appointed customs officer and magistrate. The instructions specified that the vessel was being sent "for the purpose of patrolling, exploring, and establishing the authority of the Government of Canada in the waters and islands of Hudson Bay, and the north thereof."[33]

The Low expedition spent the first year in the Hudson Bay region, wintering at Fullerton Harbor on the northwest coast and sailed northward the next summer for Smith Sound. It then proceeded south, turned westward into Lancaster Sound, and sailed into the Barrow Strait as far as Beechey Island on the southwest coast of Devon Island. Low then crossed over to Port Leopold on the south side of the Barrow Strait, where he hoisted the Canadian flag and deposited a copy of the Customs regulations in the boiler of the *Investigator's* steam launch, left there by Sir James Clarke Ross in 1849. He then sailed back to Pond Inlet, following the southshore of Lancaster Sound.

J.E. Bernier (1904–05)

In September 1904, Captain J.E. Bernier, in command of the CGS *Arctic*, with Major Moodie, as expedition leader, sailed from Quebec to patrol Hudson Bay and establish a divisional police headquarters at Churchill. They crossed the Hudson Strait and navigated Hudson Bay as far north as Cape Fullerton, where a police post had been established the year before, and they wintered there. They attempted to sail for Churchill the next summer but were prevented from doing so by ice. Moodie transferred to the *Neptune* when they met her in September and Bernier returned to Quebec with the *Arctic* for repairs.

J.E. Bernier (1906–07)

At the beginning of the century, Canada acquired a German-built ship, the *Gauss*, which had been designed for Antarctic navigation in such a way as to allow the ship to lift with the pressure of the ice because of its spoon-shaped bow, a design similar to Fritdjhof Nansen's *Fram* and Amundsen's *Gjoa*. The *Gauss* was renamed by the Canadian government as the CGS *Arctic*, which thereafter made some eight voyages to the Arctic. On seven of those voyages Captain Bernier was in command of the ship, and three of the voyages reached the Northwest Passage. In all the voyages Captain Bernier planted the Canadian flag and took formal possession for Canada of all the various areas he visited. What follows is a brief account of Bernier's first voyage in the Northwest Passage.

On 15 July 1906 the *Arctic* sailed from Quebec and proceeded directly to

Lancaster Sound, entering Navy Board Inlet and Eclipse Sound to Pond Inlet. Bernier then went back to Lancaster Sound, proceeded to Beechey Island, and continued his voyage westward along the north side of the Barrow Strait and Viscount Melville Sound as far as Arctic Point at the southeast tip of Melville Island. Captain Bernier then started his return voyage to Pond Inlet, which he completed by 10 September and during which he partly entered Peel Sound and fully explored Admiralty Inlet.

After spending the winter near Pond Inlet in Albert Harbour, Bernier sailed across the mouth of Lancaster Sound as far as Coburg Island at the entrance to Jones Sound. After a "taking of possession" ceremony at Edwards Point, Bernier returned to Lancaster Sound and at Port Leopold he made a quick sortie into Prince Regent Inlet to a point south of the Bellot Strait. Bernier returned to Lancaster Sound, navigated north to Jones Sound and to King Edward VII Point on the southeast tip of Ellesmere Island, and terminated his voyage with another formal ceremony of "taking of possession" at the Point.

J.E. Bernier (1908–09)

On 28 July 1908 the *Arctic* sailed from Quebec, made for the coast of Greenland, proceeded to Etah in Smith Sound, where she landed stores for the explorer Dr. F.A. Cook, then sailed for Lancaster Sound. She anchored at Erebus Bay on 24 August, then coasted along the south shore of Cornwallis Island, and continued west as far as Cape Providence on the south side of Melville Sound, encountering very little ice. With respect to the M'Clure Strait, Bernier reported "no ice was visible to the westward, but heavy Arctic ice was seen to the southward; we were then about half way through M'Clure Strait, and if our instructions had included making the Northwest Passage, I feel confident that it could have been made".[34]

The *Arctic* then wintered at Winter Harbour and remained there until 12 August the following year. During the winter, several journeys were made to Banks Island and the Prince of Wales Strait, as well as along the south coast of Melville Island. Sailing back from Melville Island in the summer of 1909, Bernier made attempts to go up along the east coast of Melville Island and around Byam Martin Island in order to make soundings, but without success. He did manage, however, to go up Austin Channel a considerable distance and then sailed back to Pond Inlet by Navy Board Inlet. This expedition explored no new coastline, but Bernier complied with his instructions "as to the waters to be patrolled, explored, and lands to be annexed in continuation of the two voyages already made to northern waters by the same ship, commanded by myself".[35]

J.E. Bernier (1910–11)

Having regretted the opportunity missed in his last voyage to complete the Northwest Passage, Captain Bernier obtained instructions in 1910 "to patrol Davis strait, Baffin bay, Lancaster sound, Barrow strait, Viscount Melville sound, M'Clure strait and Beaufort sea to Herschel island, thence through Behring strait to Vancouver or Victoria, B.C.". The instructions specified however that "the advisability of attempting to make the northwest passage is, however, left to your judgment after ascertaining the ice conditions on the spot".[36]

The *Arctic* sailed from Quebec on 7 July 1910 and followed much the same course as in its preceding voyage, except that it encountered much more ice than in 1908. Bernier proceeded in the Northwest Passage as far as Winter Harbour, where he stopped just long enough to erect a shelter for emergency stores, and sailed westward on 2 September. He reached Cape Dundas in the M'Clure Strait, but since there was no open water ahead, he had to make a hasty retreat eastward and then encountered large floes of polar ice around the east end of Melville Island and south of Byam Martin Island. He proceeded eastward as far as Admiralty Inlet, which he entered and set up winter quarters at Arctic Bay. The following summer Bernier took the *Arctic* to Pond Inlet, then sailed back to Lancaster Sound and into Prince Regent Inlet with the intention of reaching Hudson Bay by way of the Fury and Hecla Strait, but was prevented from doing so by heavy ice conditions. He therefore returned to Baffin Bay to visit whaling stations and then continued to Quebec. This voyage was to be the last chance for Bernier to make the Northwest Passage, which had escaped him.

Vilhjalmur Stefansson (1913–18)

Although Bernier's 1910–11 journey was the last seaborne expedition to the Arctic before World War I, an official land and sea expedition was sent out in 1913 under the leadership of Vilhjalmur Stefansson. During this five-year expedition, Stefansson practically completed the geographical discovery of the Arctic, including all remaining major islands. He brought back scientific information of various kinds, including ice conditions in numerous bodies of water, including the M'Clure Strait and the whole eastern part of Beaufort Sea.

EASTERN ARCTIC PATROL (1922–1944)

In order to ensure a better protection of Canada's interests in the Arctic, the Canadian government decided to create the Eastern Arctic Patrol. To assist in the implementation of the patrol, the government had to establish police posts and customs houses at various points, in particular along the eastern coasts of the Canadian Arctic islands.

The first Eastern Arctic Patrol was headed by J.D. Craig and was sent out in 1922 with the CGS *Arctic* under the command of Captain Bernier, who also commanded the *Arctic* for the next three Eastern Arctic patrols in 1923, 1924, and 1925. During the four voyages, at least four Royal Canadian Mounted Police posts were established along the eastern coast. On the 1923 patrol, Bernier once again entered the Northwest Passage and sailed as far as Beechey Island off the southwest coast of Devon Island.

The Eastern Arctic Patrol continued to make voyages to the Arctic every year at least up to 1944. From 1933 to 1940 inclusively, the patrol was carried out by the Hudson's Bay Company vessel, RMS *Nascopie*. In 1937, during the course of her patrol, the *Nascopie* established a Hudson Bay Post at Fort Ross at the eastern entrance of the Bellot Strait. There she met the Hudson Bay Schooner *Aklavik*, which had sailed through the strait from the west. They exchanged furs and then each ship returned the way it had come. In a limited way, it was the first internal commercial use of the Northwest Passage. This exchange was repeated in 1938.[37]

PATROLS OF THE ROYAL CANADIAN MOUNTED POLICE (1929, 1940–44)

Posts of the Royal Canadian Mounted Police began to be established with the first Eastern Arctic Patrol in 1922, and the police detachments did not lose any time in assisting in the consolidation of Canada's presence and control over the whole of the Canadian Arctic Archipelago. The presence of those police officers across the Canadian Arctic became so widely felt that it was regarded as the symbol of Canadian sovereignty and control over the whole area. During the quarter-century after the establishment of the Eastern Arctic Patrol, two of the most notable patrols by the police were directly related to the Northwest Passage. One was an overland patrol by Staff Sergeant A.H. Joy in 1929 and the other was a seaborne patrol by Staff Sergeant Henry Larsen in 1940–44.

A.H. Joy (1929)

Probably the most notable of the numerous journeys of Staff Sergeant A.H. Joy was the 1929 winter-spring patrol by sledge from Dundas Harbour at the eastern entrance of Lancaster Sound as far as Winter Harbour on Melville Island. He returned by a northeasterly route across the Queen Elizabeth Islands, crossing over the ice cap of Ellemere island and completed his journey at the

Royal Canadian Mounted Police post located at Bache Peninsula on the east coast of Ellesmere Island. During this journey he covered a total of some 1,700 miles.

Henry Larsen (1940–42, 1944)

The small *St. Roch*, built in 1928 specifically for the Royal Canadian Mounted Police, with extra-thick Douglas fir and equipped with a small 150-horse power diesel motor, became the first vessel to navigate the Northwest Passage in both directions. It was also the first vessel to transit the Northwest Passage in a single season. All this was accomplished under the command of Staff Sergeant Henry Larsen.

The first crossing from west to east was made part of the regular tour of duty by the police. The ship left Vancouver on 23 June 1940 and reached Halifax on 11 October 1942. *St. Roch* followed Routed 3A and 4 through the Bellot Strait and spent two winters en route, the first at Walker Bay at the entrance of the Prince of Wales Strait on Victoria Island, and the second at Pasley Bay on the west coast of Boothia Peninsula. Larsen's crossing was without major incident although he had a close call in his transit of the Bellot Strait when the swift current nearly flung his ship against what is now known as Magpie Rock.

The second voyage of the *St. Roch* began in Halifax on 22 July 1944 and ended in Vancouver on 16 October. It thus became the first ship to complete the Northwest Passage from east to west in a single year, in a total of 86 days. Larsen sailed through Lancaster Sound and the Barrow Strait, following Resolute Passage south of Cornwallis Island, and met with heavy ice south of Bathurst Island. He nevertheless managed to go around the north side of Byam Martin Island, then proceeded along the south coast of Melville Island as far as Winter Harbour, which he reached on 28 August. *St. Roch* then continued across Viscount Melville Sound to the Prince of Wales Strait, with practically no ice blocking its passage. After crossing the Prince of Wales Strait, Larsen paid a visit to the Hudson Bay post on Holman Island, north of Prince Albert Sound on Victoria Island, and then proceeded westward across Amundsen Gulf and along the coast without major difficulties. In an account of these two voyages, Larsen wrote that "this route will no doubt be used in the future".[38] Indeed, this is Route 1, which is the primary route envisaged by the companies currently developing hydrocarbons under the Beaufort Sea.

NAVIGATION IN THE NORTHWEST PASSAGE SINCE 1945

The relatively small degree of navigation which has taken place in the Northwest Passage since 1945 has been motivated mainly by two factors: national security and economic development. National security seems to have been the primary consideration up to 1969 and economic development after 1969. Consequently, the brief review of the full transits which have taken place in the Northwest Passage since 1945 will be divided into two periods, with the year 1969 marking the division point.

Navigation from 1945 to 1969

With the rapid development of the Cold War between the United States and the Soviet Union after World War II, the Canadian government acceded in 1947 to an American request made the previous year to establish joint weather stations in the Canadian Arctic islands. Then, in May 1955 Canada and the United States concluded an agreement to establish a Distant Early Warning (DEW) line along the northern coast of Canada. This was intended to be part of a 3,600-mile chain of radar stations, stretching from the northwestern tip of Alaska to the east coast of Greenland. These cooperative defense arrangements led to a number of crossings of the Northwest Passage by military or para-military ships.

In 1954, the year before the conclusion of the DEW line agreement, Canada had sent her naval icebreaker, HMCS *Labrador*, on a show of sovereignty and general survey mission through the passage. The *Labrador*, under the command of Captain O.C.S. Robertson, completed its westward crossing by following Route 1 through the Prince of Wales Strait. It thus became the first large ship, the first icebreaker, and the first armed Canadian vessel to complete the passage.

In 1957, during the period of construction of the DEW line installations, a squadron of three American Coast Guard icebreakers (USCGS *Storis, Spar*, and *Bramble*) crossed the Northwest Passage from west to east, following Routes 3A and 4 through the Bellot Strait and Prince Regent Inlet. The Bellot Strait had been navigated only twice: first, in 1937 by the *Aklavik* and, second, by the schooner *St. Roch* in 1942. The object of the 1957 crossing was to conduct hydrographic surveys to determine the feasibility of navigating the route by larger ships. The American ships were met at the James Ross Strait by the *Labrador*, commanded by Captain T.C. Pullen, and were escorted north in the Franklin Strait, then led safely through the dangerous Bellot Strait into Prince Regent Inlet. The objective of the exercise was thus attained.

Two submerged crossings of the Northwest Passage by American nuclear-powered submarines took place thereafter: one in 1960 by USS *Seadragon*, which crossed Route 2 in a westerly direction, and the other in 1962, by the USS *Skate*, which followed the same route in an easterly direction. The purpose of those crossings, of course, was to test the feasibility of submerged transits. The crossings took place without incident, but particular care had to be exercised in the western portion of the Barrow Strait, where certain uncharted shoals were found to exist among the small islands straddling the strait. Both these crossings took place within the context of defense arrangements between Canada and the United States, and in the case of the 1960 crossing, there was a representative of the Canadian government aboard in the person of Commodore O.C.S. Robertson, Royal Canadian Navy.

The only other crossing during this period was that of the Canadian icebreaker *John A. Macdonald* in September 1967. It followed Route 3 in a westerly direction to reach Mackenzie Bay on the Beaufort Sea and assist an American icebreaker, the USCG *Northwind*, which was beset by pack ice some 500 miles north of Point Barrow. This was the first crossing of the Northwest Passage by a Canadian Coast Guard vessel.

Navigation from 1969 to 1983

With the discovery of large oil reserves at Prudhoe Bay in 1968 on the north slope of Alaska, oil companies began to consider the possibility of using the Northwest Passage to transport oil to the American eastern seaboard. Consequently, in 1969 Humble Oil (now Exxon USA) had the S/T *Manhattan*, a huge 155,000-ton tanker, converted into an icebreaking vessel and sent through the Northwest Passage to determine the feasibility of year-round navigation. Notwithstanding the assistance of icebreakers *John A. Macdonald* and USCG *Staten Island*, *Manhattan* failed to negotiate the polar ice of the M'Clure Strait and it was decided, because of the lateness of the season, to complete the crossing westward by following the Prince of Wales Strait, thus using Route 1 instead of Route 2. On this same crossing the *Manhattan* was also assisted part of the way by the USCGS *Northwind*, which had sailed eastward from Seattle following the coastal Route 3 and had met the *Manhattan* at Thule, Greenland. On its westerly crossing with the *Manhattan*, the *Northwind* developed engine trouble halfway across Viscount Melville Sound and had to retrace its steps to Resolute and then return to Seattle by the same Route 3. On its return trip eastward, *Manhattan* followed the same Route 1 and was again escorted by the *John A. Macdonald*, as well as by the USCGS *Staten Island*. Throughout this voyage, Captain T.C. Pullen was aboard the *Manhattan* as a representative of the Canadian government.

Since the *Manhattan* voyage of 1969, a total of twenty-three ships have completed a transit of the Northwest Passage. Aside from four adventure crossings by pleasure yachts, most transits were related in some way to hydrocarbon exploration in the Canadian shelf offshore in the Beaufort Sea. With the exception of two of the yachts, all ships were of Canadian registry.

In 1970 two hydrographic ships effected crossings via Route 1: the CHS *Baffin* and the CHS *Hudson*. The transit of the passage by the *Hudson* also completed its circumnavigation of America.

In 1975 five ships completed three different routes of the passage. The CCGS *Skidegate* was redeployed to the east coast and completed the eastward crossing by following Routes 3A and 4, through the Bellot Strait and Prince Regent Inlet. The CCGS *John A. Macdonald* made a westward crossing in order to assist the CCGS *Camsell* and the commercial dredge *Beaver MacKenzie*, damaged and beset by ice off Herschel Island in the Beaufort Sea. The *John A. Macdonald* followed Route 3 through the Victoria Strait and took the same route on her return voyage. In the same year, two survey ships, the MV *Pandora II* and MV *Theta*, were redeployed to the east coast and made their eastward crossing by following Routes 3 and 5, through the Fury and Hecla Strait. They thus became the first and only ships to have completed a transit of the Northwest Passage by that route.

Two ships crossed the Northwest Passage in 1976, the *Canmar Explorer II* and the CCGS *J.E. Bernier*. The *Canmar Explorer II*, a drillship of the Dome Petroleum Company, made its westward crossing by following Route 3 through the Victoria Strait. It had to be escorted, however, by the *Louis St. Laurent* as far as Queen Maud Gulf. *J.E. Bernier*, a small icebreaking and buoy tender, followed the same route eastward without any incident.

The year 1977 saw only one transit of the Northwest Passage: by *Williwaw*, a 42-foot ketch of Dutch registry. Its captain and sole occupant, Willy de Roos, sailed the passage by following Route 3A through Peel Sound and the James Ross Strait. It was the first time that a crossing had been completed by that route since the first crossing of the passage in 1903–06. It was also the first navigation of that route in a single season.

The year 1978 saw the completion via Route 3A of a westward crossing by another yacht, the 35-foot diesel powered ketch *J.E. Bernier II*. Completion of the passage itself took two years, for the yacht, having developed motor trouble, was forced to spend the 1977 winter at Resolute. The whole voyage of the *Bernier II* actually took three years, since the yacht spent the 1976 winter at Gothaab, Greenland and the 1978 winter at Tuktoyaktuk on the Beaufort Sea.

Two more crossings took place in 1978, both in an eastward direction and both using Route 1 through the Prince of Wales Strait: the first by the CCGS *Pierre Radisson* and the second by the CCGS *John A. Macdonald*. The latter had been despatched to assist in icebreaking for the Dome Petroleum Company operations in the Beaufort Sea.

Having wintered at Summers Harbour, Cape Parry, the CCGS *John A. Macdonald* made its return voyage to the east coast in 1979 and followed the same Route 1 through the Prince of Wales Strait. Two more ships crossed the passage during this year, following the same route but in westward direction. The MV *Kigoriak*, a Dome Petroleum Company ship, effected the first transit by a commercial icebreaker. The CCGS *Louis St. Laurent* went to the assistance of the CCGS *Franklin*, which had broken a propeller in Viscount Melville Sound and was escorted to the Beaufort Sea through the Prince of Wales Strait and Amundsen Gulf, thence to the east coast via the Panama Canal.

Two crossings were completed in 1980, both in the eastward direction following Route 3A: one by the CCGS *J.E. Bernier* and the other by the MV *Pandora II.* Having reached the Dome operations in the Beaufort Sea via the Panama Canal and completed its icebreaking mission, the *Bernier* returned to Quebec City by the Northwest Passage. Along the way it escorted the survey ship MV *Pandora II* through Queen Maud gulf, the Simpson Strait, the Rae Strait, the James Ross Strait, the Franklin Strait, and Peel Sound as far as Resolute. The *Pandora* then completed its crossing without further assistance.

The year 1981 also witnessed two crossings, one by the survey ship CHS *Hudson* and the other by the *Morgan Stanley.* After completing her survey program in the Beaufort Sea, the *Hudson* made an eastward transit by following Route 3. As part of their transglobal expedition 1979–1982, British explorers Sir Ranulph Fiennes and Charlie Burton left Tuktoyaktuk on 26 July 1981 in their 18-foot open Boston whaler (bought in Vancouver) powered by two 60 H.P. outboards. Following Route 3A eastward, they arrived at Cape Sherard a month later on 26 August. In 1982 the Japanese yacht *Mermaid* finally completed her westward crossing, which took three years, following Routes 3A and 4 through Bellot Strait. During 1983, two Canadian ships effected eastward transits: one, the *Arctic Shiko*, a supply tug which followed Route 3 and, the other, *Polar Circle*, a survey ship which followed Route 3A.

SUMMARY TABLES OF NAVIGATION IN THE NORTHWEST PASSAGE

To give a comprehensive view of past navigation in the Northwest Passage, two summary tables have been prepared: Table 1 covers the full transits of the passage since 1903 and Table 2 shows the partial transits of the passage since 1977.

Full Transits of the Northwest Passage (1903–1983)

Table 1 shows all of the full transits of the Northwest Passage, beginning with the first one by Amundsen in 1903–06 and including the two known submarine crossings.

Partial Transits of the Northwest Passage (1977–1982)

An appreciable number of partial transits have been made since Amundsen's crossing of 1903, particularly by Captain Bernier between 1906 and 1922. How-

Table 1

Full Transits of the Northwest Passage (1903–1983)*

No	Year	Name of Ship	Registry	Route and Direction	Type of Ship	Nature of Voyage
1	1903–06	GJOA	Norway	3A west	herring boat	exploration
2	1940–42	ST. ROCH	Canada	3A & 4, east	schooner	patrol and exploration
3	1944	ST. ROCH	Canada	1, west	schooner	patrol and exploration
4	1954	HMCS LABRADOR	Canada	1, west	naval ice-breaker	sovereignty and survey
5	1957	USCGS STORIS	USA	3A & 4, east	icebreaker	hydrographic survey
6	1957	USCGS SPAR	USA	3A & 4, east	icebreaker	hydrographic survey
7	1957	USCGS BRAMBLE	USA	3A & 4, east	icebreaker	hydrographic survey *Note:* The three US ships were led through the narrow Bellot Strait by HMCS *Labrador*
8	1960	USS SEADRAGON	USA	2, west	nuclear submarine	exploration of sub-merged route *Note:* With Canadian representative Com-modore Robertson aboard
9	1962	USS SKATE	USA	2, east	nuclear submarine	exploration of sub-merged route *Note:* With previous consent of Canadian Govt.
10	1967	CCGS JOHN A. MACDONALD	Canada	3, west	icebreaker	1) assist CCGS *Cam-sell* in MacKenzie Bay; 2) assist USCGS *Northwind* 500 miles north of Point Bar-row
11	1969	S/T MANHATTAN	USA	1, west	ice-strength-ened tanker	test feasibility for large tanker passage *Note:* With Canadian representative Captain Tom Pullen aboard
12	1969	CCGS JOHN A. MACDONALD	Canada	1, west	icebreaker	escort and assist *Man-hattan*

(Table 1, continued)

No	Year	Name of Ship	Registry	Route and Direction	Type of Ship	Nature of Voyage
13	1969	S/T MANHATTAN	USA	1, east	ice-strengthened tanker	return passage
14	1969	USCGS NORTHWIND	USA	3, east	icebreaker	rendezvous and support *Manhattan*
15	1969	CCGS JOHN A. MACDONALD	Canada	1, east	icebreaker	support of *Manhattan*
16	1969	USCGS STATEN ISLAND	USA	1, east	icebreaker	support of *Manhattan*
17	1969	USCGS NORTHWIND	USA	3, west	icebreaker	return to Seattle
18	1970	CSS BAFFIN	Canada	1, east	survey ship	hydrographic and oceanographic survey
19	1970	CSS HUDSON	Canada	1, east	survey ship	hydrographic and oceanographic survey
20	1975	CCGS SKIDEGATE	Canada	3A & 4, east	icebreaker	redeployed to east coast
21	1975	CCGS JOHN A. MACDONALD	Canada	3, west	icebreaker	to assist CCGS *Camsell* and dredge *Beaver Mackenzie* in Beaufort Sea
22	1975	CCGS JOHN A. MACDONALD	Canada	3, east	icebreaker	return trip to east coast
23	1975	MV PANDORA II	Canada	3 & 5, east	survey ship	hydrographic survey
24	1975	MV THETA	Canada	3 & 5, east	survey ship	hydrographic survey
25	1976	CANMAR EXPLORER II	Canada	3, west	drill ship	to drilling program of Dome in Beaufort Sea *Note:* assisted by CCGS *Louis St-Laurent* as far as Queen Maud Gulf
26	1976	CCGS J.E. BERNIER	Canada	3, east	icebreaker	redeployed to east coast
27	1977	WILLIWAW	Netherlands	3A, west	yacht	adventure
28	1977–78	J.E. BERNIER II	Canada	3A, west	yacht	adventure
29	1978	CCGS PIERRE RADISSON	Canada	1, east	icebreaker	redeployed to east coast
30	1978	CCGS JOHN A. MACDONALD	Canada	1, west	icebreaker	charter to Dome in Beaufort Sea
31	1979	CCGS JOHN A. MACDONALD	Canada	1, east	icebreaker	return from charter
32	1979	MV KIGORIAK	Canada	1, west	icebreaker	support for Dome, Beaufort Sea
33	1979	CCGS LOUIS ST-LAURENT	Canada	1, west	icebreaker	to assist CCGS *Franklin* in Viscount Melville Sound

(Table 1, continued)

No	Year	Name of Ship	Registry	Route and Direction	Type of Ship	Nature of Voyage
34	1980	CCGS J.E. BERNIER	Canada	3A, east	icebreaker	returning to Quebec after icebreaking in Beaufort Sea
35	1980	MV PANDORA II	Canada	3A, east	survey	redeployed to east coast
36	1981	CSS HUDSON	Canada	3, east	survey	return to East coast after survey program off west coast
37	1981	MORGAN STANLEY**	Canada	3A, east	Boston whaler	adventure
38	1979–82	MERMAID	Japan	3A & 4, west	yacht	adventure
39	1983	ARCTIC SHIKO	Canada	3, east	tug	supply
40	1983	POLAR CIRCLE	Canada	3A, east	survey ship	hydrographic survey

* The writer is greatly indebted to Captain T.C. Pullen R.C.N. who compiled a list of transits on which this one is based.

** Ship bought in Vancouver just prior to crossing; see Ranulph Fiennes, *To the ends of the Earth*, at 158 (1983).

ever, since the reporting system NORDREG was established only in 1977 and for the sake of a greater degree of accuracy, Table 2 is limited to showing partial crossings since that year.

From 1977 to 1982 inclusively, a total of 129 ships made partial transits of the Northwest Passage. Of these, 108 were Canadian and 21 were foreign flags. Two of the Canadian ships were naval vessels and the rest include icebreakers, survey vessels, fuel tankers, general cargo ships, bulk carriers, tugs, and drillships. All the 21 foreign ships, except three yachts (2 French and 1 West German), were tankers and bulk carriers. The tankers took fuel to Rea Point on Melville Island for the Panarctic Oil Company operations and the bulk carriers transported ore from Nanisivik Mine on Strathcona Sound, south of Lancaster Sound.

Most of the ships, 115 out of 129, entered the Northwest Passage through Lancaster Sound. Virtually all the Canadian ships penetrated at least half way across the passage and 21 went as far as the western half of Viscount Melville Sound. This latter point was also reached by the 6 foreign ships (5 Finnish and one Swedish) destined for Rea Point. All the other 13 westbound foreign ships (5 Liberian, 5 Swedish, and the 3 yachts already mentioned) crossed only part of Lancaster Sound to reach Ninisivik Mine. The only foreign ships to enter the passage by the western entrance of Amundsen Gulf were two small American tankers. They went as far as the Rea Strait in Route 3A, carrying fuel to stations of the Distant Early Warning line.

Table 2

Partial Transits of the Northwest Passage (1977–1982)*

		Ships Transitting Water Bodies			
		Entry from East		Entry from West	
Route	Water Body	Canadian	Foreign	Canadian	Foreign
Route 1	Lancaster Sound	96	19[1]	0	0
	Barrow Strait	70	8[2]	0	0
	Viscount Melville Sound	21	5[3]	1	0
	Prince of Wales Strait	1	0	1	0
	Amundsen Gulf	0	0	12	2[4]
Route 2	M'Clure Strait	0	0	0	0
Route 3	Peel Sound	4	0	0	0
	Franklin Strait	3	0	0	0
	Victoria Strait	3	0	0	0
	Queen Maud Sound	0	0	11	2[4]
	Coronation Gulf	0	0	12	2[4]
Route 3A	James Ross Strait	0	0	1	0
	Rae Strait	0	0	8	2[4]
	Simpson Strait	0	0	8	2[4]
Route 4	Prince Regent Inlet	1	0	0	0
	Bellot Strait	0	0	0	0
Route 5	Hudson Strait	150	131[5]	0	0
	Foxe Basin	39	0	0	0
	Fury and Hecla Strait	0	0	0	0
	Gulf of Boothia	1[6]	0	0	0
Route 5A	This route has not been used.				

1. Ships of Finland (5), France (2), Liberia (5), Sweden (6) and West Germany (1).
2. Ships of Finland (5), Liberia (2) and Sweden (1).
3. Ships of Finland.
4. Ships of the United States.
5. No transits by foreign ships north of Foxe Channel.
6. Entry via Prince Regent Inlet and Lancaster Sound.

* The author is indebted to Captain J.Y. Clarke, Director General, Fleet Systems, Canadian Coast Guard, for the compilation of the list of partial transits on which this summary is based.

CURRENT CANADIAN ACTIVITIES IN THE NORTHWEST PASSAGE

To complete the review of the historical development of the Northwest Passage since the transfer of the Arctic islands to Canada by Great Britain in 1880, a summary of current Canadian activities follows. They involve activities mostly by the Canadian Coast Guard and Canadian Hydrographic Services but also, although to a very much lesser degree, those of the Canadian naval forces.

Coast Guard Activities

Unlike their American counterparts, the Canadian Coast Guard icebreaker ships are not military or even para-military in nature. Only three (the *Louis St. Laurent*, the *John A. Macdonald*, and the *Labrador*) are designed to allow retrofitting to accommodate defensive armament.[39] The Coast Guard itself is a component of the Department of Transport and answerable to the Canadian Maritime Transportation Administration of that department. In 1983 it was headed by a Commissioner, Andrew Collier, who had retired from the Royal Canadian Navy in 1979, but the Coast Guard is not answerable to the Department of National Defence. The idea of having a single government fleet was studied about fifteen years ago and rejected.[40]

The primary role of the Canadian Coast Guard is to provide marine aid and icebreaking services. To perform those services more efficiently in the Arctic, it has recently created a Northern Directorate, which will eventually be upgraded to a Coast Guard Arctic Region.

The specific services for which the Coast Guard is responsible in the Arctic are basically the following: marine navigational aids, icebreaking and escorting, marine search and rescue, marine emergencies, pollution prevention and control, maritime mobile communications, ports, harbors and terminals, vessel inspection, vessel traffic management, marine resupply and support and pilotage.[41] The legal implications of the implementation of these functions of the Coast Guard, in particular the enforcement of pollution prevention and control regulations, will be discussed in Chapter 8 where the legal status of the Northwest Passage is examined.

In the recent past, Coast Guard ships transiting sections of the Northwest Passage have been engaged mainly in icebreaking activities and the resupplying of Arctic communities. Icebreaking has been required not only for the Dome Petroleum Company's drilling operations in the Beaufort Sea, but also to assist various commercial vessels. For instance, in 1979 some 76 commercial vessels entered Canadian Arctic waters and 51 of them required icebreaking assistance. During that same year, the Coast Guard conducted the annual resupply in the Eastern Arctic and had to assist ships in their delivery of fuel and other commodities by providing ice-routing and icebreaking as far as Resolute Bay and Rea Point in the Parry Channel. In addition, during that year, six ships sustained damage in Arctic ice and had to be assisted. Icebreaking services are also frequently required to support ships transporting zinc concentrate from the Nanisivik mine, on Strathcona Sound off Admiralty Inlet, to Europe. Approximately six loads of concentrate are shipped yearly.

Hydrographic Service Activities[42]

The Canadian Hydrographic Service (CHS) is an element of the Ocean Science and Surveys Sector of the federal department of Fisheries and Oceans. It has the responsibility for surveying and charting all of Canada's navigable waterways and also publishing Sailing Directions, Tide and Current Tables, and Current Atlases to supplement the charts. Natural Resource Maps showing bathymetry, gravity and magnetics are also published in collaboration with the Department of Energy, Mines and Resources (EMR).

Until the end of World War II, the only charts available in the Canadian Arctic were those published by the British Admiralty, partly based on the work of the early explorers and largely based on sledge journeys at the time of the search for Franklin. The acquisition of timetrogon aerial photography of the entire Arctic during and just after the end of the war introduced a much higher degree of precision into the shoreline of the Arctic. The successive introduction of new methods of establishing horizontal control and the use of vertical air photographs by EMR led to further improvements in the mapping of the Arctic, culminating in 1968 with the publication of the last sheets of the 1:250,000 maps covering the entire archipelago.

To meet the needs of Arctic navigation, CHS published a new series of 1:500,000 navigation charts based on the best source data available; and, in the early years, differences of up to eight miles could exist between adjacent charts. With the completion of the 1:250,000 mapping, the decision was made that new charts based on the new maps and control would be in metric units.

By 1983 all the routes of the Northwest Passage were covered in metric units based on good shoreline and control, except for three parts of the southern route – the James Ross Strait to Cambridge Bay; Foxe Basin and the Fury and Hecla Strait; and the east coast of Baffin Island, south of Clyde River. Although all of the other charts are in metric units, they are not necessarily based on the latest surveys as CHS has faced to parallel requirements, first, to convert charts in fathoms to metric units and second, to incorporate new surveys into existing charts. The incorporation of new surveys may take up to four years. It will take another twenty years to produce adequate charts of the Arctic at adequate scales.

The first CHS chart of any part of the Northwest Passage covered the Mackenzie Delta and Port Brabant (near Tuktoyaktuk). It was based on a survey carried out in 1933 to permit the Hudson Bay Company to start a barge route down the Mackenzie. The next surveys were carried out in the early 1950s from the Eastern Arctic Patrol ship, *C.D. Howe.* Surveys were also carried out in the Northwest Passage in 1954 from HMCS *Labrador*. During the construction of the DEW line in 1955–57, surveys along Route 2 received a major impetus from the U.S. Navy working in the western Arctic and on the coast of Baffin Island, while hydrographers on the HMCS *Labrador* surveyed Foxe Basin and the Bellot Strait. CSS *Baffin*, the first Canadian hydrographic ship designed for work in the Arctic was commissioned in 1957, and in 1960 a survey of Lancaster Sound and the Barrow Strait was started, which was finished in 1974. In 1968 the M'Clure Strait was surveyed through-the-ice, a technique that was also used in the Beaufort Sea, Viscount Melville Sound, and the Prince of Wales Strait. The discovery of the first submarine pingo in the Beaufort Sea by CCGS *John A. Macdonald* led to a three-ship program there in 1970. These ice-cored mounds, rising to within 10 meters or less from the surface, are hard to detect as they are less than 300 meters in diameter at the top. From 1981 to 1983, a ten-mile wide corridor was surveyed through the pingo field. More than twenty pingos were found with a shoaliest depth of 19.8 meters.

One caution must be noted. While surveys exist through most of the Northwest Passage, the major exceptions being the Victoria and James Ross straits, the surveys only cover the deeper waters. It is rarely possible to deploy sounding launches in the Arctic, due to ice; therefore, few inshore areas have been surveyed. A method of using an airborne laser and air photo interpretation is being developed for use during the short periods which are ice free, but it will be many years before the inshore areas can be surveyed.

Naval Activities

Canadian naval activities have been very limited in the Canadian arctic waters, although some commentators would like to see a greater naval presence in those waters. Admiral R.W. Timbrell (ret.) stated in 1981 that "Canada has to recognize that the underwater passage through the Northwest Passage or under the Polar Cap by submarines is an acceptable task for modern day submarines, and it behooves Canada to make a contribution to deny freedom of this passage."[43] In 1982 Harriet Critchley severely criticized the Department of National Defence for ignoring the Arctic and suggested that it should "occasionally send Canadian naval vessels into the Davis-Baffin Bay area".[44] In the same year, Captain T.C. Pullen, R.C.N. (ret.), agreed that National Defence "is almost totally unaware of our maritime concerns in the Arctic",[45] but believed that "the red and white ships of our Coast Guard, not the navy, should be the custodians of our Arctic Waters".[46]

Regardless of the merits of a naval presence in Canadian Arctic waters, the fact is that naval ships are seldom seen in the Northwest Passage. Northern deployment, which is usually comprised of warship and a supply replenishment ship, normally limits itself to the Jones Sound/Lancaster Sound areas and is programmed roughly every other year.[47] It is only exceptionally that a naval ship will go as far as Resolute, such as the replenishment ship HMCS *Preserver* did in 1979.[48]

CONCLUSION

During the period of British explorations prior to the transfer of the Arctic islands to Canada in 1880, virtually all of the waters of the Canadian Archipelago were explored. The explorations, also carried out on land along the coasts or on the ice, were particularly intense during the search for the Franklin expedition between 1847 and 1859. During that period alone, over seventy search expeditions were despatched to the Canadian Arctic, about half of which spent at least one winter and some of them up to three. Although none of Her Majesty's ships actually completed the navigation of the Northwest Passage, Britain's naval officers effectively discovered all of its main routes.

In 1821 W.E. Parry discovered *Route 2* by sailing through Lancaster Sound, the Barrow Strait, Viscount Melville Sound, and entering the M'Clure Strait. Those four straits are now appropriately called Parry Channel and constitute the full length of that route. The completion of the last portion of the route was achieved by Robert M'Clure in 1852. Having sailed into the M'Clure Strait from the west and his ship having been forced by the ice to remain at Mercy Bay, he led a sled party to Winter Harbour on the south east coast of Melville Island and thus crossed the full length of the strait.

The discovery of *Route 1*, through the Prince of Wales Strait, was also made by M'Clure during his voyage of 1850–54. Having followed the coast from the Bering Strait in 1850, he crossed Amundsen Gulf and sailed north through the Prince of Wales Strait up to about 30 miles from its opening into Viscount Melville Sound. He even wintered on one of the Princess Royal Islands lying in mid-strait.

As for *Route 3*, through the Victoria Strait, and its variation Route 3A, through the James Ross Strait, the honor of its discovery has to go mainly to the ill-fated Franklin expedition. Franklin himself led his expedition through Peel Sound, the Franklin Strait, and Larsen Sound as far as the entrance to the Victoria Strait in 1847. Then, the next year, the surviving members of his expedition marched across both King William Island and the Simpson Strait to the south. The discovery of the westerly part of the route was done by Richard Colinson and his men when they sailed eastward through Amundsen Gulf, the Dolphin and Union Strait, Coronation Gulf and the Dease Strait. In searching the coasts of Victoria Island they also reached the other two bodies of water involved in this route, namely Queen Maud Gulf and the Victoria Strait.

The discovery of *Route 4* through the Bellot Strait was made in 1852 by Joseph Bellot, a lieutenant in the French navy and a member of the British expedition led by William Kennedy. He made the discovery when exploring the coast of Boothia Peninsula with a sled party. As for the northern sector of this route, Prince Regent Inlet, it had been discovered over thirty years before by W.E. Parry at the beginning of his first voyage in 1919.

Route 5, through the Fury and Hecla Strait, was discovered by the same W.E. Parry in 1822. After sailing through the Hudson Strait, Foxe Channel, and the Frozen Strait to Repulse Bay, he followed the coast of Melville Peninsula in Foxe Channel as far as the eastern entrance to the strait. Ice conditions prevented him, however, from crossing the strait westward and he was no more successful in his second attempt the following year.

After the transfer of territory from Great Britain in 1880, Canada sent out regular expeditions and patrols to the Arctic beginning in 1903, which eventually navigated all of the main routes of the Northwest Passage. Before 1945 this was done mainly by the numerous Bernier expeditions and the Royal Canadian Mounted Police patrols. From 1945 to the present, most of the navigation in the Northwest Passage has been done by Canadian ships: Coast Guard icebreakers, scientific ships and naval vessels.

Of the forty transits of the Northwest Passage which have taken place, including the first crossing by Amundsen in 1903–06, twenty-seven were by Canadian ships. Of the thirteen foreign crossings, ten were American, one Norwegian, one Dutch and one Japanese. The last three crossings were by small craft. Each followed *Route 3A and 4*, and all three were completed in either two or three years. The ten American crossings may be summarized as follows: a squadron composed of one light icebreaker and two buoy tenders following Routes 3A and 4 in 1957; two submarine crossings via Route 2 in 1960 and 1962; and the 1969 voyage of the *Manhattan* via Route 1 accompanied by two USCG icebreakers on the return part of the voyage, one of which sailed back westerly to Seattle by the same route.

Most of the twenty-sic Canadian crossings followed Route 1 or Route 3. Eleven crossings took place via Route 1, through the Prince of Wales Strait, and eleven via Route 3, through the Victoria Strait, or Route 3A through the James Ross Strait. The other four Canadian transits of the Northwest Passage were divided evenly between Route 4, through the Bellot Strait, and Route 5, through the Fury and Hecla Strait.

Chapter 4

COMMERCIAL DEVELOPMENT OF THE NORTHWEST PASSAGE

The navigation of the Northwest Passage through certain routes has been extremely limited in the past. With the exception of a small number of transits, navigation has been seasonally confined and has centered on the re-supplying of native and mining communities in the Arctic by ships of Canadian registry. With recent advances in technology, however, and the discovery of substantial mineral resources, particularly hydrocarbons, in areas adjacent to the Northwest Passage, this situation is likely to change in the future.

Re-supply operations to mining communities have already become more frequent due to limited hard mineral production and increased hydrocarbon exploration.[49] Year-round navigation, involving full transits of the Northwest Passage by Canadian and foreign flag ships, has been put forward as an option for the production phase of the development of certain hydrocarbon resources.[50]

The extent to which mining and other projects will involve increased use of the Northwest Passage and the pace at which they will proceed will depend both on the quantity of resources lying in the Arctic and on a complex network of interdependent technological, econonomic, and political factors. The quantity of a resource present will have to meet or exceed a "threshold reserve", taking into account other nearby deposits, which will provide the quantity required for minimally profitable extraction. Of significant relevance to the future use of the Northwest Passage, moreover, will be the technological and economic feasibility as well as the political acceptability of routine hydrocarbon tanker traffic through the passage.

RESOURCE POTENTIAL AND DEVELOPMENT IN ADJACENT AREAS

There is no doubt that the resource potential of the areas adjacent to the Northwest Passage is substantial.[51] However, some estimates, especially those of the commercial reserves that incorporate current economic data, are subject to significant change. In addition, the development of any reserve is subject to a host of factors, including the financial condition of the companies involved.[52]

Alaska North Slope/Beaufort Sea

There are four administratively distinct areas which constitute the Alaskan North Slope/Beaufort Sea region: the National Petroleum Reserve in Alaska (formerly known as Naval Petroleum Reserve Number 4), the Central North Slope, the National Wildlife Range, and the western Outer Continental Shelf of the Beaufort Sea, as shown in Figure 7.

Oil has been produced commercially only from the Prudhoe Bay and Kuparuk fields in the Central North Slope area. In 1982 approximately 1.5 million barrels per day (MMBpd) were produced, piped south through the Trans-Alaska pipeline to the southern Alaska coast, and shipped from there to southern markets. Proven reserves for the Prudhoe Bay field were estimated at 7,264 million barrels (MMBbls) of oil and 28,183 trillion cubic feet (TCF) of natural gas, and proven reserves for the Kuparuk field were estimated at 447 MMBbls of oil and 0.206 TCF of natural gas.[53] The potential of oil discoveries at Point Thompson on Flaxman Island and in the Lisburne group of formations underlying the main Prudhoe Bay reservoir may be significant but is currently unknown.[54]

Exploration in the National Petroleum Reserve in Alaska has led to disappointing results. Estimates of 1000 MMBbls of recoverable oil and approximately 14.3 TCF of natural gas were reported in 1979.[55] Although currently not exploited, these reserves could become commercially viable with a pipeline extension from Prudhoe Bay.[56]

Although no drilling has yet occurred in the Arctic National Wildlife Refuge, seismic testing has indicated that there is a 50 percent probability that some 400 MMBbls of oil and 6.5 TCF of natural gas exist.[57] If allowed, development is likely to be slow, since any drilling activities in the area will likely be strongly contested on ecological grounds.[58]

In the last few years, the American Outer Continental Shelf (OCS) area has seen a flurry of activity.[59] Large tracts of the OCS have been offered for lease, and if accelerated lease plans are implemented, all the American OCS areas in the Beaufort Sea may be offered for lease to industry by 1987.[60] Industry interest no doubt stems from the areas' proximity to the Trans-Alaska pipeline system and such estimates as that of the United States Geological Service; that agency stated in 1977 that there was a 50 percent probability that 3,300 MMBbls of oil and 8.8 TCF of natural gas exist in the area under less than 200 meters of water.[61]

In regard to oil development, it will be recalled that only the Prudhoe Bay and Kuparuk oil fields have been producing oil commercially and that oil has been piped south through the Trans-Alaska pipeline. It is estimated that the throughput of the pipeline could be increased by up to one third should additional reserves be found and extracted from the North Slope area.[62] Additional

Fig. 7 : MAJOR PETROLEUM AREAS OF ALASKA NORTH SLOPE / BEAUFORT SEA
Prepared for the author by the Canadian Hydrographic Service, Dept. of Fisheries and Oceans, Ottawa.
Source : National Petroleum Council, in International Petroleum Encyclopedia at P. 17 (1983)

production would have to be delivered to market via a second pipeline, or via tanker through the Bering Strait, or through the Northwest Passage. These options will be discussed in Chapter 5.

With respect to natural gas development, gas production is presently envisaged only at Prudhoe Bay. Gas would be piped through the 4780-mile Alaska Highway Gas Pipeline across Canada to the lower 48 states of the United States, assuming present financing and marketing difficulties are overcome. A total of 2,030 miles of the pipeline would be located in Canada, and, at a point south of Whitehorse, the pipeline could be joined by the Dempster Lateral Line Pipeline, which would be built to carry gas from the Mackenzie Delta, as shown in Figure 12. In 1982 the Canadian and American governments reiterated their commitment to complete the project based on private financing.[63] The target date for completion of this $40 billion project has been set at 1989,[64] but it is not likely to be met.

Although it is not possible to obtain sufficient information to make any precise estimate as to a time frame for Alaskan North Slope/Beaufort Sea oil and gas development, it seems evident that a new transportation system would have to be put in place, at least for oil production, in the likely event of additional significant oil and gas discoveries. Although energy markets were soft and hydrocarbon prices depressed in 1983, that situation may not last for an extended period of time.

In addition, considering the United States objective of increased security and self sufficiency of energy, the development of these Arctic reserves could take place in the near future. With such development in mind a number of proposals for the marine transportation of that production have been put forward. Indeed, a 1981 report prepared by the Committee on Maritime Services to Support Polar Resource Development specifically recommended that "further study be made of marine transport through the Northwest Passage to the east coast of North America from Alaska" in cooperation with Canada and other circumpolar nations.[65] These proposed transportation schemes will be reviewed in Chapter 5.

Mackenzie Delta/Beaufort Sea

The Mackenzie Delta/Beaufort Sea sedimentary basin comprises an area of about 420,000 square kilometers, as shown in Figure 8, only a quarter of which has so far been explored. Estimates of its oil potential have ranged from 5,000[66] to 38,000 MMBbls[67] and estimates of its natural gas potential have ranged from 50 TCF[68] to 320 TDF.[69] Although in 1981 the Canadian National Energy Board termed all estimates of the area's productive potential as "speculative"[70] these speculative estimates have been sufficient to spur on intense commercial exploration.[71] By 1983 no commercial discovery had been made, and the threshold

Fig. 8: MAJOR PETROLEUM AREAS OF MACKENZIE DELTA / BEAUFORT SEA

Source: Oilweek, Vol. 34, No. 15, at p. 20 (16 May 1983)

Prepared for the author by the Canadian Hydrographic Service, Dept. of Fisheries and Oceans, Ottawa.

reserves necessary to justify development had not been established.[72] It is possible, however, that this may merely reflect the 1982/83 downturn in oil price and demand since at least one operator in the region, the Dome Petroleum Company, still estimated that production might begin as early as 1989.[73] But this estimate represents an amendment to Dome's previous estimate of 1985 as the year of production and that more conservative estimates made at the same time had put the start of commercial production at 1992.[74]

In regard to the production of oil and gas from this area, it is generally agreed that Canadian and world energy price and demand, within the framework of Canadian energy policy, will, to a significant degree, determine its timing should commercial reserves be found.[75] The details of production scenarios from this area were outlined in the Environmental Impact Statement prepared by the Dome Petroleum, Esso Resources Canada, and Gulf Canada companies, and the three major proponents of Beaufort Sea/Mackenzie Delta development,[76] and were reviewed in a report of a Canadian Senate Special Committee on the Northern Pipeline.[77]

In relation to oil, Dome has estimated that production would be possible, using a tanker mode, at a threshold reserve level of 700 MMBbls and that production using a pipeline mode would require proven recoverable reserves of some 2500 MMBbls.[78] While Dome and Gulf appear to favor the marine mode and Esso appears to favor the construction of a demonstration pipeline to connect with the Norman Wells pipeline further south, shown in Figure 12, a combined system is also possible.[79] Although the Environmental Impact Statement stated in its intermediate phased development scenario that "first oil" could be produced as early as 1986 using tankers or 1987 using an overland pipeline system, this estimate was impossible to meet under 1983 economic conditions.[80]

The proponents of hydrocarbon development in the area believe that natural gas would most likely be transported to market through an overland pipeline although alternative marine transport systems have been proposed.[81] The Dempster Lateral Pipeline Project would transport gas to the Alaska Gas Pipeline Project, and the Polar Gas Project "Y" Pipeline would transport gas through the prairie provinces to eastern Canada.[82] The target date for completion of the former pipeline system was 1989[83] and the proponents of the latter pipeline, who have been seeking regulatory approval, announced in 1983 a revised plan to have their system operational by 1990, with extensions to the Beaufort Sea to be built at a later date.[84]

Canadian Arctic Islands: Oil and Gas

Estimates in 1981 put marketable gas reserves in the Canadian Arctic Islands at 18.2 TCF, and later drilling by the Panarctic Oils Company indicated the

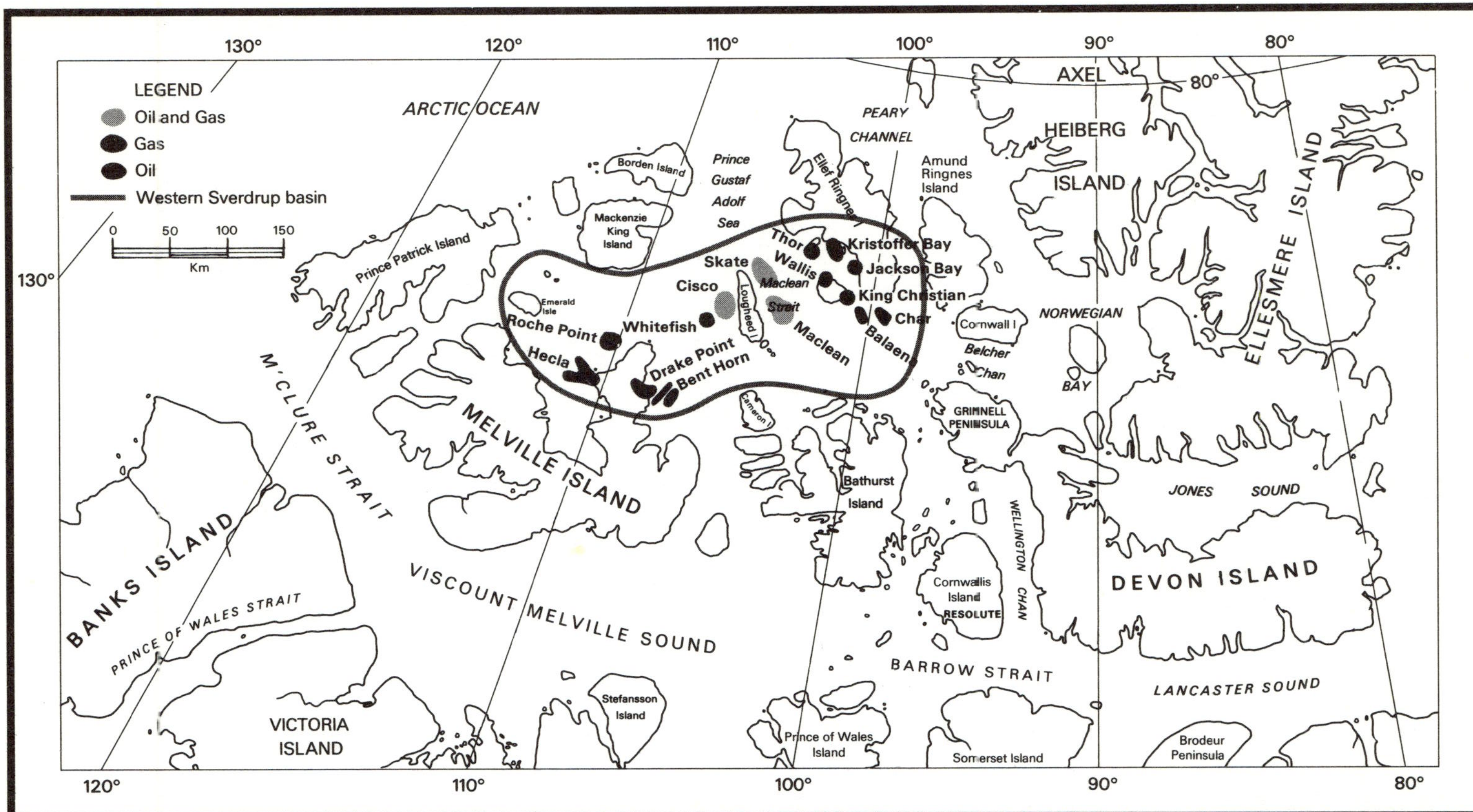

Fig. 9 MAJOR PETROLEUM AREAS OF CANADIAN ARCTIC ISLANDS
Prepared for the author by the Canadian Hydrographic Service, Dept. of Fisheries and Oceans, Ottawa.
Source: National Petroleum Council, in International Petroleum Encyclopedia at p. 27 (1983)

potential presence of some 750 MMBbls of recoverable oil.[85] Total reserves of this promising area, shown in Figure 9, may be considerably higher.[86]

Panarctic, the principal operator in the area, had hoped to deliver gas to southern markets, first using Arctic Pilot Project (APP) tankers and eventually using the northeastern branch of the Polar Gas Project "Y" Pipeline.[87] Although the APP sponsors in 1980 anticipated the gas delivery coming on steam as early as 1986, the project has been deferred.[88] As stated earlier, proponents of the Polar Gas "Y" Project Pipeline planned to have that system in operation by 1990, with later completion of the segment to the High Arctic Islands.[89] At least one author has suggested that the APP tankers may preempt the profitability of extending the pipeline to the Arctic Islands.[90]

Preliminary plans in 1982 for the shipment of any marketable reserves of crude oil from the islands envisaged a short distance of pipeline to Bridport Inlet and then shipment via ice-breaking tanker eastward through Viscount Melville Sound, the Barrow Strait, and Lancaster Sound.[91]

Canadian Arctic Islands: Hard Minerals

Although the hard mineral prospects for the area adjacent to the Northwest Passage are generally considered to be great, economic conditions have militated against the development of most of these in the near term.[92] However, four sites, shown in Figure 10, warrant mention because their current or proposed production schedules include seasonal use of sections of the passage to transport mining supplies and mineral products.

The Arvik (Polaris) lead-zinc mine, located on Little Cornwallis Island, has been in production since November 1981 and was estimated to contain enough reserves to support a 20 to 25 year operation. Shipping in 1983 required eight voyages annually but may require as many as sixteen by 1990. The Borealis mine, situated on Melville Peninsula, was scheduled to begin producing iron ore in 1985 and was estimated to contain enough ore to support an operation well into the 22nd century. Bathurst Norse mines is located about 96 kilometers south of Bathurst Inlet and was estimated to contain significant lead, zinc and silver ore deposits. One of the development options of this site would involve transportation through the southern portion of the Northwest Passage. Nanisivik Mine, on North Baffin Island, was estimated to have lead and zinc reserves sufficient for a 15-year operation. By 1983 the mine was sending out about six shipments per year.

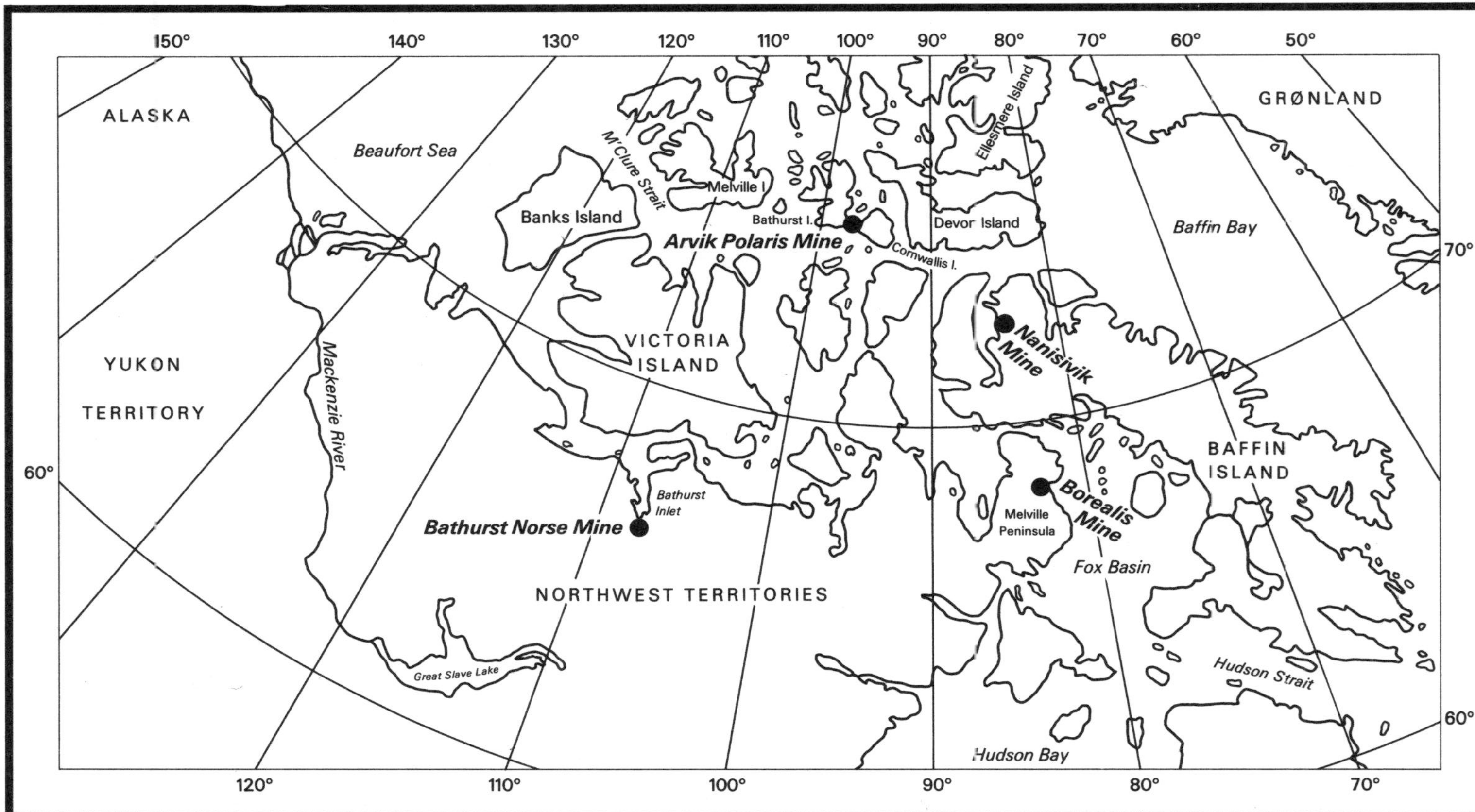

Fig. 10: MINE SITES IN THE CANADIAN ARCTIC

Prepared for the author by the Canadian Hydrographic Service, Dept. of Fisheries and Oceans, Ottawa, from a map in R.K. Keith et al., "Mining in the North" Northern Perspectives, Vol. 9, No 2, at pp 4 - 5 (1981)

RESOURCE DEVELOPMENT TECHNOLOGY

Extensive research has been done to develop socially, economically, and environmentally acceptable technology for the exploration, exploitation and transportation of Arctic resources.[93] The principal engineering problems have been associated with equipment functioning in the low temperatures and with icing. Additional obstacles are the presence, pressure, and scouring action of various sea ice features, and the thawing and refreezing of relatively unstable permafrost soils. Engineering solutions to these problems have been constrained not only by economic factors but also by the fragile nature of the Arctic ecosystem and the dependence of many northern communities on a harvest from that ecosystem. Much research on ice-structure interactions is under way.

Extensive research efforts have resulted in the development of not only Arctic modified conventional technology but also highly specialized technology designed exclusively for Arctic use. For offshore oil and gas exploration, highly specialized drillships, semi-submersible and reinforced ice platforms, and artificial islands have been designed to extend the three month drilling season otherwise permitted by the short Arctic summer.[94] Some of the highlights of past developments and remaining engineering problems are reviewed below, while details of tanker and pipeline technology relevant to the choice of transportation mode are discussed in Chapter 5.

In the Beaufort Sea-Mackenzie Delta area four drilling systems were slated for use: conventional land rigs, specially designed "platform rigs" similar to those used offshore in other parts of the world, conventional drillships, and "conical drilling units", shown in Figure 11, recently brought into use.[95] Conventional land rigs may be located either on natural islands, or on artificial islands, discussed below. Designs for the platform rigs will take into account the lessons learned through the design and operation of a variety of types of platform rigs operated in such areas as the Gulf of Mexico, the North Sea and Cook Inlet, Alaska.[96] Such structures will be anchored to the sea bottom either with steel pilings or through their own weight and designed to resist most but not all ice forces.[97] Conventional drillships in the area are being replaced to a certain extent by highly modified, polygonal, non-self-propelled drillships known as "conical drilling units".[98] The units, one of which was used by Gulf during the summer of 1983, require ice breaker and supply ship support. They are designed to operate in water depths of up to 60 meters and to withstand moving ice just over a meter in thickness.

Artificial island and associated drilling systems technology have reached a moderately advanced state and have been progressing.[99] Technology has evolved from initial "sandbag" islands, constructed in the early 1970s in less than 10 meters of water, through the "sacrificial beach" stage (where dredge material was used to construct larger islands which were highly susceptible to

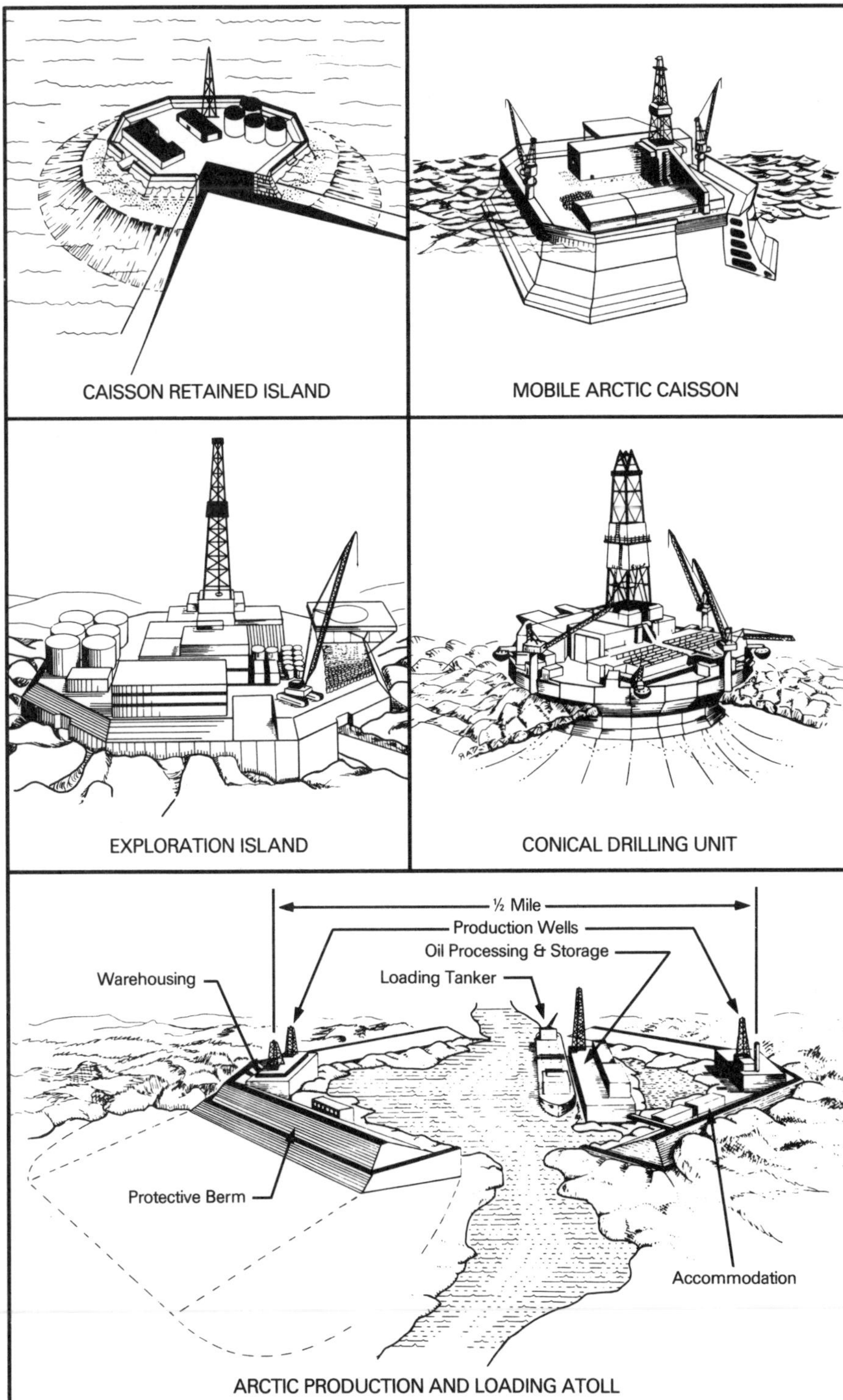

Fig. 11: EXPLORATION AND PRODUCTION SYSTEMS FOR THE BEAUFORT SEA

Prepared for the author by the Canadian Hydrographic Service, Dept. of Fisheries and Oceans, Ottawa.
Source: Beaufort Sea - Mackenzie Delta Environmental Impact Statement, Vol. 2, p. 3.11 (1982)

erosion), to the "caisson reinforced island" (CRI) stage, which has been under development. The caissons are designed to be large, movable, re-usable structures which sit on a natural or artificially elevated sea bottom and retain the sand or fill used to construct the island. They are intended to reduce greatly the amount of fill, time, and expense to construct an island, to prevent or reduce erosion, and to allow drilling in water up to 40 meters deep. Gulf has already installed one steel-reinforced concrete CRI in the Beaufort Sea at the Tarsuit site and has plans to put an octagonal steel CRI in operation in the near future. Esso planned to place its "steel doughnut" CRI in place in the summer of 1983, and Dome Petroleum constructed a "Single Steel Drilling Caisson" (SSDC) from an oil tanker, which it planned to use shortly.

One of the most technologically advanced concepts in production islands is the Arctic Production and Loading Atoll (APLA) designed to accommodate staff, oil production, processing, and storage facilities, and to provide a safe loading area for icebreaking tankers.[100] A number of alternate designs have been put forward, including some allowing operation in up to 60 meters of water.

For hydrocarbon exploration and production in the Arctic Islands area, Panarctic has developed means of drilling in over 360 meters of water from rigs placed on reinforced ice platforms and established the technical feasibility of subsea completion and production techniques.[101] Since the drilling technology is usable only where lateral movement of ice is minimal, research is being conducted to develop methods for drilling in areas of less stable ice.

In summary, it is evident that extensive research has gone into the development of specialized Arctic hydrocarbon exploration and production technology. Much of the exploration but not the production technology has already been field tested. Research is presently continuing to improve existing technology and develop new technology. Although their confidence is not universally shared,[102] proponents of the development of Arctic hydrocarbon resources appear convinced that technology is or will be sufficient to permit socially and environmentally acceptable commercial development within the very near future.

Chapter 5

MARINE TRANSPORT AND SUPPORT SYSTEMS IN THE NORTHWEST PASSAGE

In addition to the existing Trans-Alaska Pipeline, four major pipelines for the transportation of Arctic hydrocarbons have been proposed, as shown in Figure 12, and have been under active consideration. Three of them, the Alaska Highway Pipeline, the Dempster Lateral Pipeline, and the Polar Gas "Y" Pipeline, would transport gas from the Mackenzie Delta-Beaufort Sea area to southern markets. The Polar Gas "Y" Pipeline, in addition, through its northern extension, would transport gas from the Arctic Islands. The fourth pipeline system would transport oil from the northern part of the Beaufort Sea directly south to Edmonton or Rainbow, Alberta, where it would feed into the existing pipeline network.

PIPELINE SYSTEMS

The eventual adoption of any proposed pipeline system will depend on a number of factors such as the size and location of reserves, the location of markets, the price of oil and gas, the development of appropriate technology, and the routing of the pipeline. Technological solutions to permafrost instability and ice scour include cooling the hydrocarbons in buried pipeline sections to prevent a thaw of permafrost, the use of specially designed vertical support members to maintain the pipeline above permafrost, and the burying of pipeline sections below riverbeds and streambeds to prevent ice scouring. Routing has taken place under public scrutiny and has been designed to avoid sensitive wildlife areas. Considerations regarding native land claims have figured prominently in the review of routing schemes.

Alaska Highway Pipeline (Gas)

The Alaska Highway Gas Pipeline is a joint Canadian-American project designed to bring natural gas from the Alaskan North Slope area over 7,700 kilometers through southern Yukon, northern British Columbia, and Alberta to southern markets.[103] It is designed to connect with the 1200-kilometer Dempster Lateral Line near Whitehorse, discussed below, to feed gas from the Mac-

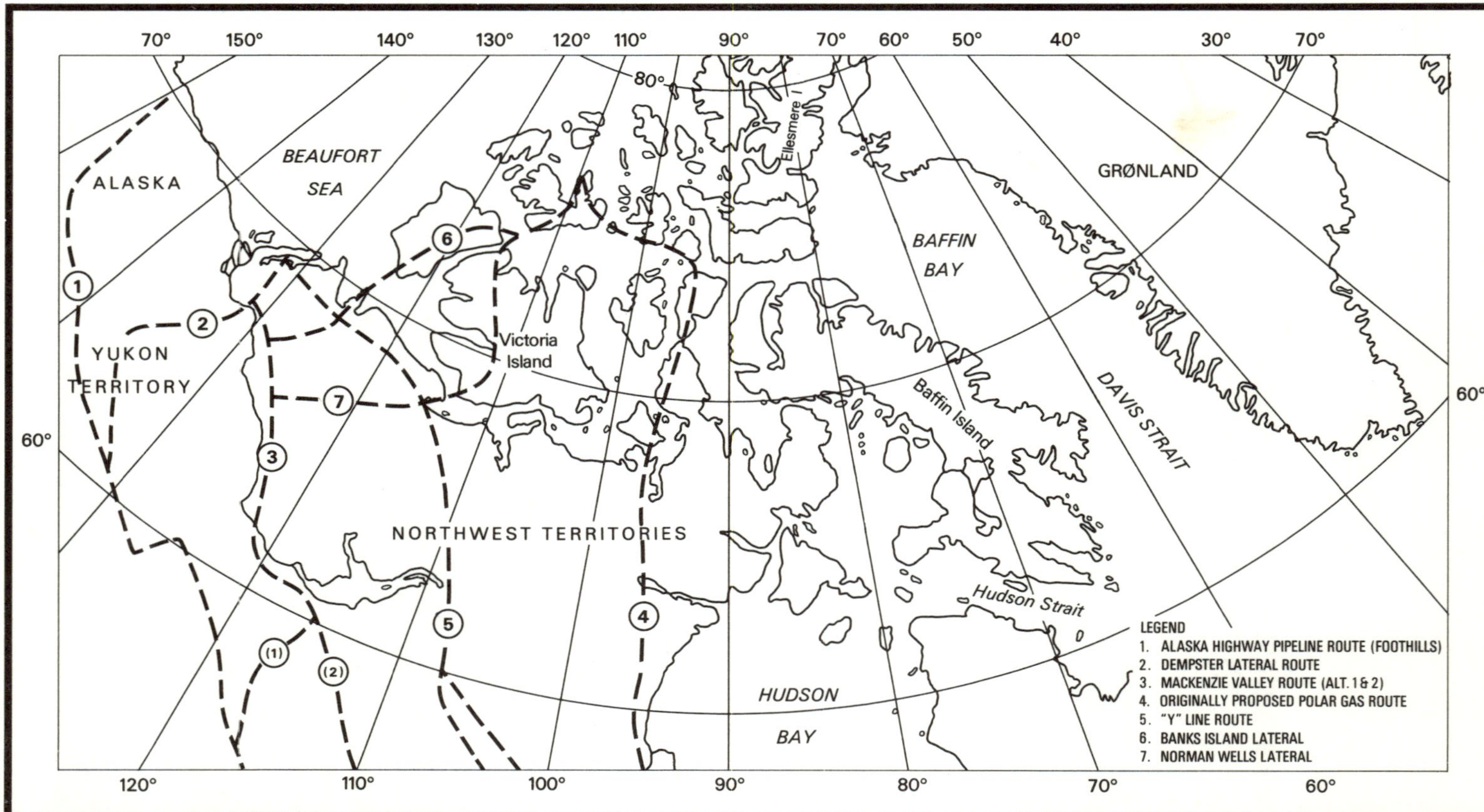

Fig 12 : POSSIBLE OIL AND GAS PIPELINES FROM THE ARCTIC

Prepared for the author by the Canadian Hydrographic Service, Dept. of Fisheries and Oceans, Ottawa.
Source : Beaufort Sea - Mackenzie Delta Environmental Impact Statement, Vol. 5, p. 11.1 (1982)

kenzie Delta area into the main pipeline with a capacity of 3.6 billion cubic feet (BCF) per day.

A number of technical, environmental, socio-economic, financial, and consequent political problems which have plagued the project appear to have been alleviated to a certain degree, but completion of the pipeline by its scheduled 1989 completion date was war from certain. Although improved economic conditions reduced the estimated cost of the U.S. portion of the pipeline from $30 billion to $20 billion, the consortium was not likely to seek firm financing commitments until the gas marketing situation in the United States had been clarified. Some doubted that the pipeline would ever be built, but the Canadian Northern Pipeline Commissioner was "reasonably optimistic" in 1983 that it would go ahead.[104]

Dempster Lateral Line (Gas)

The Dempster Lateral Line, discussed briefly above, would have the capacity to bring up to 1.2 BCF of natural gas per day to the Alaska Highway Pipeline. Gas transported by the line would be destined primarily for Canadian markets. Completion of this line was contingent on both the approval and completion of the Alaska Highway Line and the prospects of a timely completion of the Polar Gas Project Pipeline, which might compete for markets with the Dempster Lateral Line.

Polar Gas "Y" Pipeline (Gas)

The Polar Gas Project, formed in 1972, originally sought to develop optimal means of transporting natural gas from discoveries made by Panarctic Oils in the Arctic Islands. Once the project determined that a large diameter pipeline would be the most economical and efficient means of transporting the gas to market, a number of alternative routes and development plans were put forward. In 1980 the concept of a "Y" configuration pipeline, linking discoveries in the Arctic Islands and the Mackenzie Delta-Beaufort Sea to southern Canadian markets was established. In March 1983 it appeared that the project, still slated for completion by 1990, would be scaled down to bring about 0.8 BCF of gas per day from the Mackenzie Delta area. Subsequent phases of the project would be built to deliver gas from the Beaufort Sea and Arctic Island areas. Extension of the pipeline to the Arctic Islands would require marine crossings at the M'Clure Strait (about 150 kilometers) and the Dolphin and Union Strait. Plans for the complete "Y" pipeline called for its capacity to be expandable to about 3.3 BCF per day.[105]

In spite of over $80 million having been spent on this project by 1983, its implementation was far from certain. It will depend in particular on the approval of the Dempster Lateral Pipeline, which is in part a competing system, as well as on the fact that it is a highly expensive system. In addition, the possibility of the pipeline being damaged by some of the giant multi-year-old ice floes coming down the M'Clure Strait and the fact that some of its sponsors are also partners in the competing Arctic Pilot Project may militate against its full implementation.

Beaufort Sea-Edmonton Pipeline (Oil)

This pipeline, as an alternative to a tanker system, would carry oil about 2,250 kilometers south from Richards Island at the northern end of the Mackenzie Delta, along the Mackenzie Valley past Fort Simpson to Edmonton, Alberta, where it would feed into an existing pipeline system. Sub-sea pipelines, buried in the sea-bed to prevent ice scour damage, would connect production wells on artificial islands to the beginning of the main pipeline on Richards Island. According to the plan of phased development under consideration, initial production rates of 4,000 cubic meters per day could be increased to 27,500 and then 218,000 cubic meters per day with expansions of the pipeline capacity. It has been estimated that either the small (16 to 27-inch) or large (42-inch) diameter pipeline would require four years to build.[106] About one-third of the line would be elevated and two-thirds be buried at least one meter below ground. Where particularly sensitive permafrost soils would have to be crossed, the pipeline would be supported by special anchors designed to maintain the integrity of the soil. The major proponent of this pipeline is Esso Resources Canada, one of the three major operators in the Beaufort Sea.

Esso also favors the initial construction of a demonstration oil pipeline from the Beaufort Sea, which would connect with the Norman Wells oil pipeline already approved by the federal government. The Norman Wells buried pipeline, with a capacity expandable to about 48 thousand barrels a day, will follow the Mackenzie Valley from the Norman Wells oilfield 866 kilometers to Zama, Alberta, where it will join with an existing Alberta pipeline system. It was slated for completion by 1985. Estimates for completion of the entire Beaufort Sea pipeline optimistically have been put at 1987,[107] but this appears to be an impossible date. Construction of the Norman Wells pipeline would free the demonstration pipeline and allow it to be used to transport supply oil, methanol, or other products.

TANKER SYSTEMS

Three Canadian and five American proposals for tanker systems will be reviewed. One of the Canadian proposals involves the transportation of oil from the Mackenzie Delta-Beaufort Sea area, while the other two Canadian proposals involve the transportation of gas from the Arctic Islands. All six American proposals envisage the transportation of oil from the Alaskan slope through the Northwest Passage, and one of them also involves the transportation of gas.

Severe and variable ice and climatic conditions, 24-hour winter darkness, a fragile marine ecosystem, and the difficulty of oil spill cleanup under ice have been some of the problems associated with the design of a marine transportation system. These problems have been accentuated by the requirement of year-round navigation for economic reasons.

CANADIAN PROPOSALS

Dome's Icebreaking Tankers (Oil)

Although the Dome Petroleum Company has advanced a proposal for a pipeline to transport oil from the Mackenzie Delta-Beaufort Sea area, it has expressed a preference for a marine mode of transportation.[108] In 1982 Dome proposed to use either an 80,000-ton or a 200,000-ton capacity icebreaking tanker to begin production in 1987 and to use up to 16 of the larger tankers for servicing the offshore Beaufort oil fields by the year 2000, assuming an intermediate rate of development. The larger of these tankers would be an Arctic class 10, meaning that it would be permitted, under the Canadian Arctic Shipping Pollution Prevention Regulations, to navigate in any ice conditions within the Canadian Arctic at any time of the year. Class 8 icebreakers are considered sufficient for year-round navigation through Route 1 of the Northwest Passage but not Route 2.

The distinctive design characteristics of the Arctic tankers envisaged by Dome include: icebreaking capabilities to enable year-round passage throughout the Northwest Passage, a double-sided shell and double-bottomed hull to minimize risks of oil spillage in the event of a collision or grounding, separate oil and ballast tanks, replacement of air in cargo tanks with inert gases to reduce explosion risk, multiple independent propulsion systems and rudders, specialized navigation equipment for use in ice, and specialized cargo containment systems, including multiple (14) cargo tanks. The 200,000-ton tanker being considered by Dome would be 390 meters long, 52 meters wide, with a draft of 18 to 20 meters, and would develop about 100,000 horsepower. It would have a spoon-shaped bow with reamers to widen the channel cut in the ice in order to reduce hull friction. Its maximum speed would be about 23 knots in open water and about 6 knots in three meters of level ice. Loading would take place either at an Arctic production and loading atoll, described earlier, or at a single point mooring terminal, a structure similar to the caisson islands, also described earlier. The crew would be specially trained and tested and would be employed under conditions designed to reduce fatigue and boredom.

The primary shipping corridor that has been proposed is Route No. 1 through the Prince of Wales Strait, shown in Figure 13. Route No. 2, through the M'Clure Strait, has been envisaged as an alternate route. In addition, the Bering Strait Route would be favorable for shipments to Japan, a country which has often expressed interest in buying Arctic hydrocarbons. Use of such a route would of course depend, among other things, on export authorization from the Canadian National Energy Board.

Arctic Pilot Project Tankers (Gas)

The Arctic Pilot Project was designed to test the feasibility of delivering natural gas in a liquified form from the Arctic Islands to markets in Europe and eastern North America.[109] The proposed project would involve piping natural gas from fields in northern Melville Island 160 kilometers to a liquification, storage and loading facility on the south coast of the island and southern transportation of the gas most likely via two class 7 Arctic Liquid Natural Gas (LNG) tankers each with a capacity of 140,000 cubic meters.[110] If terminals in southern Canada were involved, each ship would make sixteen trips per year. In its liquified state, the gas would occupy only about one six-hundredth of its normal volume, rendering tanker transportation efficient yet potentially hazardous in the event of a rupture of a carrying tank. Production, which had been scheduled to begin as early as mid-1985, may not begin until 1990 owing to the recent fall of prices in the gas market.[111]

The ships, to be built outside Canada, would be 372 meters long, 43 meters wide, and have a draft of 11 meters. These ships would be capable of moving through seven-foot, first-year ice at a constant speed of three knots. They would be LNG tankers designed with an ice breaking bow, heavy plating, close frame spacing to resist ice-related stresses, and approximately four times the power of comparable conventional LNG carriers.

TransCanada Pipelines Project (Gas)

This project was designed to transport gas from King Christian Island to European markets via three 75,000-ton Arctic class 10 icebreakers capable of year-round navigation. The gas would come by a 77-kilometer pipeline from adjacent Ellef Ringnes Island to King Christian Island where it would be liquified and loaded into tankers.[112] Due to depressed European markets for gas, this project will probably be delayed and the original estimate of completion by the late 1980s moved to the 1990s.

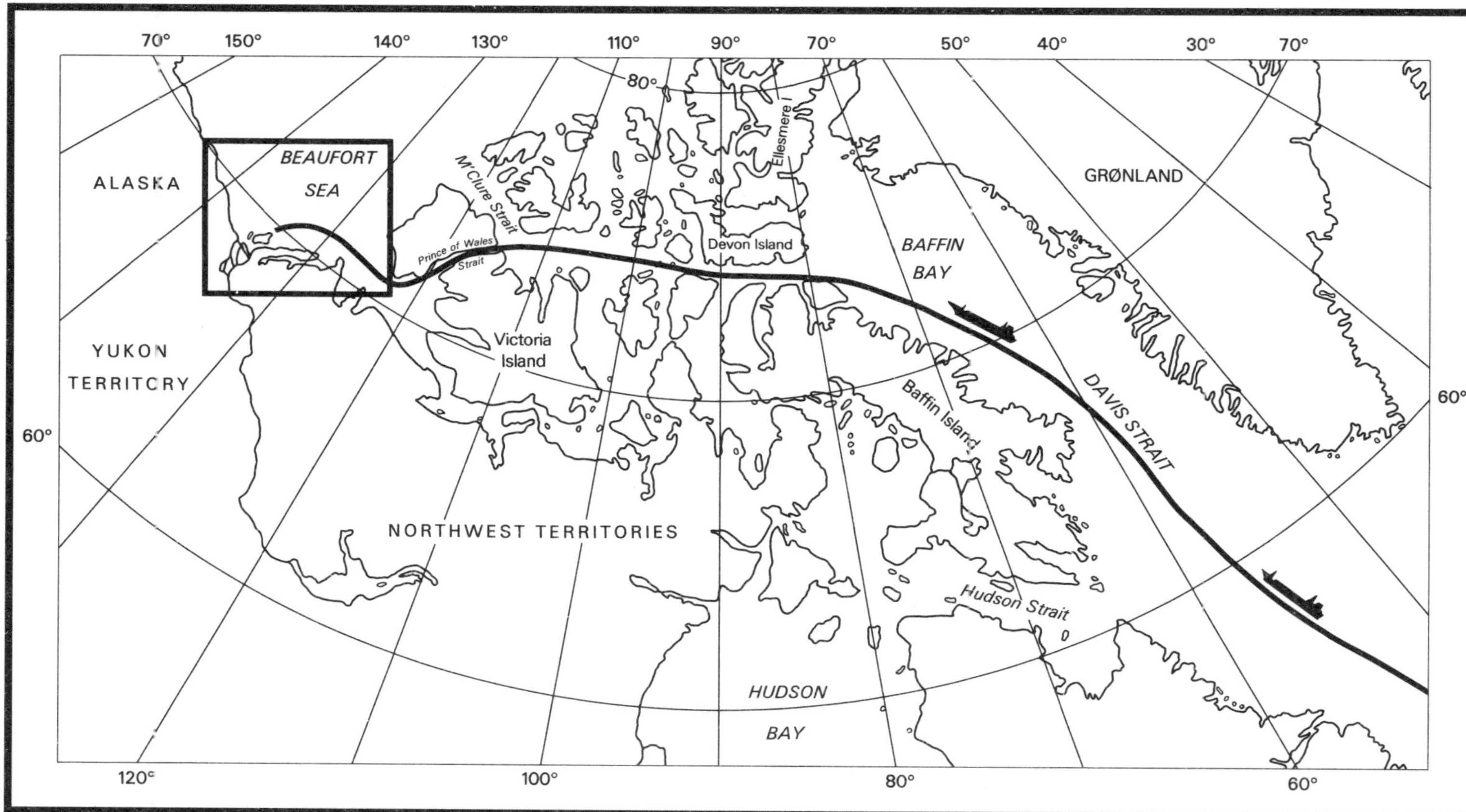

Fig. 13: ROUTE NO. 1 OF THE NORTHWEST PASSAGE (via Prince of Wales Strait)
Prepared for the author by the Canadian Hydrographic Service, Dept. of Fisheries and Oceans, Ottawa.

AMERICAN PROPOSALS

U.S. Maritime Administration (Oil)

In 1973 a study prepared for the Maritime Administration (MARAD) of the U.S. Department of Commerce recommended that MARAD and the appropriate Canadian agencies develop a marine transportation system to ship oil from the Beaufort Sea through the Northwest Passage to the American east coast.[113] The system envisaged would involve the use of twenty-one to thirty-three Arctic tankers of 245,000 dead weight tons (dwt) with offshore terminals in Prudhoe Bay, Alaska, and in Delaware Bay, on the American east coast, and possibly the use of trans-shipment ports in Greenland or Newfoundland.

The study reported favorably on the economics of such a system. It concluded that the system would be substantially more economical than an equivalent pipeline system, even if oil were piped from the American east coast to consumers in the American mid-west. A subsequent study, prepared for MARAD in 1978, concluded that the Northwest Passage would be the most acceptable route for icebreaking tankers to follow.[114]

Seatrain Lines (Oil)

In 1978 Seatrain Lines outlined a plan to use three class B tankers of 225,000 dwt to transport oil from Prudhoe Bay to the northeastern United States using the Northwest Passage.[115] Seatrain's statement, referring to the MARAD study conclusion that the Northwest Passage would be the most acceptable tanker route, specified that the tankers would navigate the route year-round and would meet the requirements of the Canadian Arctic Waters Pollution Prevention Regulations. Three such tankers, each carrying about 1.5 million barrels of oil, could average 12 round trips annually.

Globtik Tankers (Oil)

In 1980 the Chairman of the Board of Globtik Tankers presented what he termed "a rational and economical solution" for the transportation of north slope oil and gas to Canadian and American east coast markets.[116] He maintained that continuation of the present system involving transportation via the Trans-Alaska Pipeline and tanker was uneconomical and that expansion using larger tankers would not work since these would not fit through the Panama Canal and could not be navigated economically around the tip of South America. He proposed using between one and twenty-four Arctic class 10 double-hulled tankers of 350,000 dwt to transport oil from an Alaskan offshore terminal via Amundsen Gulf and Prince of Wales Strait to a trans-shipment terminal in Newfoundland. The number of tankers, of course, would depend on the amount of daily production to be transported and would be based on an assumption of 12 round trips per year per tanker.

Globtik Tankers (Gas)

In addition to the above, Globtik proposed to transport liquified natural gas from Prudhoe Bay and the Canadian Arctic Islands by using between 4 and 20 Arctic class 10 tankers with capacities of 125,000 or 165,000 cubic meters. Each tanker would make an average of 12 round trips annually.[117]

General Dynamics Submarine Tankers (Gas)

General Dynamics has proposed using either 17 non-nuclear or 14 nuclear powered submarines with 140,000 cubic meters of cargo capacity to transport liquified natural gas from the Alaskan north slope to southern markets.[118] Cargo would be carried within six cylindrical tanks. Each submarine would have a beam of 228 feet (69.5 meters), a depth of 92 feet (28.1 meters) and a maximum operating depth of 600 feet (185 meters). Nuclear submarines would have an overall length of 1,270 feet (387 meters), power capacity of 75,000 horsepower in each of its two shafts, and be capable of navigating at 15 knots. Comparable characteristics of the non-nuclear submarines would be 1,470 feet (448 meters), 50,000 horsepower, and 12 knots. Preliminary industry studies in 1981 indicated that the system would be an economically viable alternative to pipeline or icebreaking tanker systems.

Proponents of this system point to two advantages: one, that navigation is relatively unaffected by surface ice and weather conditions allowing reliable, uniform navigation, and two, that the system would have less social and environmental impact since it would not involve a constant disruption of surface ice. Those more skeptical of the system point out that these submarines would be substantially larger than the U.S. Trident (military) submarine, also built by General Dynamics, and would encounter difficulties on account of their size. Stopping distance, for instance, would be approximately three times the maximum operating range of the sonar system used to avoid bottom and under-ice obstructions, and the estimated safe operating depth of 150 meters might not exist throughout the Northwest Passage, particularly in the Barrow Strait where mid-channel depths are as shallow as 22 meters.[119]

OTHER PROPOSALS

Other proposals for the marine transportation of Arctic hydrocarbon resources have been advanced, promoted, or withdrawn by their respective proponents in the recent past. Trans Polar Shipping has designed a submarine to transport LNG.[120] Semi-submersible icebreaking tankers have been advanced as being the most economical means of moving oil through the Northwest Passage.[121] The U.S. Coast Guard some years ago announced plans to cross the Northwest Passage with heavy icebreakers during the winters of 1983 and 1985 to test support systems for proposed shipping,[122] and Japan has expressed interest in obtaining Beaufort Sea hydrocarbons on various occasions.[123] As more becomes known about the hydrocarbon reserves of the Arctic, new proposals may be expected.

CHOICE OF TRANSPORTATION MODE

The choice of transportation mode is a multi-staged decision. First, a specific Canadian transportation system must be approved by the responsible government agencies, boards, departments, and offices on the basis of a host of technical and political considerations. Then a decision must be made by the proponents to develop the resources in question and transport them to southern markets under the terms and conditions imposed by the government. Although the pipeline and the marine modes of transportation are not mutually exclusive, a basic choice has to be made. The choice of one mode, however, might still permit a limited use of the other.

Canadian government policy is clearly behind a responsible development of Arctic hydrocarbon resources.[124] In pursuit of its National Energy Program, which seeks security of the Canadian oil supply and requires more information about frontier hydrocarbon reserves, the government has negotiated a series of exploration agreements concerning the Beaufort Sea, Mackenzie Delta, and Arctic Islands areas with the operators designated for each area.[125] In addition, the Petroleum Incentives Program has given a strong monetary incentive for companies to explore Arctic frontier areas. However, before production and transportation can take place, approval will be required from a wide range of governmental bodies. These include the National Energy Board; the Departments of Transport; Indian Affairs and Northern Development; Energy Mines and Resources; Environment; Employment and Immigration; Fisheries and Oceans; the Canada Oil and Gas Lands Administration; the Federal Environmental Assessment and Review Office; and the governments of the Northwest Territories and the Yukon Territory.

Assuming that difficulties related to socio-economic and environmental impacts as well as the development of export or domestic markets can be overcome, the federal government has appeared to favor somewhat the marine mode of transportation. In a speech delivered in June 1982, Senator Jack Austin, speaking on behalf of the Minister of Indian and Northern Development, noted that the government would be instituting a five-year research and planning program in support of a "phased approach" to northern development.[126] Such an approach would favor reasonably sized demonstration project initially and larger projects if demonstraation projects prove successful. This approach would appear more disposed to approval of a marine mode of transportation since tankers could be added and their impacts could be monitored as production increased.

In addition to the tanker demonstration project, however, which was proposed by the proponents of the stalled Arctic Pilot Project, Esso has proposed a demonstration oil pipeline from the Beaufort Sea area connecting with the Norman Wells Pipeline, which was described earlier. Speaking about this project, Senator Austin noted: "Without prejudging it in any sense, I think it's fair to suggest that the successful completion of the Norman Wells-Zama Lake Pipeline – successful on the basis of reasonable criteria – will have a bearing on all future pipeline proposals for the north".[127] Construction of this pipeline has been approved and was scheduled to begin in 1984 and to be completed in 1985.

A possible indication of the future direction of government policy is contained in the March 1983 Report of Senate Special Committee on the Northern Pipeline, where it is recommended: "that transport of hydrocarbons from the Arctic region commence by tanker on a small scale and that consideration be given to various combinations of tanker and/or pipeline systems as other factors warrant".[128] That recommendation was made after hearing from numerous government, industry, and northern peoples representatives, with the Committee agreeing that under certain conditions, both pipeline and tanker systems were technically and environmentally feasible.[129] A number of factors leading to the recommendation were cited by the committee. These include: 1) federal and industry policies supporting phased development with expansion linked to demonstrated capabilities, 2) uncertain markets, 3) untested technology, 4) insufficient levels of proven reserves, 5) desirability of generation of early cash flow, 6) desirability of a system flexible enough to adapt to reserve levels and market demand, 7) need for Canada to stay in the forefront of cold ocean technology and shipbuilding of Arctic class ships, 8) desirability of sustained industrial activity and reduced inflationary pressures, 9) opportunities to monitor impacts of a gradual increase in Arctic shipping, 10) inflexibility of a large diameter pipeline system, and 11) opportunity for northern communities to absorb growth.[130]

MARINE TRAFFIC AND SUPPORT SERVICES

Projected Traffic

In light of the uncertain future of a number of the major oil and gas development projects described previously, it is not possible to make an accurate, detailed projection of marine traffic through the Northwest Passage. It is, however, possible to make three general observations with respect to future traffic outlined below.

First, it is likely that the re-supply of northern communities, and the shipment of ore from Arctic mines will continue for the foreseeable future to provide a low level of seasonal traffic through the eastern portions of the Northwest Passage.[131] Increases and decreases may be expected as mines go into and out of operation. Shipping to the Polaris Mine (about eight voyages per year) will probably not continue much past the year 2000, and shipping to Nanisivik Mine (about six voyages per year) may cease as soon as the early 1990s. Shipping to the Borealis Mine may start by 1985 and continue well into the 21st century, and shipping to Bathurst Norse mines may be developed in the near future. Changes in mineral markets will of course affect this component of navigation through the Northwest Passage.

Second, the possible scenarios of marine traffic through the Northwest Passage for oil and gas exploration and production range from those with low or no activity to those with high activity. The former would be realized in the unlikely event that discoveries of oil and gas in the Arctic turned out not to be commercially viable, or that icebreaker tanker traffic was found by the regulatory authorities to be unacceptable, or that the early development of a pipeline system or systems precluded the economic viability of a tanker system.[132] To realize a scenario with high activity would require oil and gas shipments via icebreaker tankers from Arctic areas commencing as early as 1988 (Arctic Pilot Project) or 1989 (Beaufort Sea Oil), with the number of tankers and transits of the passage escalating rapidly into the mid 1990s. Shipments of gas from the Beaufort Sea area and oil and gas from Alaska and the high Arctic Islands would begin in the early 1990s and escalate rapidly.[133] Since such a scenario would depend on a highly favorable development of considerations discussed earlier in this Chapter, its realization is also not likely. For purposes of reference, a high activity scenario that was issued by Transport Canada in August 1982 is reproduced as Table 3. However, by 1983 it was already apparent that such a scenario would not fit the future.

Third, in all probability, oil and gas related marine traffic through the Northwest Passage will fall somewhere between the two scenarios described above.[134] While commencement dates are far from certain, it is possible that oil from the Beaufort Sea could be shipped as early as 1990 and that gas from

Table 3

Most Demanding Forecast of Transits of the Northwest Passage (1986–1995)

Oil/Gas Scenario, Year Round Operation, Number of One-Way Ship Transits								
	1986	1987	1988	1990	1992	1993	1994	1995
Beaufort Sea (Oil)	—	24	48	72	96	120	144	168
Arctic Islands (Oil)	—	—	—	—	—	30	60	60
Labrador (Oil)	—	—	—	—	—	—	—	36
Arctic Islands (Gas)	30	60	60	90	120	150	180	210
Alaska	—	—	—	—	—	24	48	72

Source: Transport Canada, *Position Statement to the Beaufort Sea Environmental Assessment Panel*, 88 pp., at 12 (1982); figures assumed as of 10 September 1980.

Melville Island could be shipped as early as 1988. Shipments of oil and gas from the American Arctic and the Canadian Arctic Islands, other than Melville Island, would probably begin in the early 1990s. Regulatory approval of tanker shipments and the experience gained from a phased development of tanker traffic would facilitate moderately paced increases of both Canadian and American traffic. This type of development would accord well with industry's marine transportation development option and with the perceived government preference for a closely monitored, flexibile, and phased development. Transportation in the mid- to late 1990s would depend on the technical and financial success of the initial years of tanker operation.

In relation to gas transportation, the credibility of this scenario is enhanced by the uncertainty surrounding the financing of the Alaska Highway Gas Pipeline and the possible negative impact on the Polar Gas "Y" Pipeline that early implementation of the Arctic Pilot Project would have. In addition, Canadian development of globally competitive Arctic shipbuilding capabilities would exert strong pressure on the Canadian government to adopt a policy favoring marine transportation of both oil and gas. The credibility of this scenario, however, is diminished by the uncertain foreign gas markets and by the uncertain government approval of any gas exports.

Projected Support System

In anticipation of the potential for a considerable increase in shipping through the Northwest Passage, the Canadian government and the hydrocarbon project proponents have coordinated plans to provide for greatly increased support systems. The government has developed an Arctic Marine Services Policy to "provide for an appropriate level of services and regulation in support of marine transportation and related activities in the Canadian Arctic".[135] The policy is designed to accommodate a "most demanding" Arctic traffic scenario, although individual programs will be tailored to actual service demand. The private sector, expected to share the costs of the provision of some of these services, has developed its own plans for the provision of extensive support services. However, many of these service plans have been designed to support non-shipping exploration and production activities as well.[136]

In relation to regulation of support services, the Arctic Marine Services Policy provides a set of standards for the provision of the following services: ports, navigational aids, icebreaking, pollution control, search and rescue, communication, vessel traffic management, re-supply, and external services, such as hydrological information, ice information, and dredging assistance.[137] In addition, it defines or allocates responsibility for the provision of the above services among federal, private, and territorial bodies and provides for the establishment of specialized training programs for federal government and private employees.[138] This policy has been devised in collaboration with industry and affected government departments.

Icebreaking. Canadian government policy calls for federally controlled Arctic icebreaking capability in all areas to which the Arctic Waters Pollution Prevention Act applies and in which cargos pose a significant pollution risk, or foreign-flag ships engage in any service activity, or any activity of significant socio-economic or strategic importance is undertaken.[139] To attain this capability, authority has been given to establish a Northern Directorate within the Coast Guard which would coordinate Arctic transportation research efforts and would oversee, among other things, the development of a class 8 polar icebreaker.[140] This icebreaker, at 90,000 horsepower, would be almost four times as powerful as the CCGS *Louis St. Laurent*, in 1983 the Coast Guard's most powerful icebreaker. The principal function of the new ship would be to provide a measure of assistance to LNG and oil tankers and to provide support to Arctic supply ships. In addition, it would be involved in a wide variety of other functions, including ice surveillance, hydrographic services, pollution monitoring, search and rescue, and personnel training. Plans to increase the present icebreaker fleet would be commensurate with the rate of increased use of the Arctic waterways and would potentially include the development of a class 10 icebreaker, possibly nuclear powered, by the mid-1990s.

Industry plans for icebreaker services have been extensive although the Beaufort Sea development proposals have called for the use of class 10 icebreaking tankers which, it was claimed, would need escort services only in exceptional circumstances.[141] Non-tanker icebreakers would be used principally to support exploratory work by breaking drillships out of their ice-bound winter mooring sites and protecting them, while drilling, from damage from moving ice packs. The proponents of Beaufort Sea drilling envisage the possibility of using between 16 and 24 icebreakers by the year 2000.[142]

Weather and Ice Forecasting. Weather and ice forecasting services, essential for Arctic navigation and search and rescue in Arctic Canada, have been provided by the Atmospheric Environment Service (AES) of Environment Canada and by the private companies operating in Arctic areas. The services provided by AES involve the gathering and processing of data from satellites, long-range reconnaissance aircraft, buoys, ship and shore stations, and the provision from mid-June to late November of current ice condition reports and 30-day ice forecasts twice monthly to ships and other Arctic stations.[143] More limited service is available during the winter months. As a result of this and related work, the AES was able in 1981 to publish an *Ice Atlas* summarizing average, minimum and maximum ice conditions throughout the Canadian Arctic.[144] Information received by operators in the Arctic from the AES is generally supplemented by information received from independent data sources.[145]

Proponents of Beaufort Sea development have planned to use in the future a sophisticated environmental prediction system called REMSCAN (remote sensing, communications and navigation).[146] The system has been designed to forecast wind, ice motion and stress, wave, icing and visibility conditions on the basis of meteorological data received primarily from existing sources and from sea ice data received from a variety of radar systems. The radar systems would include currently available airborne systems, some of which would be capable of detecting ice features desite fog and freezing rain, and currently available satellite systems.[147] Government and privately sponsored research has been underway both in Canada and the United States to develop a satellite capable of all-weather high resolution ice feature detection;[148] an industry publication has predicted that such a satellite might be operational by the late 1980s.[149] In short, the capability to observe ice extent, ice movements, ice roughness and some aspects of ice thickness under all-weather conditions presently exists. However, complete ability to observe ice thickness and snow cover through satellite systems remains to be developed.[150]

Search and Rescue. Search and rescue procedures have been developed by all the operators in the Arctic regions, the Canadian Coast Guard, and the Canadian Armed Forces.[151] Although the primary emphasis of both private and government policy is the avoidance of marine casualty, a system has been established under which all three of the above groups can participate in marine search and rescue efforts. In 1982 the possibility of using a SARSAT satellite to reduce greatly the time required to locate aircraft and vessels in distress was investigated, and field assessments of offshore standby, safety, and evacuation capability have been regularly reviewed by the Canada Oil and Gas Lands Administration.

Pollution Prevention and Control. Both Canadian industry and government have expended considerable time and money to assess and reduce the risks of accidental and operational pollution of the Arctic marine environment. Risks of pollution, pollution prevention, and control systems associated with projects with federal involvement are assessed primarily through the federal Environmental Assessment and Review Process (EARP). In relation to the development of Arctic island natural gas reserves, the panel established under EARP concluded that the systems incorporated in the northern component of the proposed Arctic Pilot Project would be environmentally acceptable as long as certain recommended conditions were met.[152] These conditions included a close monitoring of the effects of year-round traffic and the routing or re-routing of tankers to avoid sensitive wildlife areas. The acceptability to the federal environmental assessment and review panel of pollution prevention and control systems proposed by the proponents of Beaufort Sea-Mackenzie Delta development had not been determined by 1983 but might be determined in the near future.[153] Taking into account the EARP conclusions, exploration and production activities involving federal lands will be subject to the environmental protection conditions incorporated in agreements with the Canada Oil and Gas Lands Administration.

All marine pollution prevention and control systems to be used in the Canadian Arctic will have to comply with environment-related federal laws and regulations, particularly the *Arctic Waters Pollution Prevention Act* and the regulations promulgated pursuant to that Act.[154] These regulations, which have been under review in light of recent technological developments, among other matters relate to standards for operational discharges, cargo spaces, and equipment of ships navigating in the Arctic. Compliance with the NORDREG vessel traffic management system and the TERMPOL code of recommended standards for the prevention of pollution around marine terminal systems has been voluntary, although compliance with the former may become mandatory in the near future.[155]

To deal with accidents threatening the marine environment, industry and government have developed a number of contingency plans, notably through joint industry-government working groups set up by the Arctic Petroleum Operators Association and Environment Canada's Arctic Marine Oil Spill Program. In their environmental impact statement, the proponents of the Beaufort Sea development went through ten scenarios involving oil spills and indicated counter measures which would, in each case, be taken to mitigate environment damage.[156] In its position statement to the Beaufort Sea Environmental Assessment Panel, Transport Canada outlined its Arctic Seas Contingency Plan, which was designed to bring together industry and government efforts to mitigate environmental damage from accidents.[157] To control any oil spills in the Beaufort Sea, Canada and the United States signed an agreement outlining a joint contingency plan.[158]

CONCLUSION

The exploitation of the vast resources of the areas adjacent to the Northwest Passage appears certain and the development of the Northwest Passage as a commercial shipping route for oil and gas seems assured. If industrial proposals to use the passage are sanctioned by the Canadian government, oil and gas tanker traffic could become a reality by about 1990. In cooperation with industry, the government has adopted an Arctic Marine Services Policy, which has been designed to accommodate the "most demanding" level of traffic. A decision by the Canadian government not to allow traffic would only run counter to the preliminary indications that it has given, but also might run afoul of United States interests seeking to develop fully Alaskan offshore reserves. Regardless of the extent of the marine traffic, the potential for such activity raises the question of the legal status of the Northwest Passage.

Chapter 6

THE LEGAL STATUS OF INTERNATIONAL STRAITS

Canada's legal position is that the Northwest Passage is comprised of internal waters. This position was articulated about the time of the voyage of the S/T *Manhattan* in 1969. In May that year, before the voyage, Prime Minister Trudeau made a formal statement in the House of Commons, in which he quoted from a 1958 declaration by the Minister of Northern Affairs that "the area to the north of Canada, including the islands and the waters between the islands . . . is *national terrain*".[159] The Prime Minister did not state expressly, however, that the waters of the Canadian Arctic Archipelago were claimed as internal waters but limited himself to acknowledging that "not all countries would accept the view that the waters between the islands of the archipelago are internal waters over which Canada has full sovereignty".[160]

In December 1969, after the voyage of the *Manhattan*, the Standing Committee on Indian Affairs and Northern Development was more explicit than the Prime Minister in its Report to the House of Commons as to what Canada's position should be. It stated: "Your Committee considers that the waters lying between the islands of the Arctic Archipelago have been, and are, subject to Canadian sovereignty historically, geographically and geologically".[161]

In December 1973 a letter from the Bureau of Legal Affairs contained what is probably the most precise statement on the status and legal basis of the waters: "Canada also claims that the waters of the Canadian Arctic Archipelago are *internal waters* of Canada, on an historical basis, although they have not been declared as such in any treaty or by any legislation".[162]

In May 1975 the Secretary of State for External Affairs, Allan MacEachen, made a statement to the Standing Committee for External Affairs and National Defence in which he said, with reference to the Single Negotiating Text of the Third UN Law of the Sea Conference, that:

> . . . the provisions define the straits as only those which are used for international navigation and exclude straits lying within the internal waters of a state. As Canada's Northwest Passage is not used for international navigation and since Arctic Waters are considered by Canada as being *internal waters*, the régime of transit does not apply to the Arctic.[163]

This official position on the Northwest Passage was clearly reiterated in October 1980 by the Honorable Mark MacGuigan, Secretary of State for External Affairs, in an address to the Canadian Council on International Law, entitled "Beyond the Law of the Sea Conference". Having referred to the new regime of transit passage through international straits, he emphasized: "And here let me make clear immediately that the Northwest Passage is not an international strait".[164]

Canada's position that the Northwest Passage is not an international strait having been made sufficiently clear, what is the validity of that position in the light of the principles of international law applicable to straits in general and those used for international navigation in particular? The question must be addressed not only in relation to the present situation but also with respect to the future, on the assumption that international shipping will eventually take place in the Northwest Passage.

DEFINITION AND CLASSIFICATION OF INTERNATIONAL STRAITS

It was believed for a while during the Third UN Law of the Sea Conference (UNCLOS) from 1974 to 1982 that the question of international straits was so difficult to resolve that it could cause a failure of the conference. Indeed, there was a fundamental difference of position on this issue between the maritime powers and the bordering states. On the one hand, the maritime powers insisted on having an unrestricted freedom of navigation for maritime commerce and strategic mobility and, on the other, the states bordering straits maintained that they had to restrict such freedom in order to protect their marine environment and national security.

Fortunately a compromise was finally reached, and a fairly comprehensive set of provisions on international straits were adopted in the UN Law of the Sea Convention, which was signed in December 1982. The convention specified the categories of international straits falling within the scope of the convention and the legal regime applicable to each category. However, no definition of an international strait was incorporated in the 1982 convention. In the words of Professor J.N. Moore, "UNCLOS has not altered or clarified the existing uncertainty in customary international law over the definition of 'straits used for international navigation'."[165] In these circumstances, it becomes imperative to determine as precisely as possible the basic characteristics of such straits.

Definition of International Straits

On the geographic element of the definition of an international strait agreement was reached in the 1958 Convention on the Territorial Sea as well as the

1982 Convention on the Law of the Sea. Although attempts at the codification of customary international law on international straits were made by a number of international bodies, such as the Institut de droit international, the International Law Association and the International Law Commission,[166] they did not achieve much success as to the "international use" element of the definition so that on this important point, guidance must be sought in the *Corfu Channel Case* of 1949, which is still the only international decision on the question.

Geographic Criterion. From a strictly geographic point of view, any narrow and natural passage between adjacent land masses, joining two parts of the high seas or two bodies of sea water, comes within the definition of a strait. From the legal point of view, this definition is unsatisfactory since it mentions no width and does not cover the overlap of territorial waters. As long as there is a strip of high seas throughout a strait, no legal problem arises and the traditional principle of the freedom of the high seas continues to apply to that strait. The strait which presents a problem is the one which is narrow enough to cause an overlap of the territorial waters of one or more states bordering the strait. This type of strait is sometimes referred to as a "territorial" strait although it is more often called a "legal" strait because it is governed by a special legal regime.

Since a 12-mile territorial sea has been permitted in international law, a legal or territorial strait means one which is 24 miles or less in width. Under the 1982 Law of the Sea Convention, such a strait must join either a part of the high seas (or the exclusive economic zone) with another part of the high seas (or another part of the exclusive economic zone), or a part of the high seas (or part of the exclusive economic zone) with the territorial sea of a foreign state. Exceptionally, a strait of more than 24 miles and used for international navigation might be considered a legal or territorial strait, if the high seas route in the middle is not suitable or convenient enough for navigation.[167]

The overlap of territorial waters in legal or territorial straits need not be complete throughout the strait since there may be enclaves or pockets of *high seas*. However, in the words of Professor R.R. Baxter, "the incongruity of the existence of such enclaves of the high seas led to the conclusion that these areas might be incorporated in the territorial sea of the States concerned."[168] Professor Baxter's conclusion was that "the application of the usual rules on the territorial sea and the high seas would suggest that international law need not make any special provision for navigation in geographic straits where the overlapping territorial seas of the littoral nations do not, as it were, block the strait."[169] This was also the conclusion reached by Professor Charles De Visscher, former judge of the International Court of Justice, who stated that the solution which appears to prevail in practice is the elimination of any pockets of high seas.[170] The result of this approach is that, if there exists only one littoral state, the pockets of high seas in the strait are assimilated to the territorial sea of that state; otherwise, the territorial waters will be divided along the median line between the littoral states.

Another problem relating to the geographic element of a legal or territorial strait is the status of *pockets of internal waters* within the strait. The 1982 Law of the Sea Convention provides that nothing in Part III on straits used for international navigation affects "any areas of internal waters within a strait, except where the establishment of a straight baseline in accordance with the method set forth in Article 7 has the effect of enclosing as internal waters areas which had not previously been considered as such."[171] Presumably, the waters of a bay or other area within a strait which would have the status of internal waters, by reason of an historic title, could never be subject to the regime of international straits. However, if areas of a strait become internal waters because of the establishment of straight baselines, those waters are assimilated to territorial waters for purposes of passage and may become subject to the legal regime applicable to international straits. The reason is, as pointed out by Professor D.P. O'Connell, that the right of passage through straits is an autonomous institution of international law and not only a corollary of a right of passage through the territorial sea.[172]

Functional Criterion. Not all straits meeting the geographic requirements of a "legal" strait can be classified as "international". Only "straits used for international navigation" fall within the scope of Part III of the 1982 Law of the Sea Convention and they are subject to the rights of passage through such straits. The right of passage, as will be explained later, normally will be "transit" passage but exceptionally may be non-suspendable "innocent" passage. The territorial waters of legal or territorial straits not used for international navigation will be subject only to the ordinary suspendable right of innocent passage applicable to any territorial waters.[173]

Considering the difference in the applicable legal regime, it may be of fundamental importance to determine the degree of use required for a strait to be considered as being "used for international navigation". Unfortunately both the 1982 Convention on the Law of the Sea and the 1958 Convention on the Territorial Sea are silent on this question. The matter was raised during the Third UN Law of the Sea Conference[174] and some delegations would have preferred to limit the new regime to straits *traditionally* used for international navigation.[175] However, it soon became obvious that no agreement could be reached and the matter was left to be resolved through customary international law. The issue of "use" is a complex one since it is necessary to determine what factors are relevant and what relative importance should be attached to those factors before deciding if a particular strait is sufficiently used to be considered international in character.

Probably the Danish jurist Eric Bruel has studied this issue in the most exhaustive manner. In his definitive two-volume treatise entitled *International Straits*, published in 1947, he suggested that the question ought to be determined on the basis of such facts as "the number of ships passing through the strait, their total tonnage, the aggregate value of their cargoes, the average size of the ship and especially whether they are distributed among a greater or small number of nations – all of which seem to give good guidance, no single factor, however, being decisive . . .".[176]

Having enumerated the relevant factors to take into account, Bruel concluded that only those straits that are of considerable importance to international maritime commerce enjoy the peculiar legal position accorded to international straits. By the qualification "international", he wrote, "is simply meant that the interest attached *to the use* of these straits is world wide."[177] He added that the number of straits endowed with this quality was limited and that the special conservatism of shipping in the use of routes made it reasonably clear what straits were considered important.

Bruel further indicated that a number of qualifying expressions had been developed over the years to point to what were considered to be international straits. The expressions mentioned were "*routes maritimes indispensables*", "*routes maritimes nécessaires à la navigation*", "*grandes routes maritimes*", "*passage habituel*", "international highways", "highways for international traffic" and "natural traffic routes".[178]

Bruel's view represented quite accurately the state of the law when the International Court of Justice in 1949 had to judge whether or not the North Corfu Channel was an international strait. The court concluded that "the North Corfu Channel should be considered as belonging to the class of international highways through which passage cannot be prohibited by a coastal State in time of peace."[179] The judgment had to weigh the arguments of the United Kingdom, which put the emphasis on the geographic criterion, and those of Albania, which insisted on the functional one.

The United Kingdom contended that "the character of the channel as an international route depends on the fact that it connects two parts of the open sea and is useful to navigation, not on the volume of traffic passing through it."[180] It adduced evidence showing that during the period from 1 April 1936 to 31 December 1937 (one year and nine months), some 2,884 ships of seven different nationalities had put in at the Port of Corfu after passing or just before passing through the channel. The court was also informed that the British Navy had regularly used the channel for some 80 years or more as had the navies of other states as well.[181]

Albania, on the other hand, contended that the Corfu Channel had very little importance for international navigation and was not a highway (*grande route*) but only a byroad (*une voie latérale et secondaire*). It contended that this secondary route was practically reserved to local navigation and cabotage and therefore did not serve for passage properly so-called.[182]

In answering the question "whether the test is to be found in the volume of traffic passing through the Strait or in its greater or lesser importance for international navigation", the court stated that "the decisive criterion is rather its geographical situation as connecting two parts of the high seas and the fact of its being used for international navigation."[183] The French text of the judgment, which is the authoritative one, reads:

> Le critère décisif paraît plutôt devoir être tiré de la situation géographique du Détroit, en tant que ce dernier met en communication deux parties de haute mer, ainsi que du fait que le Détroit est utilisé aux fins de la navigation internationale.[184]

It would, therefore, appear that in the French text a little less importance was given to the requirement that the strait be used for international navigation.

The International Court of Justice held that the fact that the North Corfu Channel was not a necessary route between two parts of the high seas but only an alternative passage could not be decisive. What was more important was that it had been a "useful route for international maritime traffic."[185] The evidence showed that it had been a very useful route for the flags of seven states: Greece, Italy, Romania, Yugoslavia, France, Albania, and the United Kingdom. The 2,884 crossings covered only the ships which had put in port and had been visited by customs. It did not include the large number of vessels which had gone through the strait without calling at the Port of Corfu. In other words, the actual use of the North Corfu Channel had been quite considerable.

Considering this decision, it is not surprising that the UN International Law Commission, in its draft convention in preparation for the 1958 Law of the Sea Conference, intended to codify the existing customary law on the point and confined the right of non-suspendable innocent passage to straits "*normally* used for international navigation between two parts of the high seas."[186] The qualifying adverb "normally", however, was not retained in the Territorial Sea Convention of 1958 and is absent from the 1982 Law of the Sea Convention. Consequently there is no indication whatever in conventional law as to what degree of use for international navigation is required before a strait can qualify as an international strait. It is obvious that the actual use has to be considerable, although it might not have to be as extensive as it was in the *Corfu Channel Case*. As pointed out by G.C. Fitzmaurice, "in the *Corfu Case*, the Court clearly thought that the Channel was used to an *important* extent."[187]

As for the factors relating to use, the court did not seem to have considered two of the factors mentioned by Bruel, namely, the total tonnage and the aggregate value of their cargos. It did not take into account, however, the two other factors, namely, the number of ships passing through the strait and the number of flag states represented by those ships. It also appears to have considered the evidence presented by the United Kingdom "that the British Navy has regularly used this Channel for eighty years or more, and that it has also been used by the navies of other States."[188]

Having regard to the above, perhaps the only effect of deleting the qualifying adverb "normally" from the International Law Commission draft, which had probably been intended to cover such regular use such as was made by the British Navy for some eighty years, was to remove the necessity of such regular use for that long period of time. In other words, the simple phrase "used for international navigation" would represent a somewhat modified codification of the *Corfu Channel Case* principle in that it would not include the regular use by the British Navy but only the 2,884 crossings or more made by the ships of seven states during a 21-month period. Regardless of the precise reasons for the insertion and the removal of the word "normally", it seems clear that before a strait may be considered international, proof must be made that it has *a history as a useful route for international maritime traffic* similar to that shown to exist in the North Corfu Channel.

This conclusion is in accord with the interpretation generally given to the judgment of the International Court of Justice. For instance, Professor Baxter wrote that "international waterways must be considered to be those rivers, canals, and straits which are *used to a substantial extent* by the commercial shipping or warships belonging to states other than the riparian nation or nations."[189] As to the criteria applied by the court in the *Corfu Channel Case*, Professor Baxter concluded that "the test applied by the Court lays more emphasis on the practices of shipping than on geographic necessities."[190]

The importance of the functional element was also emphasized by Professor O'Connell in the following passage:

> When it is said, then, that a strait in law is a passage of territorial sea linking two areas of high sea this is not to be taken literally, but rather construed as meaning a passage which ordinarily carries the bulk of international traffic not destined for ports on the relevant coastlines. *The test of what is a strait*, unlike the test of what is a bay, is *not so much geographical, therefore, as functional.*[191]

Professor O'Connell re-emphasized the importance of the functional criterion in his most authoritative study, *The International Law of the Sea*, published posthumously in 1982. In his opinion, the *Corfu Channel Case* established "that not all straits linking two parts of the high seas are international straits, but *only those which are important as communication links.*"[192] He concluded that "the real significance of the Case is its treatment of the qualities that give a strait this importance." In his view, "it is clear that it need not be the only or an indispensable or a necessary avenue, but equally clear that mere potential utility is insufficient."[193]

On the basis of the above analysis, as to the functional criterion in the determination of what is an international strait, the following propositions may be formulated:

(1) actual use of a strait, in opposition to mere potential use, is necessary;
(2) the strait does not have to constitute a necessary route for international navigation and may be only an alternative one;
(3) the strait must have a history as a useful route for international maritime traffic, and episodic or infrequent transit is insufficient;
(4) the sufficiency of the use is determined mainly, although not exclusively, by reference to two factors, namely, the number of ships using the strait and the number of flags represented; and
(5) the numbers of ships and flags should normally reach the order of magnitude shown to exist in the *Corfu Channel Case*, but the location of the strait and other relevant circumstances might render lower numbers sufficient.

Classification of International Straits

The 1982 Convention on the Law of the Sea covers at least five categories of international straits and provides for four different legal regimes. This rather complex situation is mainly the result of a compromise as to the type of passage which should be permitted in international straits. The historical background of this compromise has been covered by a number of writers[194] and only a very brief summary is given here.

On the one hand, the maritime powers insisted on treating international straits as an autonomous legal institution, divorced from the territorial sea and providing for the same freedom of navigation and overflight as on the high seas.[195] On the other hand, a coastal state group (Cyprus, Greece, Indonesia, Malaysia, Morocco, Philippines, Spain and Yemen) wished to keep international straits linked to the territorial sea, limiting the right of passage to one of non-suspendable innocent passage and requiring prior notification or authorization for warships.[196]

The compromise articles, entitled "Passage of Straits Used for International Navigation", were introduced by the United Kingdom at Caracas in 1974.[197] The proposal made two important changes – at least in point of form – to the draft articles previously introduced by the United States and the Soviet Union. It removed the provocative words "the same freedom of navigation as on the high seas," to qualify the type of passage applicable, and coined the phrase "transit passage" to replace them. In addition, it limited the application of "transit passage" to straits joining two parts of the high seas and retained the innocent passage rule for straits joining one part of the high seas with the territorial sea of a foreign state. The substance of the United Kingdom proposal was incorporated in the Negotiating Text of 1975 and, in spite of periodic objections on the part of some of the coastal states, remained intact in the subsequent texts of the conference, including the 1982 convention.

The five categories of international straits provided for, aside from those already governed by long-standing conventions,[198] may be described according to Figure 14 as follows:

(1) International straits with a route of high seas (or exclusive economic zone) of "similar convenience" within them will be subject to freedoms of navigation and overflight applicable to the high seas and exclusive economic zone.[199] The determining criterion of "similar convenience" refers to "navigational and hydrographical characteristics".[200] Such straits join parts of high seas or exclusive economic zones.
(2) International straits with a route of high seas (or exclusive economic zone) not of "similar convenience" will be governed by the right of transit passage.[201] This category of straits is provided for by implication in Article 36, which states that "this Part does not apply to a strait used for international navigation if there exists through the strait a route through the high seas or through an exclusive economic zone of similar convenience." If the condition for the exclusion of such straits is not met, they are included in the application of Part III on international straits and subject to the right of transit passage. These straits join parts of high seas or exclusive economic zones.
(3) International straits with a high seas (or exclusive economic zone) route of "similar convenience" seaward of an island (which forms the strait) of the coastal state are subject to the right of non-suspendable innocent passage.[202] The question of "similar convenience" is always in relation to navigational and hydrographical factors. These straits join parts of high seas or exclusive economic zones.
(4) International straits joining a part of the high seas (or an exclusive economic zone) with the territorial sea of a foreign state are governed by the traditional right of non-suspendable innocent passage.[203]
(5) International straits joining a part of the high seas (or an exclusive economic zone) with another part of the high seas (or exclusive economic zone) and not included in the previous categories are subject to the right of transit passage.

The categories of international straits just outlined would seem to be exhaustive, except for the possibility that a strait comprised exclusively of internal

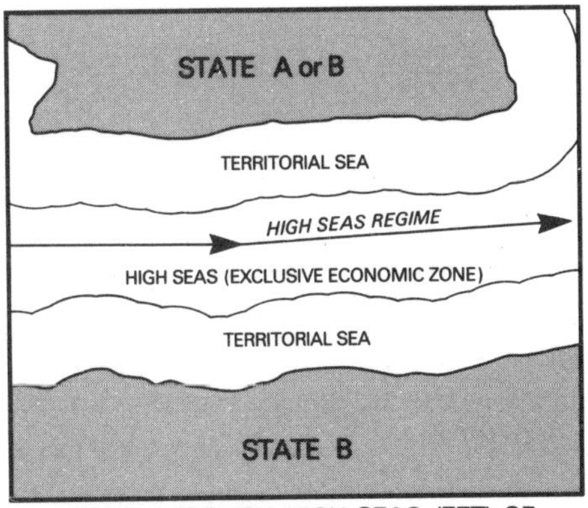

ROUTE THROUGH HIGH SEAS (EEZ) OF SIMILAR CONVENIENCE – ARTICLE 36

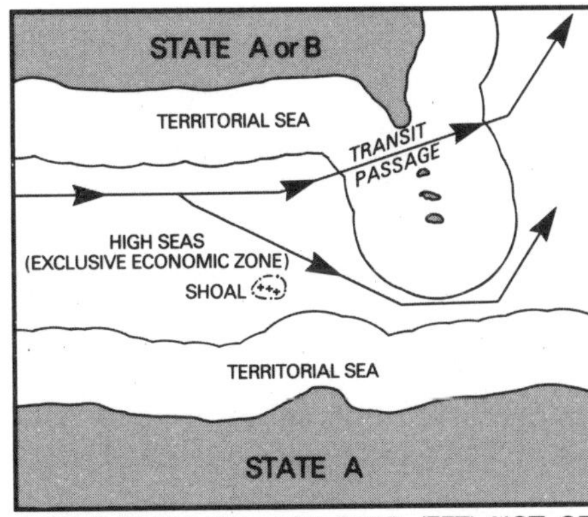

ROUTE THROUGH HIGH SEAS (EEZ) NOT OF SIMILAR CONVENIENCE – ARTICLE 36

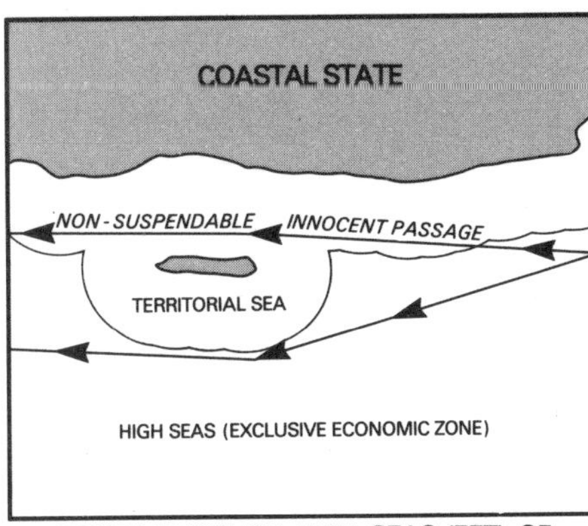

ROUTE THROUGH HIGH SEAS (EEZ) OF SIMILAR CONVENIENCE SEAWARD OF ISLAND – ARTICLES 38 (1) AND 45 (1) (A)

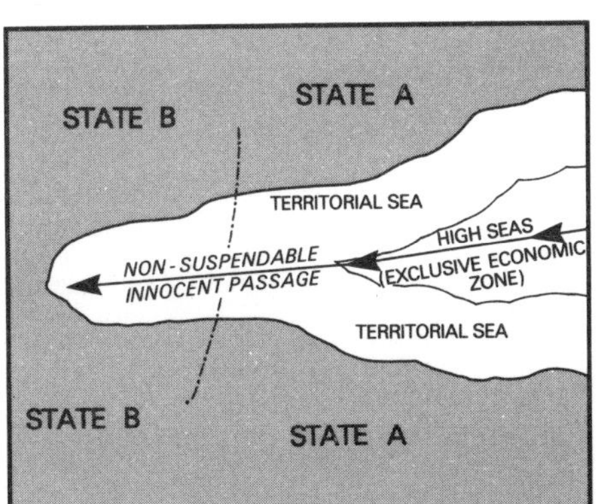

ROUTE JOINING HIGH SEAS (EEZ) WITH TERRITORIAL SEA OF FOREIGN STATE – ARTICLE 45 (1) (B)

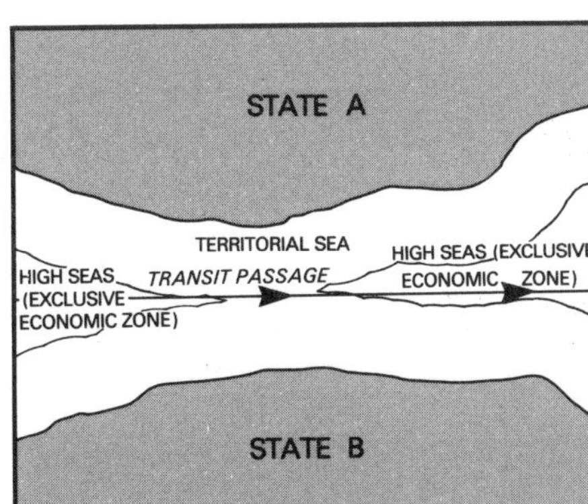

ROUTE JOINING HIGH SEAS (EEZ) WITH HIGH SEAS (EEZ) – ARTICLES 37 AND 38 (2)

Fig. 14: INTERNATIONAL STRAITS IN 1982 LAW OF THE SEA CONVENTION

Prepared for the author by John Cooper, Technical Advisor to Dept. of External Affairs, Ottawa.

waters might be used for international navigation. Two different legal situations might result, depending on the legal basis for the status of the waters. If the waters are internal because of the establishment of straight baselines, they are assimilated to territorial waters for the purposes of passage and either transit passage or non-suspendable innocent passage would apply as already discussed. If the waters are internal by reason of historic title, no right of passage applies and the strait would normally not be capable of becoming an international strait. The only possible exception to the latter legal status would result from the coastal state permitting foreign use of the strait without adequate conditions attached. A right of passage would then result from the acquisition of a servitude, rather than from the status of the waters *per se*.

Chapter 7

THE LEGAL STATUS OF THE NORTHWEST PASSAGE

Three main questions must be answered in the examination of the legal status of the Northwest Passage: 1) is it an international strait? 2) what right of passage, if any, is applicable to it? and 3) what right of protection over the Northwest Passage does Canada have as the littoral state?

THE NORTHWEST PASSAGE: AN INTERNATIONAL STRAIT?

Applying the definition reviewed in Chapter 6, two criteria, geographic and functional, must be met by the Northwest Passage before it can be classified as an international strait.

Geographic Criterion

For the first criterion to be met in the Northwest Passage the geography must be such that the passage links two parts of the high seas (or exclusive economic zones) and comprises an overlap of Canada's territorial waters. The first element of this criterion is present since the eastern end of the passage leads to Baffin Bay, the Davis Strait, the Labrador Sea, and the Atlantic Ocean, and the western end leads to the Beaufort Sea, the Chukchi Sea, the Bering Strait and the Pacific Ocean. It has occasionally been suggested that the Beaufort Sea, which is part of the Atlantic Ocean, should not be considered as high seas because of the presence of ice.[204] The above suggestion would seem to be based on the assumption that the Arctic Ocean, including the Beaufort Sea, is covered by some kind of permanent ice cap which would constitute a complete barrier to navigation. Such is not the case, however, as was shown in Chapter 1. The pack ice, comprised of ice floes and in constant motion, does not extend to the continental coast of Canada and Alaska for about three months of the year. Consequently Route 2 (through Amundsen Gulf) of the Northwest Passage leads to an open sea during that period at least. In addition, as noted in Chapter 4, navigation through winter ice has now been proven to be technologically feasible.

As for the second element of the criterion, namely, that there be an overlap of territorial waters, all the Northwest Passage routes described in Chapter 1 involve passages through such an overlap. The existence of areas of territorial waters presumes, of course, that the waters of the Canadian Arctic Archipelago are not internal waters. In this respect, although Canada has not drawn straight baselines around the archipelago, it claims that the waters of the archipelago generally, and those of the Northwest Passage in particular, are internal in nature by virtue of an historic title. However, since Canada has never formally defined or delimited its claim under the Territorial Sea and Fishing Zones Act by the establishment of straight baselines, the precise status and extent of that claim is unclear. In these circumstances, and without prejudging in any way the validity of the claim, the hypothesis or supposition presented here is that the waters of the Northwest Passage are not internal. This supposition applies particularly to Routes 1 and 2 of the passage, as described in Chapter 1.

On the basis of that supposition, the extension of Canada's territorial waters to 12 miles in 1970 resulted in an overlap of territorial waters in the middle of the Northwest Passage, namely, in the western portion of the Barrow Strait. Because of the presence of five islands lying across the strait, the widest inter-island area in the strait is Kettle Passage, between Lowther and Young Islands, which is 15½ miles, as shown in Figure 3. Consequently, even if one were to consider the Northwest Passage as being only Route 2 (through the M'Clure Strait), the passage would still qualify as a legal (territorial) strait.

In addition, Route 1, through the Prince of Wales Strait, has always had an overlap of territorial waters because the presence of the Princess Royal Islands at about the middle of the strait narrows the strait to less than six miles, as shown in Figure 3. All the other routes of the Northwest Passage must also go through narrows of less than six miles.

Considering for the moment only Routes 1 and 2, in which deep-draft navigation is possible, the effect of the 1970 legislation was to establish a second gateway of territorial waters in the Northwest Passage. This effect was explained by the Canadian Secretary of State for External Affairs at the time of the introduction of the bill in the House of Commons in the following terms:

> Since the 12-mile territorial sea is well established in international law, the effect of this Bill on the Northwest Passage is that under any sensible view of the law, Barrow Strait, as well as the Prince of Wales Strait, are subject to complete Canadian sovereignty.[205]

The legal result of the legislation was explained in similar terms by the Legal Adviser of the Department of External Affairs, a few days later, as follows:

> This has implications for Barrow Strait, for example, where the 12-mile territorial sea has the effect of giving Canada sovereignty from shore to shore.

To put it simply, we have undisputed control – undisputed in the legal sense – over two of the gateways through the Northwest Passage.[206]

The quoted statements would seem to imply that, at least before 1970, Canada recognized the possibility that a strip of high seas might exist throughout Route 2 of the Northwest Passage. This was probably the view of the United States in 1969 when the *Manhattan* attempted to cross the Northwest Passage by attempting to navigate the M'Clure Strait instead of the Prince of Wales Strait.

The above review, in the light of the stated assumption, leads to the conclusion that the Northwest Passage constitutes a legal (territorial) strait, in that it connects two parts of the high seas and has an overlap of territorial waters in all of its routes, including Routes 1 and 2, which offer the greatest potential for deep-draft navigation.

Areas of high seas which, under the present assumption, would remain in the Northwest Passage would be assimilated to territorial waters.

Functional Criterion

Pursuant to the test applied by the International Court of Justice in the *Corfu Channel Case*, that an international strait must have had an appreciable history as a useful route for international maritime traffic, as evidenced mainly by the number of ships using the strait and the number of flags represented, reference should be made to Chapters 2 and 3 where all of the crossings of the Northwest Passage have been reviewed.

Throughout the 80-year history of attempted exploratory navigation in the Northwest Passage, only 40 complete transits of the passage have taken place and of these, 27 were by Canadian ships.[207] Of the 13 foreign crossings, 10 were American, 1 Norwegian, 1 Dutch, and 1 Japanese. The Norwegian historic crossing was made with a herring boat, and the Dutch and Japanese adventures took place in pleasure yachts.

Three of the American transits were made by a squadron of icebreakers in 1957, performing hydrographic surveys during the joint Canadian-American establishment of the Distant Early Warning System, and all three ships were led through the narrow Barrow Strait by HMCS *Labrador*. Two American submarine crossings took place to test the feasibility of submerged transits of the Northwest Passage. The USS *Seadragon* in 1960 had a Canadian representative aboard in the person of Commodore O.C.S. Robertson, and the USS *Skate* in 1962 made its crossing within the context of US-Canada defense arrangements. The other five American transits were made in 1969, when the S/T *Manhattan* tanker loaded with water made its feasibility voyage in Route 1 and was accompanied for part of the voyage by the US icebreakers *Staten Island* and *North-*

wind. It had a Canadian representative aboard in the person of Captain T.C. Pullen and was escorted by the Canadian icebreaker *John A. Macdonald*.

A threefold conclusion follows from the above review: first, there were only 11 foreign transits during the 80-year period; second, all the transits were experimental; and third, they were made with Canada's consent or acquiescence, either express or implied. In these circumstances, it is obvious that by no stretch of the imagination could the Northwest Passage pass the threshold test for it to be classified as an international strait. Those who maintain that the passage may be so classified obviously confuse *actual use* with *potential use*. The latter is the criterion used by American courts to determine whether a waterway is navigable or not. In such cases, as explained by Professor Baxter, it is the capacity for navigation which is the effective criterion,[208] but it is not the criterion of actual use applied in international law.

RIGHT OF PASSAGE IN THE NORTHWEST PASSAGE

Applying the supposition that the waters of the Northwest Passage should be considered as territorial waters, the right of innocent passage applies as in any territorial waters. This is so regardless of the fact that those waters lie within a strait, although not used for international navigation, joining two parts of the high seas.

The right of innocent passage is a right in the strict sense of the term and not simply a privilege or a tolerance. It has been recognized in customary international law since the latter part of the 19th century,[209] by the Territorial Sea Convention of 1958,[210] and by the 1982 Convention on the Law of the Sea.[211] Indeed, it is this right of innocent passage which traditionally distinguishes the legal status of internal waters, over which a state has absolute sovereignty, from that of territorial waters, where the sovereignty of the coastal state is subject to this restriction. It is only since the 1958 Territorial Sea Convention that the newly enclosed internal waters of a coastal archipelago have been subject to the right of innocent passage.

To understand the meaning and the scope of the right of innocent passage both in general, and with reference to its application to the Northwest Passage, two points at least must be addressed: (1) the meaning of innocent passage and (2) the passage of warships.

Innocent Passage

In the 1958 Convention on the Territorial Sea and Contiguous Zone, passage was defined as innocent "so long as it is not prejudicial to the peace, good order or security of the coastal State."[212] In the 1982 Convention on the Law of the

Sea the same definition of "innocent" is retained, except that it specifies a series of activities which are considered to be non-innocent. Eleven such activities are listed and relate to the following: use of force; violation of customs, fiscal, immigration, and sanitary laws; wilful and serious pollution; fishing; research and survey; and interference with communications. Any other activity not bearing on passage is also prohibited.[213]

All the activities specifically mentioned require an overt act. This is consonant with the view of the International Court of Justice in the *Corfu Channel Case* that it is the manner of passage rather than its purpose which is the determining factor.[214] The passage becomes prejudicial to the coastal state only if the foreign ship engages in any of the specific activities mentioned.

It would also seem that the requirement of an overt act would not make it possible, as it was under the 1958 convention, to consider a sub-standard tanker threatening the coastal state with pollution damage as being *per se* non-innocent. This interpretation is supported by the fact that one of the specific activities listed is "an act of wilful and serious pollution contrary to this Convention."[215] Consequently, not only must there be an actual act of pollution, but the pollution must also be wilful and serious.

The list of prohibited activities is not an exhaustive one, however, since it includes "any other activity not having a direct bearing upon passage". This residual clause is compatible with the obligation that the passage must take place, not only in conformity with the Convention but also "with other rules of international law".[216] It is also in accord with the new definition of "passage", which specifies that the act of navigation through the territorial sea must be "continuous and expeditious".[217] The only exceptions to this are stopping and anchoring insofar as they are incidental to navigation or are rendered necessary by *force majeure* or for rendering assistance.

A remaining point of interest is the burden of proof of a non-innocent activity. Under the 1958 convention, there seemed to be a presumption of innocence in favor of the ship, since the text simply said that "passage is innocent so long as it is not prejudicial to the peace, good order or security of the coastal State."[218] Since the same wording is retained in the 1982 convention, the only difference being the list of activities, the presumption probably still applies.[219] If it does, the coastal state should be able to regulate the passage of ships in such a way that it can point to a breach of its protective regulations as proof of the non-innocence of the passage.

To sum up the meaning of innocent passage, the following propositions may be stated:

(1) passage is innocent so long as a ship does not engae in any of the specifically prohibited activities or any other activity not directly related to passage;
(2) prohibited activities are expressed in the form of overt acts; and

(3) it is not clear if the burden of proving that an activity is not innocent is on the coastal state or on the ship, but it seems to be on the coastal state.

Passage of Warships

The question whether or not warships benefit from the right of innocent passage[220] has been a very controversial one, although less so in recent years. In the *Corfu Channel Case* of 1949, the International Court of Justice carefully avoided pronouncing itself on the question of innocent passage of warships through the territorial sea as such; it confined its judgment to the strict question at issue, namely, the right of innocent passage of warships through international straits in peacetime.

Judge Krylov, however, did deal with the question in his dissenting opinion, agreeing with Professor Gidel, that the passage of warships was not a right but rather a tolerance. He also referred with approval to the view expressed by Elihu Root, agent for the United States government in the North Atlantic Fisheries Arbitration of 1910, that warships possessed no right of innocent passage because they constituted a menace and threatened the coastal state.[221]

In preparing the draft of the 1958 Convention on the Territorial Sea and Contiguous Zone, the International Law Commission fully debated the question of passage of warships. It began by granting passage to warships without prior authorization or notification but, due to the strong opposition of certain members and the comments received from governments, it provided in its final draft article that prior authorization was necessary. It specified, however, that such authorization should normally be granted.[222]

At the 1958 Geneva Conference on the Law of the Sea, after much debate, no specific provision on the right of innocent passage of warships was retained, but all provisions relating to innocent passage were made applicable to all ships.[223] The conference also approved a special article providing for the expulsion of warships from the territorial sea in case of refusal to comply with the regulations of the coastal state.[224]

As a result of the above, the right of innocent passage in favor of warships in territorial waters continued to be questioned after the conference, and the Soviet Union attached a reservation which provided for prior authorization to its ratification of the Territorial Sea Convention. The reservation was consonant with the interpretation put on the convention by Professor G. Tunkin and other Soviet jurists.[225] On the other hand, the overwhelming view of international lawyers and commentators is that the convention does grant the right of innocent passage to warships.[226]

On this question, the well-known legal historian Professor J.H.W. Verzijl made a thorough review of the proceedings and deliberations of the 1958 conference, both in committee and in plenary sessions, and came to the following conclusion:

After the rejection of the exceptional provision for passing warships, their freedom of passage is clearly covered by the general rules in subsection A "applicable to all ships." No falling back upon a pretended contrary rule of customary law, said to allow a coastal State to prevent the passage of warships without its authorization, a rule, – for the rest, resolutely opposed by others – would seem to be of any judicial avail against the explicit provisions and the logical context of Section III of Part I of the first Convention.[227]

In spite of the controversy on the proper interpretation of the 1958 Territorial Sea Convention relating to the right of innocent passage of warships, the 1982 Convention on the Law of the Sea followed exactly the same approach. In Part II, on the territorial sea and contiguous zone, Section III, entitled "Innocent Passage in the Territorial Sea", begins with subsection A, "Rules Applicable to all Ships". This subsection is of general application to *all* ships and makes no mention of warships in particular. However, as in 1958, the new convention contains the same article permitting the expulsion of a warship which does not comply with the regulations of the coastal state concerning passage through its territorial sea and disregards a request for compliance.[228]

The controversy on warships is not over. At the last session of the Third UN Law of the Sea Conference in December 1982, a number of coastal states attempted to present an amendment which would have required prior notification or authorization for the passage of warships. However, because of the opposition of the great maritime powers, in particular the Soviet Union (somewhat contrary to its reservation to the 1958 Convention), the proposed amendment was conditionally withdrawn. The condition was that the president of the conference would read a statement in plenary that the withdrawal was without prejudice to the views of states which maintained that prior notification for the innocent passage of warships was required under international law.[229]

As to the right of innocent passage on the part of submarines, both the 1958 and 1982 conventions provide that submarines have an obligation to navigate on the surface and show their flag. In 1982 the text enlarges this obligation to "other underwater vehicles".[230] Considering the fact that the innocent passage of submarines would normally be warships, it is an additional reason to conclude that the intention of the drafters of both the 1958 and the 1982 conventions was to make the right of innocent passage applicable to warships.

CANADA'S RIGHT OF PROTECTION IN THE NORTHWEST PASSAGE

As a state bordering the Northwest Passage, Canada has the right to take a certain number of protective measures to regulate the exercise of innocent passage in that waterway. In addition, because the Northwest Passage is situated in an ice-covered area, Canada has a special right to adopt and enforce regulations for the protection of its marine environment.

General Right of Protection

The 1958 Convention on the Territorial Sea and the Contiguous Zone confined itself to providing that the coastal state could take the necessary steps in its territorial sea to prevent passage which was not innocent and, if it was essential for the protection of its security, to suspend temporarily the innocent passage of foreign ships. The 1982 Convention on the Law of the Sea is much more complete in specifying the protective rights of the coastal state.

The 1982 convention contains a list of matters for which the coastal state may adopt laws and regulations, and the list is in effect the counterpart of the list of prohibited activities on the part of the ship.[231] Unlike the latter, however, the list of coastal state powers appears to be an exhaustive list. It covers the safety of navigation, navigational aids, cables and pipelines, living resources and fisheries, preservation of the marine environment, scientific research, and customs, fiscal, immigration and sanitary laws. In addition, the coastal state may designate sea lanes and establish traffic separation schemes requiring foreign ships, particularly tankers, to confine their passage to such lanes.

The coastal state must be careful not to hamper the innocent passage of foreign ships through its territorial sea and, in particular, must not impose requirements which have the practical effect of denying or impairing the right of innocent passage.[232] It may, however, take the necessary steps to prevent passage which is not innocent and may also, if it is essential for the protection of its security, suspend temporarily in specified areas the innocent passage of foreign ships.[233]

Of special interest is the right to adopt laws and regulations for "the preservation of the marine environment of the coastal State and the prevention, reduction and control of pollution thereof."[234] There are two important limitations, however, to this regulatory power. First, it is specifically provided that such laws and regulations shall not hamper innocent passage of foreign vessels.[235] Second, none of the laws of the coastal state can apply to the design, construction, manning or equipment of foreign ships, unless they are giving effect to generally accepted international rules or standards.[236]

With the above limitations, it is evident that the powers of the coastal state to regulate the passage of tankers in its territorial sea (or straits not used for international navigation) are normally severely confined. Indeed, since the passage of a foreign ship remains innocent so long as it does not engage in "any act of wilful and serious pollution,"[237] the regulatory power of the coastal state is limited to preventing such an act. Since coastal state powers are specifically enumerated in the convention, it is difficult to argue that more extensive powers could be derived from "other rules of international law" preserved by Article 21.

Most enforcement powers with respect to the preservation of its marine environment are vested in the flag state, with limited concurrent jurisdiction in favor of the coastal and port states. It is only when there are clear grounds for believing that a ship has violated its anti-pollution laws during passage through its territorial sea that a coastal state may physically inspect the ship in question and go so far as to detain the vessel and institute proceedings. Even then, such a violation would have to be a wilful and serious act of pollution before the coastal state could proceed with any action. In other words, the coastal state would have to wait until the pollution had actually occurred before it could enforce its national laws and regulations relating to pollution.

In spite of the limitations on the powers of the coastal state to prevent and control pollution within its territorial sea, Canada enjoys considerably enlarged powers by virtue of a special provision applicable to ice-covered areas, under which falls of course, the Northwest Passage.

Special Right of Protection

Somewhat disappointed at the limited scope of application of the 1969 Brussels Convention Relating to Intervention on the High Seas to prevent oil pollution damage, which had prevented a coastal state from taking any protective measure until after a maritime casualty, Canada adopted its Arctic Waters Pollution Prevention Act in 1970. The Act provided for the establishment of shipping safety control zones in Arctic waters and for regulations prescribing certain standards of hull and fuel tank construction, navigational aids, manning of the ship, pilotage, ice-breaking assistance, and maximum cargo quantity. The shipping safety control zones were, in fact, established in 1972, and the standards which must be met for navigation in those various zones were specified.

The United States strongly objected to Canada's claim of jurisdiction over foreign ships on the high seas up to 100 miles from Canada's coast. This prompted Canada to embark upon intense diplomatic efforts in a number of international fora to obtain recognition of international law principles which would serve as basis for its legislation. These efforts were pursued mainly at three international conferences: the Stockholm Conference on the Human Environment of 1972, the London Conference of the International Maritime Consultative Organization on the Prevention of Pollution by Ships in 1973, and the United Nations Third Law of the Sea Conference which began its substantive work in 1974.

At the 1975 session of the Law of the Sea Conference, a special Arctic clause was inserted in the first Negotiating Text. It provided that coastal states could adopt special protective measures in areas within their exclusive economic zone where exceptional hazards to navigation prevailed and marine pollution could cause irreversible disturbance of ecological balance. In 1976 the provision was enlarged to enable coastal states themselves to enforce such protective measures, instead of leaving the enforcement to the flag state.

The above provision was retained without change in the subsequent Negotiating Texts of 1977, 1979, and 1980, as well as in the Convention on the Law of the Sea itself, signed in December 1982. The special Arctic clause in question reads as follows:

> Coastal States have the right to adopt and enforce non-discriminatory laws and regulations for the prevention, reduction and control of marine pollution from vessels in ice-covered areas within the limits of the exclusive economic zone, where particularly severe climatic conditions and the presence of ice covering such areas for most of the year create obstructions or exceptional hazards to navigation, and pollution of the marine environment would cause major harm to or irreversible disturbance of the ecological balance. Such laws and regulations shall have due regard to navigation and the protection and preservation of the marine environment based on the best available scientific evidence.[238]

There are at least five elements in this special clause which should be highlighted. First, the coastal state not only has the right to adopt special protective measures, but it may also enforce them against foreign ships. Second, the permitted regulations may be of a preventive nature and may, therefore, apply to the design, construction, manning, and equipment of foreign ships. Third, this right applies within the limits of the 200-mile exclusive zone and, therefore, *a fortiori*, to the limits of the territorial sea. Fourth, such measures may only be taken in areas where ice is present most of the year, where it creates exceptional hazards to navigation, and where pollution could cause major harm to, or irreversible disturbance of, the ecological balance. Fifth, the regulations of the coastal state must have due regard to the imperatives of navigation and the best scientific data available relating to the protection of the marine environment.

The first two elements mentioned above circumscribe the extent of the right conferred on the coastal state, whereas the other three define the physical requirements for the valid exercise of that right. In addition, it is important to note that the exercise of that right by the coastal state is not subject to any control whatever by the International Maritime Consultative Organization.

The special Arctic clause removes any doubt as to the international validity of Canada's 1970 legislation and, having regard to the wide consensus which the clause has received, particularly on the part of other Arctic states, it may now be regarded as accepted in customary international law.[239] The question whether the Arctic clause would continue to apply if the Northwest Passage were to become an international strait will be discussed in the next chapter.

Chapter 8

THE FUTURE LEGAL STATUS OF THE NORTHWEST PASSAGE

In examining what the legal status of the Northwest Passage may be in the future, three basic questions must be answered: 1) could the Northwest Passage become an international strait? 2) what right of passage would apply in that event? and 3) what right of protection would Canada have?

THE NORTHWEST PASSAGE: AN INTERNATIONAL STRAIT?

The answer to the question of whether the Northwest Passage is an international strait depends, in turn, on the answer to two other questions: 1) will there be sufficient international shipping in the Northwest Passage? and 2) could Canada take measures to prevent the internationalization of the passage?

Sufficient International Shipping

In spite of all the uncertainties about the future commercial development of Arctic resources and the projected marine traffic discussed in Chapter 4, one conclusion would seem inescapable: international shipping will eventually take place through the Northwest Passage. Such shipping has already begun in part of the passage to transport minerals from Nanisivik Mine, south of Lancaster Sound, and Polaris Mine, north of the Barrow Strait. In addition, it seems to be only a question of time before shipping of gas from Melville Island, north of Viscount Melville Sound, and the shipping of oil from the Beaufort Sea along the full length of the Northwest Passage will take place. This oil would probably come from both the Canadian and the Alaskan side of the Beaufort Sea. Realistic estimates for the beginning of Beaufort Sea oil shipping are between 1990 and 1995.

Assuming that international shipping will take place, would this result in the internationalization of the passage? More precisely, will the number of foreign flags and foreign transits be sufficient to put the Northwest Passage in the category of straits being used for international navigation? The answer to those questions is probably yes. It would seem that the only uncertainty is the time at which this would take place, which depends on the intensity of the use. On this point, it will be recalled that the threshold used in the *Corfu Channel Case* was fairly high, but a sufficient use for the Northwest Passage might be considerably lower because of the remoteness of the region and the absence of alternative routes.

Canadian Measures to Deny International Character

In 1983 an official of the Department of Transport stated that it was relatively easy to implement a domestic or coastal shipping policy which reserved Canadian coastal trade to Canadian ships, but such would not be the case for an international shipping policy.[240] The difficulty was summed up as follows:

> The definition of a Canadian policy and the ways of achieving high Canadian content is a much more difficult proposition when applied to international movements. Export and import movements out of the Arctic go beyond the unilateral control of Canada and our policy cannot be defined in ignorance of market forces or exceed boundaries of our national jurisdiction through a variety of extraterritorial considerations.[241]

In other words, the insistence on using Canadian flags – supposing for a moment Canada had the necessary ships – would risk retaliation and could perhaps jeopardize the viability of the projects being developed. However, the government might deem it appropriate "to request all companies wanting to do business in the Canadian Arctic to submit in advance a well-defined transportation plan that could be assessed in terms of Canadian capability and Canadian content."[242]

In addition to the above, it is conceivable that Canada might wish to take a certain number of measures to deny any international character of the Northwest Passage, such as a legislative confirmation of its sovereignty claim over those waters, the development of what might be termed a technological sovereignty, and perhaps also the conclusion of user agreements with shipping states.

Sovereignty through Legislation. In keeping with a number of measures of functional jurisdiction adopted since 1970, Canada might decide to adopt legislation to provide an adequate basis for its claim to sovereignty over the waters of the Arctic Archipelago. The best approach for Canada to follow would be to encircle the archipelago with straight baselines, from which it would then draw its territorial sea. As additional support for the enclosed waters to become legally "internal", Canada could invoke the historical use of those waters by its Inuit population.[243] This was the approach followed by Norway to justify its straigt baseline system along its coast of jagged islands, which was approved by the International Court of Justice in the *Anglo-Norwegian Fisheries Case* in 1951.[244]

It would seem preferable for Canada to rely on the customary law applied in the *Fisheries Case* rather than on the codifying provisions of the 1958 Convention on the Territorial Sea and retained in the 1982 Convention on the Law of the Sea. The first reason is that the legal result would be preferable, in that Canada would have complete sovereignty over the enclosed waters, although it might permit innocent passage which would be subject to Canadian regulations. In the second place, there would appear to be more flexibility under the court's judgment than under the convention to meet the geographic requirements for the application of the strait baseline system. Canada could emphasize the very special geographic and physical characteristics of its Arctic Archipelago, leading to the conclusion that those islands ought to be considered as an integral part of the mainland of Canada for the purpose of delimiting territorial waters.

The International Court of Justice was quite receptive to this type of argument in the *Fisheries Case* and admitted that the "drawing of straight baselines must be adapted to the special conditions obtaining in different regions."[245] An important part of the special conditions prevailing in the Canadian Arctic is the fact that the waters of the archipelago are frozen solid for some nine months of the year, thus enhancing the physical unity of the archipelago and reducing the logic of attempting to delimit territorial waters around the islands individually.

Of course, the above would entail drawing a certain number of baselines of considerable length, particularly across Amundsen Gulf and the M'Clure Strait at the western end of the passage, and Lancaster Sound at its eastern entrance. It is in this respect that Canada could invoke the historical use of those waters, as did Norway in 1951. In particular, Canada is in a position to rely on the fact that it performed a number of manifestations of sovereignty, such as the collection of customs in the western Arctic and the enforcement of fisheries and whaling legislation in the eastern Arctic, beginning in 1903 and 1904 respectively. Canada could also invoke the exclusive sea-ice use for hunting and fishing by its Inuit for at least 4,000 years, which it has protected by the adoption of such measures as the creation of the Arctic Islands Preserve in 1926 and the enactment of the Arctic Waters Pollution Prevention Act in 1970.

Technological Sovereignty. Legal sovereignty is very important, but to make it credible it has to be accompanied by technological sovereignty. As one Canadian official put it recently, "the Arctic has to be won in fact as well as in law". In other words, if Canada is to exercise the necessary control to maintain the sovereignty it claims to have acquired over the waters of the Northwest Passage, it must develop a full range of sea and land based services to ensure that its control is factual and effective.

The Department of Transport, in its 1982 position statement to the Beaufort Sea Environment Assessment Panel, seemed to have recognized the importance of effective control when it stated that it should be able to provide the following services: marine navigational aids, icebreaking and escorting, marine search and rescue, marine emergencies/pollution control, marine mobile communications services, ports, harbors and terminals, vessel inspection services, vessel traffic management, marine re-supply administration and support, pilotage, and training.[246] The position paper specified that these services would be in addition to those such as hydrography, oceanography, ice properties, ice distribution and movements, meteorology, dredging implementation, and customs services, which other government departments would continue to provide.

Of all the above services, perhaps the most important ones for the exercise of effective control are icebreaking and pilotage. Of course, these are services for which a coastal state is entitled to charge foreign shippers. This was the plan of the Soviet Union in 1967, when it invited certain foreign shippers to use the Northeast Arctic Passage and distributed to them a brochure setting out the rates to be charged.[247] Apparently the Soviet offer was not accepted, but the important fact is that the Soviet Union insisted upon providing those necessary services to any interested foreign shipper. In addition, the regulations of the Northern Sea Route Administration provide for compulsory icebreaker escort and pilotage for all vessels in most of the straits constituting the Northeast Arctic Passage.[248]

With the necessary technological tools at its disposal, Canada could establish and enforce a transit management system which could become the primary means at its disposal to ensure effective control over foreign shipping.

User Agreements. Presuming it had acquired both the legal and factual control of the waters of the Northwest Passage, Canada would be in a position to insist upon the conclusion of bilateral agreements for the use of the passage by foreign shippers. Those agreements would, of course, recognize Canada's control over the passage and provide for the conditions to be met by foreign shippers, such as the use of Canadian icebreaking and pilotage services.

If one can judge from the reaction of certain American participants at a 1981 workshop on Arctic Ocean issues, such an agreement would not be too difficult to conclude with the United States. A summary of the proceedings stated that "an American participant agreed with an earlier speaker (also an American) that it might be diplomatically feasible for the United States and Canada to negotiate a bilateral treaty that spelled out specific conditions of transit through the Passage for commercial vessels.[249]

The conclusion of user agreements would follow logically from declarations made by Canada in 1969 and 1970. The Prime Minister stated in 1969 that "to close off those waters and to deny passage to all foreign vessels in the name of Canadian sovereignty, as some commentators have suggested, would be as senseless as placing barriers across the entrances of Halifax and Vancouver harbours.[250] Again, in its Note of 1970 to the United States, the Canadian government reierated "its determination to open up the Northwest Passage to safe navigation for the shipping of all nations subject, however, to necessary conditions required to protect the delicate ecological balance of the Canadian Arctic."[251]

THE NORTHWEST PASSAGE: AN INTERNATIONAL REGIME?

To analyze rights of passage that might be applied to the Northwest Passage were it to beome an international strait, two main points must be addressed, namely: 1) the meaning of transit passage; and 2) whether or not it is applicable to warships. The discussion will be limited to the right of transit passage applicable to straits used for international navigation, but the right of sea lanes passage applicable to the waters of an archipelagic state is basically the same.

Transit Passage

The definition of transit passage in the 1982 Law of the Sea Convention is practically a verbatim reproduction of the one found in the proposal of the United Kingdom of 1974 and reads as follows:

> Transit passage means the exercise in accordance with this Part of the freedom of navigation and overflight solely for the purpose of continuous and expeditious transit of the strait between one part of the high seas or an exclusive economic zone and another part of the high seas or an exclusive economic zone.[252]

Since the expression "transit passage" replaced that of "free passage", which the United States and the Soviet Union had in their proposals,[253] the question arises as to whether this new right of passage is more restrictive than the one which the two great powers wanted. More specifically, what are the limitations of "the freedom of navigation and overflight" in international straits as distinguished from the same freedoms on the high seas? The definition contains two limitations: first, the freedom has to be exercised "in accordance with this Part", and second, it must be "solely for the purpose of continuous and expeditious transit". These limitations are expressed in the form of duties imposed on ships and aircraft during transit and are found in articles 39, 40 and 41.

Article 39 specifies certain duties for ships and aircraft, either together or separately. Both ships and aircraft must proceed through the strait without delay, refrain from any threat or use of force, and refrain from any activity not incidental to their normal modes of transit unless rendered necessary by *force majeure* or distress. In addition, there is a duty imposed on ships to comply with the generally accepted international regulations relating to safety at sea and pollution prevention and control.

Article 40 prohibits ships from carrying out research and survey activities without the prior authorization of the bordering states, and Article 41 requires them to respect applicable sea lanes and traffic separation schemes.

Such is the extent of the limitations imposed by the 1982 Convention on the freedom of navigation through international straits. Unlike the case of the exercise of the right of innocent passage, there is no list of prohibited activities applicable to the exercise of the right of transit passage. In these circumstances, one must conclude that the removal of the words "the same freedom of navigation as on the high seas", qualifying the type of the passage applicable to international straits, and their replacement by the limitations just discussed, did not change the essential nature of the right originally contemplated.

Passage of Warships

The question whether the right of transit passage applies to warships passing through international straits is no more expressly covered by the 1982 convention than the question of the right of innocent passage for warships passing through the territorial sea. The absence of any mention of the subject is even more complete in the articles on transit passage, in that there is no provision whatever relating to submarines. Does this indicate that the maritime powers abandoned their original insistence on the freedom of navigation and overflight "through and over" straits used for international navigation?[254] In introducing the United States proposal on the subject in 1971, the head of the American delegation specified that this was a "limited but vital right."[255]

It would be very difficult to conclude that there has been such an abandonment in light of a number of statements made by the maritime powers after 1971. The United States, in particular, made it quite clear on numerous occasions at the Third UN Law of the Sea Conference that it could not agree to an extension of a 12-mile territorial sea by coastal states, thus eliminating a strip of high seas from 113 straits (according to its own estimate), unless it retained the freedom of navigation and overflight through and over such straits for its ships and aircraft.

This condition was emphasized not only by the United States delegation at the conference, but also by the Secretary of State outside the conference. In a prepared speech delivered to the Annual Meeting of the American Bar Association in August 1975, the US Secretary of State, Henry Kissinger, stated:

After years of dispute and contradictory international practice, the Law of the Sea Conference is approaching a consensus on the twelve-mile territorial limit. We are prepared to accept this solution, provided that the unimpeded transit rights through and over straits used for international navigation are guaranteed.[256]

The Secretary of State concluded on this question by saying "we will not join in any agreement which leaves any uncertainty about the right to use world communication routes without interference".[257]

In spite of the above, however, a controversy has arisen among a number of American international lawyers who were asked in July 1976 by US Senator Barry Goldwater whether the Negotiating Text would guarantee the submerged transit of submarines through straits.[258] The main source of the controversy appeared to stem from the permissible use of supplementary means of interpretation, including the preparatory work of the convention and the circumstances of its conclusion. Supplementary means are specifically provided for in the Vienna Convention on the Law of Treaties and may be used either to confirm the meaning of the terms of a treaty interpreted in their context or to determine that meaning when it appears ambiguous or manifestly absurd.[259] It seems clear, in full agreement with the interpretation of several international lawyers, that the right of submerged transit by submarines may be deduced from a study of the text of the 1982 convention itself and is most clearly confirmed by an examination of the circumstances surrounding the conclusion of the convention.[260]

Like innocent passage, made applicable to all ships in the territorial sea by the 1982 convention, the right of transit passage is also made applicable to all ships and aircraft in international straits. Whereas this result was obtained by the simple use of a heading, "Rules Applicable to All Ships", for the right of innocent passage, the scope of application of the right of transit passage was made considerably more explicit in a special article which provides that "all ships and aircraft enjoy the right of transit passage, which shall not be impeded".[261] The applicability of this right to all ships was reinforced by a subsequent provision limiting the laws and regulations which may be adopted by bordering states. This limitation specifies that "such laws and regulations shall not discriminate in form or in fact among foreign ships."[262] One cannot conclude from this alone, however, that submarines have an unambiguous right of free transit.

The ambiguity or obscurity of the provisions already referred to is clarified in that part of Article 39 which specifies the common duties of ships and aircraft while exercising their right of transit passage. That article provides that they shall "refrain from any activities other than those incidental to their *normal modes* of continuous and expeditious transit unless rendered necessary by *force majeure* or by distress."[263]

As succinctly pointed out by Professor O'Connell, "since submarines are by definition underwater vehicles, submerged passage is a 'normal mode' of operation for such craft".[264] And the reason for the express prohibition against submerged passage in the territorial sea and the implied permission for submerged transit in international straits "rests on the essentially different juridical character of the territorial sea from straits".[265]

Professor William T. Burke had already reached in 1977 a similar interpretation of the meaning of normal mode of passage.

> In this view a submarine is in a normal mode of passage when it operates submerged and its obligations are measured in that light. On the other hand, the submarine might pass on the surface and its obligations would then take that mode into account. The important point is that Article 38 does not authorize the coastal State to determine what is a "normal" mode of transit each time a vehicle approaches a strait. It does specify that a vessel in transit passage, in whatever mode it determines to use in light of its operating characteristics and other relevant features of the context, shall only engage in conduct which is an incident of such mode of passage.[266]

The above interpretation, based solely on the terms of the Informal Composite Negotiating Text and the ordinary meaning of those terms in their context, is fully confirmed by an examination of the circumstances of the conclusion of the 1982 convention. True, the preparatory work is not very satisfactory in that it does not include a complete record of the proceedings of the Law of the Sea Convention, but the circumstances of the conclusion of the convention and as they appeared throughout the conference, unquestionably confirm the textual interpretation given above.

Professor J.N. Moore served for a while as the United States Ambassador to the Conference and headed the US team that participated in the development of the navigation and security provisions. Summarizing the circumstances prevailing at the conference on this question, Professor Moore has concluded:

> This evidence includes repeated statements by the United States, the Soviet Union, and other maritime States concerning the essentiality of transit passage (including submerged transit and other incidents), followed by absence of objections to the ICNT text by these parties; efforts by extreme strait States to reopen the text and prohibit submerged transit or overflight of straits; common and uncontradicted use of special terms during negotiations such as "freedom of navigation" and "in the normal mode" to include submerged transit; and on-the-record exchange indicating that the United Kingdom's transit passage text contemplated overflight and submerged transit.[267]

For anyone who followed the conference closely on the issue of straits, the above analysis of the circumstances appears unassailable.

There are two possible types of international straits where only the right of innocent passage would apply, and consequently a submarine would have to surface if it chose to venture in those routes: first, where there is a high seas route of "similar convenience" seaward of an island of the coastal state, which forms the strait joining two parts of the high seas or of exclusive economic zones; and second, in international straits which join a part of the high seas or of an exclusive economic zone with the territorial sea of a foreign state.[268]

CANADA'S PROTECTIVE RIGHTS OVER THE NORTHWEST PASSAGE

Even if the Northwest Passage were to become an international strait, Canada would have two sets of protective rights in relation to the exercise of transit passage by foreign ships. It would have certain general rights given to all states bordering international straits and it would continue to benefit from the special right of coastal states bordering ice-covered areas.

General Right of Protection

Bordering states are given a certain regulatory authority relating to transit passage in international straits, which is strictly limited to what is permitted, by the 1982 Law of the Sea Convention. There is no reference here to "other rules of international law", as there is in Part II of the convention relating to innocent passage.[269] The convention contains three provisions which may confer powers on bordering states: Articles 40, 41 and 42.

Article 40 contains an implied power in favor of the coastal state to adopt regulations prohibiting research and survey activities without its prior authorization. This power is implied from a specific prohibition against foreign ships engaging in such activities.[270] Article 41 empowers bordering states to designate sea lanes and prescribe traffic separation schemes. Such power is carefully circumscribed, however, since those sea lanes and traffic separation schemes must conform to generally accepted international regulations and must be approved by the competent international organization.

Article 42 contains a more general power to adopt laws and regulations with respect to the four following matters: 1) the safety of navigation and the regulation of maritime traffic, as provided in Article 41; 2) the prevention of pollution, by giving effect to applicable international regulations; 3) the prevention of fishing; and 4) the loading or unloading of any commodity, currency, or person in contravention of customs, fiscal, immigration, or sanitary regulations of the bordering state.

The above represents the complete list of subject matters over which bordering states have some regulatory authority. The only other possibility for them to obtain more protection, in respect of the safety of navigation and the prevention of pollution would be by agreement with user states.[271]

Enforcement powers, as distinguished from the regulatory powers, of the bordering state, are expressly denied the coastal state except in one instance. The only case where the bordering state "may take appropriate enforcement measures" is where a warship, or a government ship on non-commercial service, has committed a violation of the laws and regulations of the coastal state pertaining to the safety of navigation or the prevention of pollution, where the latter are in conformity with applicable regulations. The violation must be such that it is "causing or threatening major damage to the marine environment of the straits".[272] In other words, only in the case of actual or threatened major damage to the marine environment may the coastal state take enforcement action. Otherwise, the traditional jurisdiction of the flag state applies.

Special Right of Protection

As indicated at the end of Chapter 7, Canada's Arctic Waters Pollution Prevention Act and Regulations have been validated internationally by a special ice-covered areas clause incorporated in the 1982 convention, namely Article 234. But would Canada continue to benefit from that special clause if the Northwest Passage were to become an international strait? The answer has to be affirmative.

Article 234 would continue to apply. Indeed, that article constitutes a special section (Section 8 of Part XII) by itself, and its application is not excluded, as are some of the other sections in Part XII on "Protection and Preservation of the Marine Environment", from straits used for international navigation. The last article of Part XII (Art. 233) of the convention provides that "nothing in sections 5, 6 and 7 affects the legal regime of straits used for international navigation." The only exception to this relates to "major damage to the marine environment of the straits" by military and government ships, discussed above under enforcement powers.

The three sections which do not specifically affect the regime of international straits are those relating to "international rules and national legislation to prevent, reduce and control pollution of the marine environment" (Section 5), "enforcement" (Section 6), and "safeguards" (Section 7). If it had been the intention to apply the legal regime of international straits to those straits lying in ice-covered areas, Section 8 entitled "Ice-covered Areas" would have been added to the enumeration of sections specifically excluded in Article 233. This not being the case, Section 8, comprised of that unique provision (Article 234), stands in a completely independent position and is unaffected by the provisions relating to standards, enforcement, and safeguards.

The above interpretation would appear to be shared by Professor Moore, when he stated that the 1982 convention had not altered the existing uncertainty in customary international law as to the definition of straits used for international navigation and added "still, the Arctic straits controversy (including the Northwest Passage question) may be diffused by the ice-covered areas understanding embodied in Articles 234, 236, and 296, which would apply 'within the limits of the exclusive economic zone'."[273] In other words, he believed that the controversy as to whether or not the Northwest Passage is an international strait lost its importance because of the understanding embodied in the special ice-covered areas provision which continues to apply.

Since the 1982 convention was not in force at the beginning of 1984, the question whether the Arctic clause has become part of customary international law should be examined. First, the application of this special clause is limited to the exclusive economic zone, which concept received the widest possible support at the Law of the Sea Conference and has been adopted by a great number of states in their national legislation. As for the special rights of the Arctic states in the ice-covered areas within that zone, a wide and positive consensus on those rights has clearly emerged since the concept was first introduced at the Geneva session of the conference in 1975.[274]

In addition, the two series of straits mainly affected by this special provision, namely the Northwest Passage of Canada and the Northeast Passage of the Soviet Union, have both been the subject of special protective legislation. Canada adopted its legislation in 1970, and the Soviet Union did the same in 1971.[275] Although the United States protested Canada's legislation in 1970, its delegation eventually shared the consensus for Article 234 at the conference. The other Arctic states, Norway and Denmark, have not objected the Canadian legislation, and neither did the Soviet Union since its own legislation is very similar to that of Canada. In these circumstances and considering the wide consensus of states on this special provision, particularly on the part of the Arctic states, it may be regarded as part of customary international law.

CONCLUSION

By way of conclusion on the legal status of the Northwest Passage, six main propositions may be formulated:

(1) An international strait is one which has been used for international maritime traffic, the sufficiency of the use being determined mainly by reference to the number of foreign ships having crossed the strait and the number of flags represented.
(2) The Northwest Passage is not an international strait, because it has never been used for international navigation.

(3) The Northwest Passage is a legal or territorial strait, since there is an overlap of territorial waters in its various routes, based on the supposition that the waters of the passage are not "internal".
(4) The right of innocent passage in favor of all ships applies in the Northwest Passage, but such right is subject to two limitations: first, it is suspendable by Canada if such suspension is essential for the protection of its security; second, because of the presence of ice virtually year-round and the possibility of major harm to the fragile marine environment of the Arctic, Canada may adopt and enforce special standards relating to the design, construction, manning, and equipment of foreign ships.
(5) Since international shipping through the Northwest Passage may begin around 1990, the passage could become an international strait unless Canada succeeds in taking appropriate preventive measures and in exercising adequate control over foreign ships.
(6) If the Northwest Passage were to become an international strait, the right of transit passage provided by the 1982 Law of the Sea Convention, when in force, would apply in favor of all ships, including submarines in their normal submerged mode of navigation and this right could not be suspended or impeded.

Chapter 9

COMMERCIAL DEVELOPMENT AND ENVIRONMENTAL POLICY

Much debate has surrounded the impacts upon the environment that might be associated with increased shipping, particularly by oil and gas tankers, through the Northwest Passage. This chapter outlines that debate by an examination of the following: 1) the issue of ecologically sensitive areas; 2) the potential impacts of year-round shipping on those areas; and 3) the policy implications.

ECOLOGICALLY SENSITIVE AREAS

By 1982 a large number of marine and coastal sites along or adjacent to the Northwest Passage had been proposed by government departments and national organizations to be preserved or specially managed because of their significant biological attributes. A number of the sites have been given special protective legal status. These include four migratory bird sanctuaries in the Beaufort Sea region, part of the Yukon coastal area, the Reindeer Grazing Reserve adjacent to the Beaufort Sea, the Banks Island Federal Migratory Bird Sanctuary No. 2, the Bylot Island Federal Migratory Bird Sanctuary, the Auyvittug National Park on eastern Baffin Island, and the Polar Bear Pass National Wildlife Area.[276] The latter sites, as well as sites under active consideration of special legal status and sites proposed as international ecological sites by the International Biological Program (IBP),[277] are depicted in Figure 15.

The criteria used to select each of the depicted sites has varied, reflecting the objectives of each of the departments or organizations involved. Most of the sites were selected primarily because of a perceived desirability of preserving the local, regional or global ecological balance. Bird sanctuary sites have been selected to preserve critical zones which support significant bird populations. National Park sites have been selected through intergovernmental consultation on the basis of a "natural regions concept".[278] The selection process includes the identification and analysis of natural areas of Canadian significance (NACS). The IBP Ecological Sites were selected with the object, among other things, of aiding governments "in providing for the preservation of these biologically important areas."[279] Part of the Yukon coastal area was temporarily

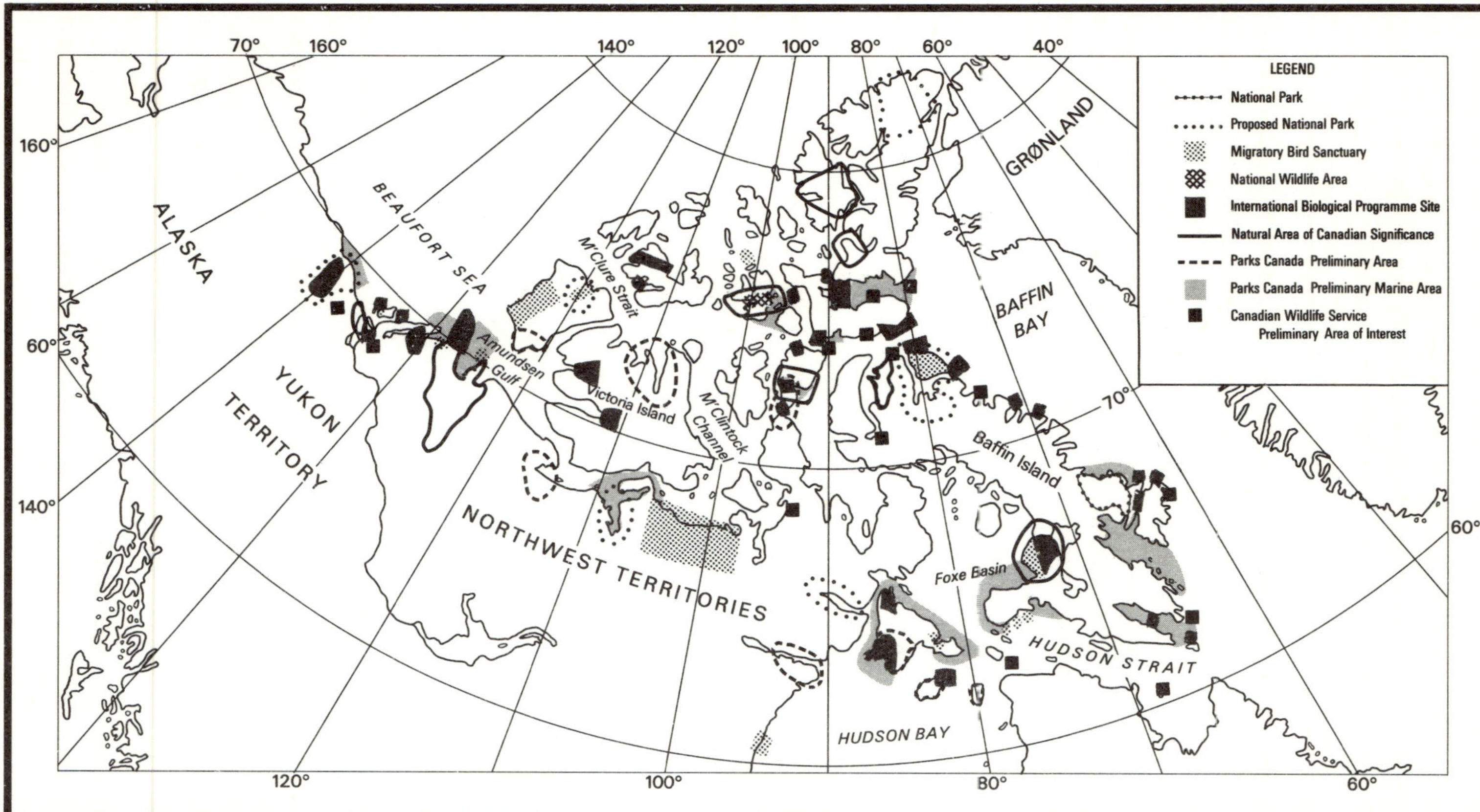

Fig. 15 : ECOLOGICALLY SIGNIFICANT AREAS OF THE CANADIAN ARCTIC

Prepared for the author by the Canadian Hydrographic Service, Dept. of Fisheries and Oceans, Ottawa, based on information received from the Environmental Assessment Division, Dept. of Indian and Northern Affairs, Ottawa withdrawn by Order in Council from further development partly because of the importance of the island area as a caribou calving ground and the importance of the coastal area as a staging and breeding ground for many waterfowl.[280]

Other regions and sites have not been specifically proposed or selected for special treatment but are generally acknowledged to be ecologically significant. Polynyas, or areas of open water bounded by fast ice or by fast ice and land, are recognized as important areas for marine mammals during the winter. They are particularly important areas for marine mammals and birds during the years when spring ice break-up is delayed or open leads are not available. These areas are essential for marine mammals during the winter to provide air access for breathing.[281] The recurrent leads which form in the eastern Beaufort Sea are considered as important spring habitats for a number of migrant waterfowl, and are used by some whales as migration corridors.[282] In fact, generally the seaward edge of the landfast ice has been shown to support a diverse and productive wildlife community.[283]

Lancaster Sound is the region which has possibly been the most extensively studied and which is probably the most widely acknowledged as a region of unique ecological importance. Within the region, the International Biological Program has proposed eight ecological sites and the Canadian Wildlife Service administers the Bylot Island Migratory Bird Sanctuary. In addition, Parks Canada has identified a number of areas of significance, and the UNESCO World Heritage Program, administered in Canada by Parks Canada, has suggested that all Lancaster Sound become a World Heritage Area, a designation given to protect areas of world wide ecological significance.[284]

Lancaster Sound itself is one of the most biologically productive regions in the entire Arctic, supporting unrivalled populations of seabirds, mammals, and marine organisms. The ecological balance of the region is to a large extent determined by the ice regime, since the interface between the landfast and drifting ice provides a critical habitat for the ringed seal, polar bear, and Arctic fox during the winter and many kinds of waterfowl just prior to the spring break-up.[285] In addition, the landfast ice which occurs in the central and western portions of the Barrow Strait provides a platform across which the Arctic fox, caribou, and musk ox cross during the winter.[286] During the relatively short Arctic summer, Lancaster Sound becomes ice free and supports a total of about one-third of Canada's eastern Arctic breeding seabirds, many tens of thousands of ducks, geese and shorebirds, most of the world's narwhal population, one-third of North America's white whale population, and significant walrus, harp seal, ringed seal, bearded seal and hooded seal populations.[287] Because of the marine Arctic food web, these populations of highly visible animals are directly or indirectly dependent on the productivity of certain fish, primarily Arctic cod, and small invertebrates which, in turn, are dependent on the productivity of populations of microscopic marine plants.[288] These populations, together with populations of migrating animals and occasional visitors to the region, form an ecologically balanced system in this region.

IMPACTS OF YEAR-ROUND SHIPPING

The potential impacts of year-round shipping on the ecological balance of the various Arctic regions and on the Arctic as a whole must be gauged both in terms of their severity, from the ecological point of view, and their probability of occurrence. Those which would be particularly severe – gas, fire, or oil spill impacts, for example – and those which would be particularly likely, such as routine winter ice-breaking impacts, have naturally been the subject of the most discussion.

It should be remembered, however, that the true impact of year-round shipping cannot be known, with any appreciable degree of certainty, unless and until such shipping actually takes place under carefully monitored conditions.[289]

IMPACTS OF ROUTINE SHIPPING OPERATIONS

It is generally acknowledged that ecological impacts from routine shipping operations could potentially result from the creation of artificial leads and the disruption and direct contact between tankers and marine seals, noise generated by tankers and associated ice reconnaissance aircraft flights, and operational waste discharge from tankers.[290] However, the exact nature and ecological significance of these impacts have been a subject of considerable controversy, with resource companies lining up on one side[291] and environmental groups and native associations lining up on the other.[292]

Tanker Tracks and Ice Regimes

Studies reported in the Beaufort Sea-Mackenzie Delta Environmental Impact Statement indicate that open water tracks of one to two kilometers are normally left by Canadian Coast Guard and industry Class 4 icebreakers, passing through loose pack ice; also, ice rubble tracks are left by a class 4 industry icebreaker, passing through close pack and land fast ice.[293] Longer and wider tracks would presumably be left behind class 10 icebreaking tankers. Although it has been suggested that the open water tracks could attract certain whales which could become trapped when the tracks froze over, it is not at all clear that this would occur, primarily because whales are not usually present in the areas and at the relevant times.[294] It has also been suggested that the rubble tracks would hinder natural migrations of Peary caribou and musk ox across

Parry Channel. In the Beaufort Sea Environmental Impact Statement, it was asserted that such hindrance would not occur.[295] Even if it did, the Arctic Pilot Project Environmental Assessment Panel speculated that it would not likely be serious in relation to a maintenance of the native caribou populations.[296]

Informed public concern has also focussed on the possibility that ice-breaking tanker tracks through landfast ice in the Barrow Strait and Lancaster Sound could delay fall freeze-up, hasten spring break-up, cause the ice edge to be located further west than normal, and, as a result, affect the delicate ecological balance of the region.[297] Although the Beaufort Sea development proponents concluded that the impact of shipping on the ice regime and dependent ecological balance probably would be negligible and almost indistinguishable from natural variation,[298] this conclusion was called into question in a technical review submitted by the Department of Fisheries and Oceans to the Beaufort Sea Environmental Assessment Panel.[299] The potential impact, therefore, remains unclear.

Ice Platforms and Tanker Contacts

Shipping development proponents have noted that "the hooded seal and the ringed seal are considered particularly vulnerable to potential physical impacts of ice breaking because they use the ice as a platform for breeding."[300] Mortality would occur primarily due to crushing and to exposure of seal pups to cold water during the vulnerable first weeks of life. Since mortality would be expected to vary with the width of the shipping corridor and the degree to which the corridor passed through concentrated breeding areas, corridors would be maintained as narrow as possible and would be located to avoid sensitive fast ice areas. Assuming that such impact mitigation measures could be taken, the proponents of the Beaufort Sea development estimate that ice platform disruption and direct contact impacts from year-round shipping would range from minor to moderate with respect to regional ringed seal populations, from negligible to minor with respect to regional bearded seal populations, and would be negligible with respect to regional hooded seal populations.[301] Obviously impacts within shipping corridors would be much higher.[302]

Tanker and Flight Noise

Concern has been voiced about the impact on marine mammals and birds from noise produced by tanker navigation and ice reconnaissance flights.[303] Auditory signals are used by most if not all marine mammals and birds for communication purposes and by some marine mammals, particularly whales, for underwater orientation. Underwater noise could interfere with these communication and orientation functions, possibly causing disruptive changes of behavior, desertions of portions of habitat, or disorientation of whales. Disturbance of marine mammals and birds from atmospheric and underwater noise would depend on the level and type (frequency) of noise reaching the animals and the ability of the animals to distinguish the noise from any natural background noise. The Beaufort Sea Environmental Impact Statement noted that, when possible, noise would not be generated near sensitive areas and that other steps would be taken to minimize disturbance by operational noise.

Considerable controversy exists relating both to the level of noise which would be generated by tanker traffic and to the effect that noise generation would have on Arctic animal populations. On the basis of a study of levels of noise source, attentuation, background noise, and hearing sensitivity, proponents of tanker traffic have predicted that the impacts of tanker noise on all marine mammals except narwhals and ringed seals, would range from negligible to minor. Effects on the latter would range from negligible to moderate.[304] However, government department and native group submissions to the Beaufort Sea Environmental Assessment Panel seriously questioned such predictions.[305] The submissions asserted that the knowledge of noise levels, hearing sensitivity, and particularly the cumulative effects of chronic noise and other disruptions was not sufficient to provide the basis for an accurate prediction of biological impacts. They further asserted that the methodology used to determine probable impacts was, in general, one in which many questionable assumptions were made but not enunciated.[306]

Operational Waste Discharge

Tankers operating along the Northwest Passage would discharge treated sewage, warm cooling water, combustion gases and particulates into the environment as they proceeded.[307] Since these effluents and emissions would be rapidly dispersed, development proponents concluded that only negligible and short term local impacts would result.[308] This expectation has been subject to the same general criticisms enunciated earlier, namely, the impact assessment methodology and the lack of attention paid to cumulative effects.[309]

RISKS AND IMPACTS OF SHIPPING ACCIDENTS

Oil Tanker Accidents

Although probabilities have been attached to the occurrence of oil tanker accidents in the Northwest Passage and its approaches, the actual risk of a serious accident is very difficult to calculate.[310] Since numerous studies have shown that the most frequent cause of tanker accidents is undoubtedly human error,[311] the training and reliability of the operating crew would normally affect the accident risk more than any other single factor. Additional factors to be considered include exposure to severe climatic conditions and ice-covered areas which create exceptional hazards to navigation, operation during extended periods of reduced visibility and winter darkness, and the number and quality of safety features designed into each tanker.

Nevertheless, with the design and equipment features planned for the 200,000 dwt class 10 icebreaking tankers, the tanker proponents have estimated that its spill risk would be "120 to 160 times less than that of a conventional well maintained tanker operating on a southern Canadian route."[312] No other spill risks were presented in their Environmental Impact Statement. However, Ray Lemberg, an independent consultant to the Beaufort Sea Environmental Assessment Panel, calculated that the annual risk of a major tanker spill involving up to 1.5 million barrels of oil occurring by 1990 would be about 1.8 percent and by the year 2000 about 4.8 percent.[313]

The amount and spreading of oil spilled as a result of a tanker accident would depend on the degree to which tanker design features and mitigative measures were successful in reducing the spillage and spreading.[314] The type of accident, i.e., explosion, grounding, or collision between two tankers or a tanker and an iceberg, would determine the total amount of oil which could potentially be spilled. The location and time of the spill would determine, subject to mitigative measures being taken, the degree of spread of such spill.

In general, oil spilled on open water spreads rapidly, as a result of dispersive forces, wind, currents, and wave action.[315] The oil weathers with the light fractions evaporating rapidly and the heavy fractions weathering in the water column. The latter weathering includes the formation of oil-water emulsions, the mixing or dissolution of parts of the oil with the water column, the sinking of oil droplets through their attachment to suspended sediment, and the very slow eventual oxidation and biodegradation of the oil. The heaviest oil fractions eventually end up as "tarballs", which may be suspended in the water column or may settle onto bottom sediments.

Oil spilled onto, under, or around sea ice behaves in a different manner, although it weathers in a similar manner if it eventually enters open water.[316] The spread of oil spilled onto sea ice is generally reduced in relation to the roughness of the ice and the amount of snow on top of the ice. Oil which is spilled or which is pushed by currents under growing first year ice either move with under-ice currents or be incorporated into the growing ice sheet, depending on the currents and on the roughness of the under-ice surface. It may enter open water leads directly or as a result of the separation of contaminated ice. During the spring, oil under or incorporated within first year ice seeps through the ice to form pools on the ice surface subject to weathering. Once break-up occurs, this oil may be released into the water column as a tarry residue or as a sheen trailing from melting ice floes. Oil under multi-year ice spreads like oil under first year ice, except that more oil may be contained under multi-year ice and migration of oil up through the ice takes longer than similar migration through first year ice.

To reduce the amount and spreading of oil spilled, a number of design features have been incorporated into the tanker transportation system and a number of oil spill counter measure systems have been developed or are currently undergoing development. Tanker system design features include those described in Chapter 5.[317] Oil spill counter-measure systems are theoretically simple but are not actually simple to implement.[318] In theory, the spill is reported, tracked, and the appropriate contingency plans are put into action. A number of such plans involving industry, territorial, provincial, federal governments, and the United States and Danish governments have been established.[319] The plans generally involve measures to contain the spill using aritificial or natural (ice) barriers and subsequently to remove the oil by skimmering, pumping, or incineration. Some plans also involve the dispersal of the slick using government approved chemical dispersants, although the ecological use of this method would not be appropriate in many cases.[320] Finally, the plans call for the collected oil to be incinerated or buried and shorelines to be restored if required. In the Arctic, however, such factors as remoteness, the presence of ice, and extreme low temperatures make implementation of contingency plans difficult. Problems exist concerning equipment availability, administrative coordination, industry-government cooperation, and the functioning of people and equipment in extreme low temperatures.[321]

The short term (less than five year) impact that a major oil spill would have on certain organisms may be reasonably estimated on the basis of a large number of laboratory experiments and field observations of accidental and intentional experimental oil spills.[322] These studies have shown that short term impacts may be severe, varying with the timing and duration of the oil spill, the type of oil spilled, the sensitivity of the organisms to the oil, the ability and tendency of the organisms to avoid the oil, and the ability of impacted populations to recover through increased recruitment from their own or neighboring populations. Under-ice and planktonic (foating) organisms would, in general, suffer heavy mortality.[323] Avoidance would not be possible and population recovery would occur more slowly than for a similar spill in more southern waters because of reduced reproductive rates in the Arctic. Impacts on mature fish would probably not be as severe.[324] Avoidance behavior has been shown to be variable. Impact would include mortality, physiological and behavioral abnormalities, and tainting. Impacts on benthic (sea bottom) organisms would be variable, with benthic crustacea (shrimp-like organisms) being among the most vulnerable.[325] This is significant in that these crustacea are the preferred food for a variety of fish, birds, and marine mammals.

The direct impact of a major spill would be particularly severe on contacted seabirds, since small amounts of oil lead to greatly increased stress and greatly reduced insulation and waterproofing.[326] This is supported by a 1980 study which concluded that "extremely small amounts of oil contamination may result in the death of seabirds under harsh environmental conditions, and consequently, the threat to the concentration of seabirds that winter in the north environs is much more severe than previously recognized."[327] Impacts would be worst in cases where oil contacted large numbers of birds in any of many leads or in open water during springtime in Lancaster Sound. Recovery would, in many cases, take many years due to the low reproductive rates of many species. Impacts on populations of endangered species might be permanent.

Impacts of an oil spill on marine mammals would be variable.[328] Although some mammals would recognize and avoid an oil slick or oil contaminated beach, this would not be universally the case. Oil fouling of mammals has been shown to cause poisoning, sticking of flippers, blockage of breathing and feeding openings, and a severe reduction of insulation for some fur bearing mammals. All of these impacts increase stress and may lead to mortality. Indirect impacts of a spill would include increased stresses in avoiding contaminated areas, the reduction in food supply in the impacted areas, and the impacts of spill dispersants which might be used. Serious impacts on young ringed seals would occur if oil were spilled in Amundsen Gulf, the west coast of Banks Island, or in other primary pupping areas. Polar bears and Arctic foxes would be impacted through direct contact with spilled oil or through ingestion of tainted seal prey. Impacts on polar bears might be most serious during winter and spring when they hunt ringed seals in the transition zone between the landfast and pack ice. Recovery of endangered species like the bowhead whale might not be possible.

Medium and long term impacts are considerably harder to predict, since time would allow a number of complex, incompletely understood, ecological processes to take place, and the uncertainties inherent in short term impact prediction would be multiplied.[329] However, a number of factors indicate that the impact of an oil spill in the Arctic would last longer and be of greater magnitude than the impact of a similar southern oil spill. First, oil incorporated in ice or sediments would decompose at an extremely slow rate and would thus remain toxic for many years.[330] Second, the low reproductive rates of Arctic organisms would, in general, cause populations to recover at much slower rates in the Arctic than in more southern climates.[331] Third, the diversity of organisms in the Arctic is low and many of the organisms which do occur there live close to the limit of their environmental tolerance, for Arctic food chains are relatively short. All these facts contribute to the relative instability of Arctic ecosystems.[332]

Gas Tanker Accidents

In assessing the risk of accidents from surface gas tankers transiting the Northwest Passage, similar considerations to those mentioned in reference to oil tanker accidents would apply. However, as noted in the 1980 Report of the Environmental Assessment Panel for the Arctic Pilot Project, "the past history of LNG carrier operations suggests that there is little risk of serious damage from on board human error or equipment failure . . . major collision-caused damage (is) unlikely. The hazard . . . posed by sea ice is considered low . . . as is that posed by grounding."[333]

Since an LNG tanker would carry a limited amount of fuel oil besides its LNG cargo, spills of both substances would be possible. The behavior of oil in the Arctic marine environment and its impact on the ecology of the Arctic was discussed earlier. The behavior of liquified natural gas coming from a ruptured LNG carrier would involve not only the marine but the terrestrial environment as well. The highly compressed (over 600 atmospheres) and cooled (about $-162°C$) gas escaping from an LNG tanker would either escape rapidly as a super-cooled liquid or more slowly as a vaporized gas, depending on the nature of the accident.[334] In a rapid spill, an area of up to one kilometer around a ship might be covered by LNG before vaporization took place. Upon vaporization, the gas would mix with air, drift downwind and eventually rise as it warmed. If no source of ignition were encountered by the vapor cloud, it would eventually dissipate. If a source of ignition were encountered before the gas became too dissipated, a large fire or explosion could result. The size of the latter would vary and so would safe distances. It has been calculated, for example, that a distance of about 10 kilometers from the site of a spill of slightly less than one-half the 140,000 cubic meter gas carried would constitute a safe distance.[335] Safe distances based on spills of larger amounts or on spills from the collision of two LNG tankers would, of course, be greater.

Direct ecological impacts from an LNG spill would include mortality of wildlife from freezing, asphyxiation, burning, percussion from explosion shock wave and sub-lethal impacts from freezing, fume inhalation, burning and percussion.[336] Indirect impacts would include those on predators, prey, and on the physical environment. Depending on the timing and location of an accident, its impact could range from negligible to highly significant. An accident at an inopportune time in Lancaster Sound, for example, could seriously damage migratory bird and marine mammal populations.

APPRAISAL AND POLICY IMPLICATIONS

From the above discussion it may be concluded that both routine shipping operations and shipping accidents involving oil or gas tankers passing through the Northwest Passage would have potentially significant short term and long term impacts. Not all these impacts, particularly the cumulative and long term impacts, can be predicted with a great degree of certainty. Impacts on ecologically significant areas like the recurring plynyas and the Lancaster Sound region could cause major harm or potentially irreversible damage to the ecological balance of those areas.

Subtle but ecologically significant chronic impacts, observable only through careful monitoring, could result from year-round shipping. Even assuming that impact mitigative measures could be implemented at all times, a significant impact on certain seal and whale populations in the Northwest Passage would be likely. The extent of this impact and the degree to which cumulative impacts would affect other populations and the Arctic ecosystem as a whole cannot be predicted accurately at this time.

The most dramatic and easily observable impact would be that following an oil spill in such a highly productive and ecologically significant area as Lancaster Sound, an area in which weather and ice conditions often make navigation potentially hazardous. Such an oil spill during peak breeding and feeding periods would take a high toll of marine birds and some marine mammals. Recovery, if possible, would probably be slow. Impacts on other, less visible, components of the Arctic ecosystem might also be severe, with the speed of recovery varying on the basis of a number of factors.

The basic policy implication of this is clear. If Canada wishes to prevent major harm to, or irreversible disturbance of, the ecological balance of the Arctic marine environment in areas adjacent to the Northwest Passage, it must maintain both *de jure* and *de facto* control over commercial shipping through the passage. The ability of Canada to maintain this control in the face of current project proposals by the oil and gas industry and recent developments was discussed in Chapter 4.

Canada has been exercising jurisdiction over Arctic shipping primarily through the Arctic Waters Pollution Prevention Act, the Canada Shipping Act, and the regulations and orders promulgated under those Acts.[337] The Pollution Prevention Act requires that vessel operators in the Arctic establish to the satisfaction of the Department of Transport their financial responsibility to the extent of their potential liability for pollution damage and clean-up costs.[338] It also requires that ships navigating through the Arctic comply with such construction, design, and operation standards as set out by the regulation.[339] Special requirements are imposed on ships carrying more than 483 cubic meters of oil.[340] The Pollution Prevention Act applies only to a 100-mile nautical belt of Canadian Arctic offshore waters, whereas the Shipping Act applies to areas between 100 and 200 nautical miles off the Canadian Arctic Coat.[341] Thus, although Part XX of the Canada Shipping Act and its regulations impose a duty to comply with certain construction design and operation standards on vessels operating in the Arctic, these requirements apply, on any interpretation of the status of the Canadian Arctic waters, only to the approaches to the Northwest Passage.

In 1980 a study by the Canadian Arctic Resources Committee, a public interest group, concluded that "Canadian Arctic shipping standards are stringent and technically sound. If they were enforced, they would probably reduce the threat of pollution to a level as low as that achieved elsewhere."[342] Since that time, the Coast Guard has undertaken to update these standards.[343] Compliance with these updated standards, as well as the now voluntary NORDREG vessel traffic management system, may be made mandatory in the near future.[344]

The Canadian government must, however, clarify its policy with regard to northern development if it is to exercise adequate control over that development. In 1972 Jean Chrétien, Minister of Indian Affairs and Northern Development, presented a policy statement, entitled *Canada's North 1970–1980*, noting that "the needs of the people in the North are more important than resource development and . . . (that) the maintenance of ecological balance is essential."[345] In response to Middle East events in the early 1970s, the government moved to a "need to know" policy favoring accelerated exploration for northern hydrocarbon reserves.[346] In 1980 the *National Energy Program* was instituted. The program had three major objectives: security of supply, fairness in pricing and revenue sharing, and an increase in Canadian participation in the energy industry.[347] In 1982 the Department of Transport released its Arctic Marine Services Policy designed to accommodate support services for increased resource related navigation through the Northwest Passage.[348] In late 1982 the Department of Indian Affairs and Northern Development released a draft discussion paper outlining a *Comprehensive Conservation Policy and Strategy for the Northwest Territories and Yukon.*[349] The paper emphasized that any development policy should reflect a commitment to "balanced development", balanced, that is, between resource, social and cultural, and environmental considerations. However, if the government does not specifically decide whether it will sanction either limited or extensive tanker navigation through the Northwest Passage, the government's decision may be pre-empted by the insistence of industrial interests on a sanctioning of the latter option.

Chapter 10

COMMERCIAL DEVELOPMENT AND INUIT POLICY

Development of the Northwest Passage as a commercial navigation route and the possible internationalization of the passage would obviously have an impact on the culture, economy, and aboriginal rights of the Inuit who have lived for centuries in the areas adjacent to the passage.

CANADA'S INUIT POPULATION

Approximately 23,000 Canadian Inuit live in small communities in the Mackenzie Delta, the Arctic Islands, the areas adjacent to the Northwest Passage, and the shores of Hudson and Ungava Bays and Labrador.[350] This essentially nomadic native people makes extensive use of the land, sea-ice, and near-shore open water areas for hunting and fishing. The extent and intensity of this use is depicted on Figure 16, made from a compilation of highly detailed accounts by individuals of their hunting and fishing expeditions. The Inuit are currently engaged in negotiations with the federal government with respect to their claims to these land and marine areas.

Inuit Culture

Inuit exploitation of the natural environment has been central to traditional and modern Inuit culture, as noted in the 1982 formal submission of the Inuit Tapirisat of Canada, a national Inuit organization, and the Baffin Region and Labrador Inuit Associations to the Senate Northern Pipeline Committee:

> Inuit culture is derived from and organized in support of a hunting/fishing mode of existence. Hunting is therefore central to the social, economic and ideological orientation of the people . . . Country food, the harvest of the natural fruits of the land and sea, in addition to the significance of the harvest itself, is very important for the physical and psychological health of Inuit.[351]

The acquisition of detailed knowledge about the sea ice environment and the

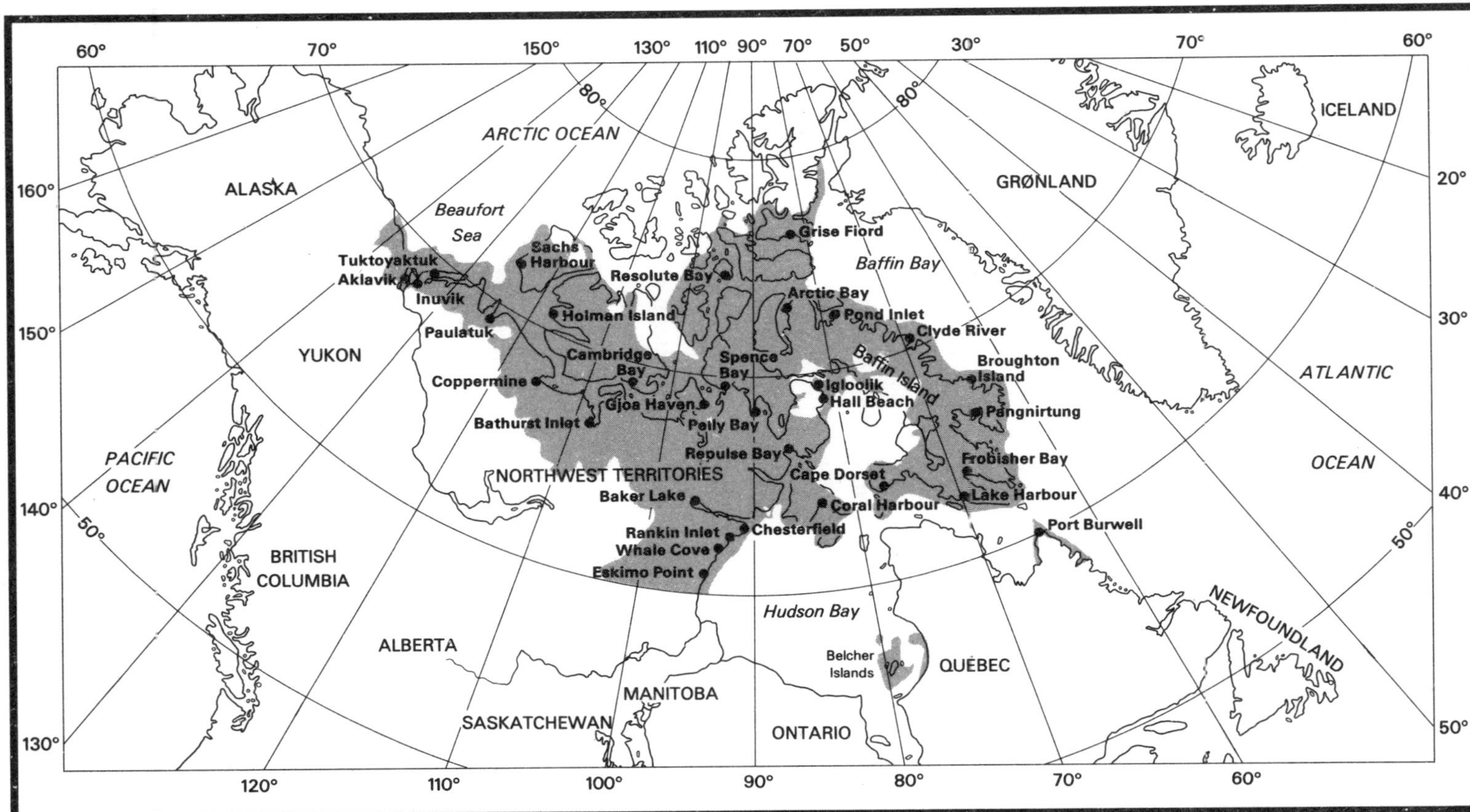

Fig. 16: EXTENT OF THE SEA ICE USE BY THE INUIT

Prepared for the author by the Canadian Hydrographic Service, Dept. of Fisheries and Oceans, Ottawa.
Source: Report on Inuit Land Use and Occupancy Project, Vol. 3, at p. 153 (1976)

utilization of that knowledge to facilitate safe traveling and successful hunting is an integral part of Inuit culture.[362] Acquisition takes place through many years of observation of sea ice conditions and of utilization by more experienced hunters and travelers. With experience, Inuit hunters learn to describe ice conditions and motion with extreme subtlety, using the multitude of words which the Inuit have attached to ice, which behaves in different ways, can support different weights, or may more or less harbor hunted animals.

The cultural significance of hunting in the evolving Inuit culture has been exemplified by a published account of a polar bear hunt made with the use of modern snowmobiles and rifles.[353] The hunting party consisted of all members of an extended family from a small Inuit settlement on Somerset Island. Three significant aspects of Inuit culture involving cooperation, teaching, and an almost religious respect for wildlife were exhibited. First, the hunt was made possible only through cooperative effort. This effort took the form of sharing a polar bear quota and the combined effort of a number of hunters in the stalking of the bear. Particular deference was paid to the advice of the elder member of the hunting party. Second, the hunt was used as a means of instructing the younger members in the ways of the Inuit as well as the technicalities of the hunt. Third, during the stalking and even slaughtering of the bear, the hunters maintained a solemn respect for the bear, the breach of which, they believed, could bring future misfortune to their hunts. This respect extended as far as the imposition of a strict prohibition against even ridiculing or belittling the bear.

Inuit culture has evolved to incorporate certain non-Inuit religious beliefs and technological convenience introduced by contact with missionaries, traders, whalers, and, more recently, resource company representatives and technicians.[354] It should be noted, however, that this incorporation has to some extent been selective. In general, the Inuit have chosen to take advantage of those inventions, like snowmobiles and rifles, compatible with a hunting/fishing mode of existence, and have rejected, to a large extent, those institutions, like structured wage employment, incompatible with such a way of life.[355] Some Inuit, however, have not rejected the introduction of such goods as convenience foods and alcohol, goods not consistent with their way of life.

Inuit Economy

Wage employment and the harvesting of renewable natural resources for sale, sharing and personal consumption, constitute the core of the Inuit economy.[356] However, it is difficult, if not impossible, to make quantitative comparisons between the cash or market economy and the non-cash economy, because monetary values cannot easily or realistically be attached to items which have not traditionally entered into a market economy. Until recently, the entire basis of the Inuit economy has not been market-oriented.

Wage employment, in general, has been associated with the periodic construction of modern northern resource development and living facilities, as well as a limited number of permanent government and private generated jobs, primarily in the larger northern communities.[357] Controversy exists, however, with respect to the availability of wage employment to the Inuit and their demand for such employment. The Inuit Tapirisat of Canada, for example, has criticized the estimate made by the proponents of the Arctic Pilot Project that Inuit demands for industrial jobs are being "grossly exaggerated"[358] and has implicitly made the same criticism of similar estimates by proponents of Beaufort Sea development.[359]

The harvesting of renewable natural resources, particularly marine mammals, has been and continues to be a key element in the Inuit economy.[360] Harvest of fur and ivory bearing animals may generate cash income or may be used by the Inuit to clothe and feed themselves, since imported food and clothing is expensive and often ill-suited to Inuit needs of a high protein diet and warm clothing.

Estimates of the total annual Canadian harvest from the Parry Channel, Baffin Bay and the Davis Strait area are listed in Table 4. All the figures, except those for polar bear and Arctic fox, represent only a minimum estimate of animals harvested, since not all animals harvested for domestic use are reported.[361] Ringed seals, the most heavily harvested seal, are taken both for food and for pelts. Over 80 percent of the narwhal are taken near Pond Inlet or Arctic Bay on Northern Baffin Island, where sale of the ivory provides a considerable cash income. Sale of polar bear skins and Arctic fox pelts also provide significant cash income for a number of Inuit communities.

In the Beaufort Sea-Mackenzie Delta area, resource harvesting patterns have been more heavily influenced by the proximity of oil and gas exploration activities[362] In the communities of Inuvik, Aklavik, and Tuktoyaktuk, comprising the "Mackenzie economy" of the Mackenzie River Delta, harvesting is mostly for domestic use, with limited export of Arctic fox and polar bear skins. Cash income is largely derived from wage employment. In the communities of Sachs Harbour, Paulatuk and Holman, comprising the "rim economy" of the Amundsen Gulf area, the export of seal skins, Arctic fox pelts, and polar bear hides constitutes a primary source of Inuit cash income. Commercial and domestic fishing is relatively limited. Harvest data, which have been summarized in Table 5, must be interpreted as minimum estimates since not all harvested animals are reported.

The importance of the harvest of various species from this area varies strongly among communities.[363] For instance, the sea harvest is an important element of the economy of the Holman community, but not of the Tuktoyaktuk community. Walrus and the bowhead whale are harvested off the Alaskan coast, but not within the eastern Beaufort Sea or Amundsen Gulf areas. Narwhal are

Table 4

Approximate Minimum Annual Canadian Harvest of Marine Mammals in Parry Channel, Baffin Bay, and the Davis Strait

Species	Number Taken
Ringed seal	20 – 30,000
Harp seal	1 – 1,500
Hooded seal	<20
Bearded seal	300 – 400
Harbour seal	<20
Walrus	100 – 150
White whale	100 – 200
Narwhal	300 – 400
Polar Bear	125 – 150
Arctic Fox	2 – 9,000

Source: *Beaufort EIS*, Vol. 38, Table 2.51.

Table 5

Approximate Minimum Canadian Annual Harvest of Marine Mammals in the Beaufort Sea and Amundsen Gulf Areas

Species	Number Taken or Exported	
	Mackenzie economy	Rim economy
all seals*	59	2429
White whale*	133	?
Polar bear**	21	36
Arctic fox**	1732	5631
all ducks*	2100	?
all geese*	1000	?

* number taken

** number exported

Source: *Beaufort EIS* (1982), Vol. 3A at 3.65-3.75 (yearly averages calculated from all data for the years 1970 through 1981 reported in the above source).

not harvested in this area at all. The sale of polar bear skins are important, however, to the economy of Tuktoyaktuk and the rim economy communities, since each hide is worth, on average, over twenty five times the value of a ringed seal skin. Arctic fox trapping is particularly important to the cash economy of Sachs Harbour and Holman, although other communities also export a significant number of furs. Commercial fishing in the area is extremely limited, and domestic fishing has declined due to the decrease in demand of food for sled dogs.

IMPACTS OF YEAR-ROUND SHIPPING

The potential socio-economic impacts of year-round shipping on the Canadian Inuit stem largely from the potential impact that shipping would have on the ecological balance and, therefore, the availability of renewable natural resources. Also, one must consider the potential impact that shipping would have on Inuit land claim negotiations with the federal government. Other potential impacts stem from increased contact between the Inuit and non-Inuit cultures and from the potential for wage employment which would result from such shipping and its support services. However, since these impacts would result more directly from increased shipping, they are not addressed here. In addition, since it would be difficult, and indeed artificial, to separate impacts on Inuit culture and on the Inuit economy due to impacts on the harvesting of renewable resources, these impacts are considered together.

Socio-Economic Impacts

A decrease in the harvesting of renewable resources would constitute a significant socio-economic impact on the Inuit, since "Inuit culture is derived from and organized around a hunting/fishing mode of existence" and "Inuit quickly experience a loss of well-being physically as well as psychologically resulting from an absence of fresh (traditional) food in their diet."[364] This decrease could arise from decreased accessible prey populations or from decreased Inuit hunting effort.

As noted previously, decreases in populations of harvested resources could result directly from the passage, noise generation, and waste discharge of tankers navigating through the Northwest Passage, from the accidental release of oil or gas into the Arctic environment, or from the noise associated with ice reconnaissance flights. The most serious socio-economic impacts would result from damage to species harvested in significant numbers by the Inuit, like the ringed seal, and from impacts to animals, like the Arctic fox, polar bear, narwhal, and white whale, the harvest of which is of significant cultural or cash-economy importance. Not only would decreased availability of the harvested species have a direct short-term socio-economic impact, but such decreases would reduce the ability of the Inuit to recover from the boom and bust cash economic cycle associated with the development of specific non-renewable development projects.

The proponents of Beaufort Sea development, assuming mitigative routing measures to be effective, acknowledge that the impact of tanker and aircraft passage on ringed seal and narwhal populations would not be negligible.[365] The potential impact of such passage on exploited bird and whale populations seems unclear, as does the potential impact on exploited Arctic fox and polar bear populations. It should be noted, however, that polar bear populations may be dependent on particular seal populations and that impacts on such seal populations as the one at Bridgport Inlet, where the APP loading terminal has been proposed, might significantly affect the bear populations.[366]

These potential impacts appear even more significant in light of the following assessment of the potential success of mitigative routing plans by Captain T.C. Pullen, a leading authority in the field of Arctic navigation:

> [Conservationists and environmentalists] desire to impose controls and assorted regulations over shipping using Parry Channel year-round including traffic lanes and "no go" zones. Mariners, however, cannot manoeuver their ships along "tram lines" because ice prevents this in many instances and to achieve this must steer a sinuous course. This is of course, a state of affairs which conflicts with traffic lanes and traffic control.[367]

Although concern has been voiced by the Inuit that ship tracks would prevent them from crossing the ice in the Barrow Strait area during the winter months to trap and hunt polar bear, activities requiring extensive use of the sea-ice, the proponents of Beaufort Sea development assert that tracks would freeze over sufficiently quickly to allow crossings to be made on a regular basis.[368] In addition, they have stated that they would undertake studies to determine the safest methods of crossing.[369]

Potential impacts on the Inuit cash economy would include those on cash generating resource harvesting and on opportunities created directly and indirectly for Inuit employment. Studies have shown that wage employment is not only compatible with resource harvesting, but wage employment may actually increase resource harvesting efficiency.[370] This would occur where wage employment allowed the purchase of modern snow transportation vehicles and modern firearms. Although, as noted earlier, controversy exists with respect to the availability of industrial employment positions for the Inuit and the Inuit demand for such employment, development proponents have expressed a willingness to train Inuit for such employment, especially in the Beaufort Sea area.[371]

Impacts on Rights to Offshore Areas

The extent of Inuit rights in offshore areas of the Arctic is a controversial issue, the settlement of which has been the subject of extensive negotiations between the Inuit and the federal and territorial governments during the past decade.[372] The Inuit have asserted on numerous occasions that the development of year-round shipping through the Northwest Passage would be prejudicial to the just conclusion of those negotiations.[373]

Inuit rights to offshore areas have been said to arise from Imperial and Canadian federal enactments and the common law.[374] With regard to government enactments, although it has been argued that the Royal Proclamation of 1763, the 1926 Order establishing the Arctic Islands Game Preserve, and the Arctic Waters Pollution Prevention Act of 1970 have all given rise to, or acknowledged the existence of, Inuit rights,[375] it is not at all clear that these enactments could form the basis of an Inuit claim to offshore areas.[376]

With regard to the common law, the possibility of an aboriginal title is recognized but it is not altogether clear under what conditions such title may arise and, particularly, may continue to exist. In the leading case of *Calder et al. v. Attorney-General of British Columbia* of 1973, the Supreme Court of Canada refused to grant a declaration "that the aboriginal title, otherwise known as the Indian title, of the plaintiffs has never been lawfully extinguished."[377] The six judges who addressed the substantive question agreed that an aboriginal title existed at common law in favor of the Nishga Nation but were evenly divided on whether it had been extinguished. Three were satisfied that proclamations and ordinances issued by the Governor and the Legislative Council of the former colony of British Columbia had extinguished the aboriginal title whereas the other three maintained that any such extinguishment was beyond the powers of the Governor and the Council.[378] The seventh judge refused the declaratory relief on the procedural ground that, in British Columbia, consent was still necessary in a proceeding against the Crown and no such consent had been given.[379] The appeal from the Court of Appeal of British Columbia was therefore dismissed by a decision of four to three.

In the *Baker Lake* case of 1979, Mr. Justice Mahoney of the Federal Court of Canada, trial division, recognized the existence of an aboriginal title to the Baker Lake area, west of Hudson Bay, in favor of the local Inuit community. In so holding, he was satisfied that the following elements, which plaintiffs must prove to establish an aboriginal title cognizable at common law, were present:

1. That they and their ancestors were members of an organized society.
2. That the organized society occupied the specific territory over which they assert the aboriginal title.

3 That the occupation was to the exclusion of other organized societies.
4 That the occupation was an established fact at the time sovereignty was asserted by England.[380]

The federal court judge further held that the aboriginal title had not been extinguished by the Royal grant of Rupert's Land to the Hudson's Bay Company in 1670 nor by any subsequent legislation of the Parliament of Canada. He did not agree with the plaintiffs' argument, however, that Parliament's intention to extinguish an aboriginal title must be set forth explicitly in the pertinent legislation.[381]

Although both the above cases are relevant in the proof of Inuit rights to offshore areas, it must be noted that title to such areas was not actually involved. Consequently, the extent to which those decisions may be relied upon for Inuit offshore rights remains uncertain.

Perhaps as a result of the *Calder Case*, the federal government agreed in 1973 to enter into comprehensive aboriginal title claims negotiations. Although the Inuit have put forward claims to offshore areas[382] and some maps, issued under the authority of the Department of Indian Affairs and Northern Development (DIAND), have included offshore as well as terrestrial areas as accepted for negotiation,[383] official government policy statements have been silent on the issue of Inuit claims to offshore areas.[384] In addition, in the James Bay and Northern Quebec Agreement, the only comprehensive claim yet settled, and the Inuvialiut Agreement-in-Principle (an agreement applying to the western Arctic region) have not dealt with the issue of title to offshore areas.[385] It is possible, however, that the government could in future consider invoking the settlement of Inuit claims to the offshore to reinforce its own claim to those areas under international law.[386]

As well as proceeding with comprehensive claim negotiations, the Inuit have also been engaged in a process to divide the Northwest Territories.[387] The process began in 1974 and gained momentum until 1982, when the Inuit voted overwhelmingly in a plebiscite in favor of the creation of Nunavut, "our land" in the Inuit language. Proposals for the offshore were released in April 1983 by the Nunavut Constitutional Forum, the vehicle by which proposals for the creation of the Nunavut government were being worked out, with recommendations that

> . . . a Nunavut government have particular powers in relation to the fast ice zone, its management, exploitation within it and benefits from its development, and that a functional division of powers respecting the offshore be worked out with the federal government taking into consideration the marine nature of Nunavut, the revenue requirements of a Nunavut government, the dependence of Inuit on the Arctic seas and the health of the marine envi-

ronment, and the employment and economic benefits which could accrue to the people of Nunavut from offshore development.[388]

In addition to the above, the Inuit have participated in development of a management plan for the Lancaster Sound area, have intervened before regulatory boards, and have been involved in constitutional lobbying efforts to clearly establish and preserve their rights. Their representatives firmly believe that the sanctioning of year-round commercial traffic through the Northwest Passage would jeopardize their efforts. Specifically, it would reduce the options available to the federal government with regard to granting wildlife harvesting and management rights, land and offshore management rights and resource ownership rights.[389]

APPRAISAL AND POLICY IMPLICATIONS

It follows from the above review that many environmental impacts of year-round shipping discussed in the previous chapter would also result in impacts on the Inuit culture and economy, since the latter are intimately linked with the environment through the cultural and economic importance attached to the harvesting of wildlife resources. Impacts on certain widely harvested species, like the ringed seal, and certain monetarily valuable species, like the narwhal, Arctic fox, and polar bear, would be particularly significant. Efforts to mitigate the impacts on such animals as the ringed seal might not be successful, since tankers might not be able to navigate around ice platform areas important for seal breeding.

The impact that year-round shipping would have on the Inuit wage economy is unclear. Although it has been shown that wage employment does not decrease renewable resource harvesting, the demand of the Inuit for such wage employment has been the subject of controversy. However, before such shipping could begin it would have to be sanctioned by the Canadian government.[390] Such sanctioning could have a significant impact on the options available to the government in its negotiations with the Inuit for a just settlement of their aboriginal claim to offshore areas. Moreover, such approval would have a possible impact on the future status of the Northwest Passage.

In light of the above impacts, it appears that the government should follow a two-track policy with regard to Inuit rights in the areas of the Northwest Passage. First, in order to strengthen its claim to the passage waters and the Arctic archipelago waters in general, Canada should endeavor to settle outstanding Inuit claims with all possible expediency. Second, it should take appropriate measures to ensure that Canadian sovereignty over all those waters is appropriately established and maintained. Only in this way will the government be able to protect the rights and way of life of Canada's indigenous Inuit population.

Chapter 11

CANADA'S NATIONAL SECURITY IN THE ARCTIC

Should the Northwest Passage be developed and become an international strait, a number of questions about Canadian national security would arise as a result of the right of transit passage, including submerged passage for submarines, which commercial and military ships would enjoy in the Arctic. Because of the strategic importance of the Arctic, Canada must ask itself if its national security would be sufficiently protected, especially with respect to submarine activities in adjacent waters, and if that protection should not be adequate, whether there might be a need for Canada to exercise a greater surveillance of the waters of the Arctic Archipelago, including those of the Northwest Passage. In light of the potential for commercial tanker traffic through the Northwest Passage by 1990, the development of an adequate ice-breaking capability may also be required.

STRATEGIC IMPORTANCE OF THE ARCTIC

The strategic significance of the Arctic was brought home forcefully after World War II, when the war-time alliance between the United States and the Soviet Union broke down, and they found themselves facing each other across the Arctic Ocean and the narrow Bering Strait. Canada, for its part, realized that it was in the rather uncomfortable position of being located between the land masses of those two superpowers.

Canada's delicate position became quite evident in 1946, when the United States asked permission to establish weather stations on Canadian Arctic islands. At the same time, an interdepartmental committee in Washington recommended "that the Army make flights over the unexplored area west and northwest of Grant's Land to determine whether (as many Arctic authorities believe) islands exist which might be claimed by the United States".[391] Permission to establish the weather stations was postponed for a number of reasons, including apparent fears on the part of Canada that such establishment might be interpreted as challenging Canada's sovereignty over some of the islands.[392] Canada's reluctance was expressed in very clear terms in a June 1946 letter from Lester B. Pearson, then Canadian Ambassador to Washington, to the

Acting Under-Secretary of State for External Affairs.[393] Pearson also expressed his reluctance a month later in *Foreign Affairs*:

> The Canadian government, while ready to co-operate to the fullest extent with the United States and other countries in the development of the whole Arctic, accepts responsibility for its own sector. There is no reason for sharing that responsibility except as part of any regional or general international arrangement for co-operation and control which may be worked out within the framework of the Charter of the United Nations.[394]

Canada's conditional permission was eventually granted, and weather stations were established between 1947 and 1950 at Eureka, Resolute, Mould Bay, Isaachsen, and Alert. Under the terms of the agreement, the weather stations were to be joint ones, with Canada providing all the permanent buildings and installations. The commanding officer at each station was to be a Canadian, with an American executive officer under him. Originally only about half the personnel in each station was Canadian, but all the weather stations were eventually taken over by Canada between 1970 and 1972.[395] Canada had assumed responsibility for all sea supply by about 1955.

As a result of the tense relations between the two superpowers and Canada's strategic position in the Arctic, Canada entered into a number of bilateral and multilateral arrangements for continental and regional defense. In 1955 Canada and the United States agreed to establish a Distant Early Warning (DEW) line along the 70th parallel, consisting of a series of radar stations designed to detect a possible bomber attack by the Soviet Union. This was followed in 1958 by the establishment of a long-range bomber interceptor system, the North American Air (changed to "Aerospace" in 1981) Defense (NORAD) system, with headquarters in Colorado Springs.[396] With the development of long-range intercontinental ballistic missiles in the late 1950s, the United States decided to add another warning system, the Ballistic Missile Early Warning System (BMEWS). Canada, however, did not participate in the establishment of this new warning system since its stations were located in Alaska, Greenland and Great Britain.

The strategic importance of the Arctic also has been demonstrated by the stationing of the Soviet northern fleet at Murmansk and other ports on the Kola Peninsula, some of which are less than 100 miles from the Norwegian border. Harriet Critchley, a noted non-government defense analyst, has summarized the components and capability of this fleet in the following terms:

> As of mid-1978, the fleet included approximately fifty-five major surface combat ships, 120 naval submarines, and sixty ballistic missile-carrying submarines. Three types of nuclear-powered submarines are assigned to this and

> other fleets of the Soviet Navy. Attack submarines and cruise missile submarines (both are designated as SSNs) have the mission of attacking an adversary's surface shipping and submarines at sea. Ballistic missile submarines (SSBNs), armed with long-range missiles with nuclear warheads, have major military installations, industrial complexes, and urban centres as probable targets in the event of a nuclear war.[397]

From the Barents Sea, the Soviet Union may deploy its submarines either through the North Atlantic or through the Arctic Ocean. Development through the North Atlantic is monitored and could be opposed at the Geenland-Iceland-United Kingdom (GIUK) "choke point" patrolled by the North Atlantic Treaty Organization (NATO), although the Soviet Union is now equipped with the long-range SS-N-8 missiles and its use of that gap might no longer be necessary.

Deployment through the Arctic Ocean, therefore, might prove more advantageous for the Soviets, since it has been established that submarines can now operate under the ice virtually in the same way as they do under open water. They can easily surface in leads or polynyas in the ice pack and, if necessary, actually break through an ice cover of considerable thickness. The major advantage of under-ice deployment, however, would be the difficulty of surveillance. As stated in the Canadian White Paper on Defense of 1971, "although Canada has a good capability to detect submarines in the temperate zone, it has only very limited capability to detect submarine activity in the Arctic."[398] It would thus be possible for submarines to enter the Canadian Arctic waters, and perhaps even reach the open water of the Atlantic, via three main routes: first, through the Nares Strait between Greenland and Ellesmere Island; second, through a number of channels in the Queen Elizabeth Islands group which lead to the Northwest Passage; and third, through the M'Clure Strait at the western end of the Northwest Passage. These possibilities were acknowledged as far back as 1973 by the Deputy-Minister of Canada's Department of National Defense, when he stated that, "to the extent the ability of the West to detect and track submarines coming through the Greenland-Iceland-UK passage improves, alternate routes to the Atlantic through the Arctic could become attractive."[399]

In addition, the potential presence of western submarines in Arctic seas, coupled with the current and imminent development of the immense energy resources of the Arctic states, would add considerably to the strategic importance of the region.

SUBMARINE ACTIVITIES IN THE ARCTIC

Shortly after World War II, the United States began experiments in the Arctic, first in the Kennedy and Robeson channels and then in the Chukchi Sea, to develop under-ice submarine navigational capabilities. In 1957 the USS *Nautilus* attempted to reach the North Pole by way of the Greenland Sea but had to turn back at 87°N when her gyrocompasses ceased to function. In August of the following year, however, the *Nautilus* cruised without difficulty from the Bering Sea across the Arctic Ocean to the Greenland Sea, passing beneath the geographic North Pole. In the words of her captain, "she had blazed a new submerged Northwest Passage, vastly decreasing the sea travel time for nuclear submarines from the Pacific to the Atlantic, one that could be used even if the Panama Canal were closed."[400]

This first crossing was followed closely by a number of other submerged crossings. In 1958 and 1962, the USS *Skate* made crossings, surfacing a number of times without any difficulty. The year 1960 also marked the testing by the United States of the feasibility of winter submarine navigation with the 31-day cruise of the *Sargo* under the ice of the Arctic Basin during January and February. It was reported that the *Sargo* surfaced some 20 times during the cruise, twice through ice three feet thick.[401] In autumn of the same year, the USS *Seadragon*, using vertical scanning sonar, made the first east to west submerged crossing of the Northwest Passage. It was reported that the "sonar gave continuous information on: overhead ice thickness, sub-to-ice distance, sub-to-bottom distance, location of holes in the ice (called polynyas), details of polynya outline ridges to allow surfacing, and also provided continuous spotting of icebergs."[402] The facility of the passage was confirmed by the Commander of the *Seadragon* who stated that "Islands and shoals were carefully and accurately plotted on the chart. There was a channel there deep enough for any future nuclear submarine to follow, winter or summer, favorable ice or not."[403] This east to west crossing was followed in 1962 by the west to east transit of the USS *Skate*, proving that underwater navigation through the Northwest Passage was possible in either direction. These passages and other publicly acknowledged passages through Arctic waters are listed in Table 6.

THE PROTECTION OF CANADA'S SOVEREIGNTY

The protection of Canada's sovereignty in the Arctic, particularly as it relates to submarine activities, has been the subject of increasing government attention. In 1969 the general theory that Canada's proximity to the United States made it necessary for the latter to defend Canada in order to defend itself – sometimes referred to as the "free ride" theory – was categorically rejected

Table 6

Known Submarine Operations in the Arctic (1931–1981)[404]

Date	Submarine	Nationality	Area	Purpose
Aug 1931	*Nautilus*	USA	northwest of Svalbard	oceanographic test
1937	*Kresnogvardeyets*	USSR	Denmark Strait	oceanographic test
1939-45	U-boats	Germany	along Northern Sea Route	warfare
1946	*USS Atule* (SS-403)	USA	Kennedy/Robeson Channel	environmental & scientific data
1947	*USS Boarfish* (SS-327)	USA	Chukchi Sea	study pack ice
1948	*USS Carp* (SS-338)	USA	Chukchi Sea	surfacing in polynyas
1952	*USS Redfish* (SS-395)	USA	Beaufort Sea	acoustic data
1953	*USS Redfish*	USA	Beaufort Sea	acoustic data
1957	*USS Nautilus* (SSN-571)	USA	Svalbard	scientific research
Aug 1958	*USS Nautilus* (SSN-571)	USA	North Pole	transit of Arctic Ocean and surfacing
Aug 1958	*USS Skate* (SSN-758)	USA	North Pole	transit of Arctic Ocean and surfacing
Jan-Feb 1960	*USS Sargo* (SSN-583)	USA	Chukchi Sea	testing piloting sonar
Aug 1960	*USS Seadragon* (SSN-584)	USA	Northwest Passage	east to west transit test under-ice sonar
June 1962	*Leninskiy Komsomol*	USSR	North Pole	
July 1962	*USS Skate* (SSN-578)	USA	Northwest Passage and North Pole	west to east transit
July 1962	*USS Seadragon* (SSN-584)	USA	North Pole	
Feb 1967	*USS Queenfish*	USA	Baffin Bay	first single-screw nuclear submarine operations in and under the ice
Apr-May 1969	*USS Whale* *USS Sargo*	USA USA	Arctic Basin	surfacing through thick ice; ridge-busting experiments
Aug 1970	*USS Queenfish*	USA	Arctic Basin Siberian Shelf	hydrographic surveys

(Table 6, continued)

Date	Submarine	Nationality	Area	Purpose
Nov 1971	*HMS Dreadnought*	UK	Arctic Basin North Pole	first UK Arctic operation
Feb-Mar 1971	*USS Trepang*	USA	Denmark Strait Greenland Sea	hydrographic surveys
Mar-Apr 1972	*USS Hawkbill* *USS Seadragon*	USA USA	Northern Bering Sea	oceanographic surveys
Mar 1975	*USS Bluefish*	USA	Greenland Sea Arctic Basin	hydrographic surveys
Mar 1976	*USS Gurnard*	USA	Arctic Basin Beaufort Sea	shallow-water oceanographic operations
Sep 1976	*HMS Sovereign*	UK	Arctic Basin	oceanographic surveys
Mar 1977	*USS Flying Fish*	USA	Arctic Basin	oceanographic & hydrographic surveys
Oct 1978	*USS Pintado*	USA	Arctic Basin	oceanographic & hydrographic surveys
Mar 1979	*USS Archerfish*	USA	Baffin Bay Nares Strait	Oceanographic & hydrographic surveys
Nov 1981	*USS Silversides*	USA	Greenland Sea Arctic Basin	

by the House of Commons Standing Committee on External Affairs and National Defense. The committee stated that "Canada must be prepared to incur reasonable expenditures for its own defence in order to maintain its independence and freedom of action as a nation, and to ensure that Canadian interests are taken into account when continental defence measures are being taken."[405]

Two years after the release of the committee's report, the government published its *White Paper on Defense*, in which the first of four major areas of activity for Canadian forces was identified as the "surveillance of our own territory and coastlines, i.e., the protection of our sovereignty."[406] The White Paper stated that surveillance over Arctic land and waters was being carried out by long-range patrol aircraft and by ships, but that surveillance by the latter was restricted to ice-free periods of the year.[407] The White Paper also addressed itself specifically to the question of submarines and concluded that "although Canada has a good capability to detect submarines in its waters in the temperate zone, it has only very limited capability to detect submarine activity in the

Arctic.[408] The White Paper added that the government was undertaking research to determine the costs and feasibility of "a limited subsurface system to give warning of any unusual maritime activity."[409]

During the Defense Structure Review of 1975, the major roles of the Canadian forces were more clearly delineated.[410] Although the wording of the roles has varied slightly from year to year, the substance has not changed significantly. As described in 1983, the first two of the four roles specifically involved the surveillance and defense of the Arctic. A task assigned under Role 1, "the protection of Canada and Canadian national interests at home and abroad (short title, sovereignty)", is "to provide surveillance of land and sea areas north of 60°N latitude to reinforce Canadian presence, and to detect and identify unauthorized activities."[411] Under Role 2, "the defence of North America in cooperation with the United States", a further task is assigned, namely "to conduct subsurface surveillance, in conjunction with U.S. forces, of shallow and deep water areas of the sea approaches to North America, including the Canadian Arctic and the Denmark Strait, to provide a continuing intelligence picture of potentially hostile submarine activities."[412]

The definition of these tasks has not necessarily meant that they have been fully implemented, since adequate resources may not have been assigned. Indeed, in the 1982 Annual Report of the Department of National Defense, there is no mention whatever of any naval activity in the Arctic waters properly so called. The most northerly operations reported for that year were those of the submersible HMCS *Cormorant*, in August, off the coast of Labrador.[413]

The question of the adequacy of the measures taken to protect Canada's sovereignty in the Arctic was extensively reviewed by the Sub-Committee on National Defense of the Senate Committee on Foreign Affairs in its report of May 1983. After hearing from some one hundred government and non-government witnesses, the Sub-Committee came to the conclusion that the protection of Canada's sovereignty, particularly in the Arctic, had been too narrowly interpreted.

> Sovereignty is more than a concept to be repetitively proclaimed. It must be continuously asserted and exercised in tangible and visible fashion. Canada's geography dictates a need for these efforts, particularly in the Arctic and on the country's extended sea frontiers along the east and west coast. Through inertia, encroachments on sovereignty can easily be invited from friend or foe. Canada's strategic geographic position, for example, virtually guarantees that if Canada were to be unwilling or unable to provide in some measure for its own defence, the United States would be obliged to fill that vacuum at the expense of Canadian sovereignty.[414]

Having thus concluded, the Senate Sub-Committee recommended that the formulation of the first role of the Canadian armed forces, that is, the protection of Canadian sovereignty, "be recast so as to include specific reference to the defence of Canada."[415] It also recommended that the description of military tasks "be reformulated immediately so as to give appropriate emphasis to the defence of Canada; to clarify priorities; to show performance criteria; to indicate dedicated sources; and to identify their geographic distribution."[416]

APPRAISAL AND POLICY IMPLICATIONS

Considering the concern posed for Canada's sovereignty by submarine activities in the Arctic, the implication is clear that Canada should develop a greater surveillance of, and ice-breaking capability for, the Northwest Passage. If Canada is not in a position to do this on its own, those objectives might be obtained through closer cooperation with some of its Arctic neighbors.

Surveillance of the Northwest Passage

Canada's surveillance of the Arctic waters has been limited. About sixteen sets of reconnaissance overflight missions, each about three to four days long, have been undertaken yearly.[417] Besides these flights, the only military presence in the Arctic has been limited to occasional training exercises and the presence of the Canadian Rangers, a special reserve unit composed of native northerners. Operation "Sovereignty Viking", for example, was conducted by the Second Battalion of the Princess Patricia's Canadian Light Infantry off Resolute Bay from February to April 1982. It was reported that "the unit conducted both mounted and dismounted sovereignty and surveillance patrols on Cornwallis Island, NWT and the surrounding ice pack."[418] The Canadian Rangers, numbering 650 in 1983, have been organized into 12 to 50-man patrols in 34 different locations throughout the Northwest Territories, Northern Manitoba and Quebec. They are commanded by native Ranger Sergeants, each annually supplied with small-arms ammunition. Their role is "to provide a military presence in sparsely settled Northern coastal and isolated areas which cannot conveniently or economically be covered by other elements of the regular or reserved force."[419] There has been virtually no Canadian naval presence in the Arctic.[420]

The relative lack of Arctic surveillance capability has been criticized by defense specialist Nicholas Tracy, who has asserted that "surveillance is the *sine qua non* of national defence at any level."[421] Tracy, watchful of potential conflicting United States interests in opening the Northwest Passage to relatively unrestricted navigation, has presented the necessity for Canada to ensure her own surveillance in the following terms:

> Adequate surveillance . . . is a necessary means of preventing the challenge of Canadian sovereignty by Canada's friends. Specifically, it is only by providing an adequate level of military surveillance that Canada can obviate the need of the United States to undertake the surveillance herself.[422]

The necessity for Canada to develop surveillance and protection capability has also been recognized by the Sub-Committee on National Defense of the Senate Committee on Foreign Relations. In its 1983 Report the Sub-Committee criticized the government's reluctance to provide Maritime Command with surveillance equipment:

> . . . the failure to provide MARCOM with additional equipment designed for the purpose of sovereignty surveillance and its related war-time tasks becomes truly baffling when the enormous additions to Canada's maritime jurisdictional claims since publication of *Defence in the 70s* are taken into account.[423]

The Sub-Committee found that "there is a requirement for Canada's maritime forces to be equipped to perform a sea-denial role in waters over which Canada claims jurisdiction."[424]

The Senate Sub-Committee also addressed itself specifically to the question of surveillance of the Northwest Passage. It believed that "adequate surveillance of the Northwest Passage could be provided, for the time being, by conventionally powered submarines stationed at the entrance and the exit of the Passage",[425] and that installation of an economically and technically feasible bottom-based sonar system might also be desirable.[426] It stated in addition that "should the frequency of nuclear submarine transits through Arctic waters rise substantially, Canada might have to contemplate obtaining nuclear submarines of its own," noting that asking its allies to patrol the area would hold "real dangers" since Canada's claim to Arctic waters were not undisputed by the United States.[427]

In addition, the Sub-Committee suggested that "consideration should be given to constructing new Coast Guard icebreakers so that they can take military helicopters and containerized weapons systems if necessary."[428] In other words, the Coast Guard would remain a civilian organization and would continue to assist in asserting Canadian sovereignty, but there would be a greater coordination of activities between the Navy and the Coast Guard. In order to ensure this, the Sub-Committee recommended "that the practice be established of regularly seconding some Maritime Command personnel to the Coast Guard for practice and training in Arctic navigation."[429]

Considering that the Maritime Command should gradually increase its activities in the Arctic and would find it useful to have a central supply and repair base, the Committee recommended that "the government examine the need for a year-round Arctic base to provide support for air, land and sea operations of all departments with responsibilities in the North."[430] Such a base, if located on Devon Island, could also service as a surveillance center at the entrance of the Northwest Passage, and as an air force interceptor element in order to improve Canada's air identification parameter.[431]

Ice-breaking Capability for the Northwest Passage

In its report, the Senate Sub-Committee attached considerable importance to the presence of icebreakers in the Arctic to substantiate Canada's claim to the waters of the Northwest Passage. It stated in particular,

> . . . Canada should strengthen its case by maintaining a significant maritime presence there. The country must be table to control access to and enforce its jurisdictional claims over Arctic waters. In peace time, this presence should be provided by icebreakers with capabilities equal or superior to those of commercial vessels now being designed for use in the North (and likely to grow in numbers as commercial exploitation of Arctic resources increases).[432]

The Sub-Committee added that class 8 Polar icebreakers would undoubtedly be required in the next five to seven years and that Canada should give consideration to building a Polar class 10 icebreaker. In 1983 none of Canada's eight 1200 and above class icebreakers were capable of operating in the Arctic for more than three to four months of the year. Only three, the *Louis St. Laurent*, the *John A. Macdonald*, and the *Labrador* were capable of being retrofitted for military use, and only the *Louis St. Laurent* was suitable for use in ice covered areas up to Zone 6. However, it is evident from Figure 17 and Table 7 that even the *Louis St. Laurent* would not be able to navigate Routes 1 and 2 of the Northwest Passage. This situation was in stark contrast with that of the Soviet Union, which has been building its icebreaker fleet and by 1983 had the largest and most powerful one in the world.[433]

To remedy this situation, the Canadian government approved funds for the design but not the construction of a class 1400 Polar-8 icebreaker adequate for navigation via Route 2 of the Northwest Passage. Even if funds for construction should be approved, the Commissioner of the Coast Guard admitted in 1982 that one vessel would not be sufficient for year-round surveillance and control of foreign shipping.[434]

Table 7

List of Ship Categories for Shipping Safety Control Zones

Column I Category	Column II Zone 1	Column III Zone 2	Column IV Zone 3	Column V Zone 4	Column VI Zone 5	Column VII Zone 6	Column VIII Zone 7	Column IX Zone 8
Arctic Class 10 1.	All Year	All Year	All Year	All Year	All Year	All Year	All Year	All Year
Arctic Class 8 2.	Jul. 1 to Oct. 15	All Year	All Year	All Year	All Year	All Year	All Year	All Year
Arctic Class 7 3.	Aug. 1 to Sept. 30	Aug. 1 to Nov. 30	Jul. 1 to Dec. 31	Jul. 1 to Dec. 15	Jul. 1 to Dec. 15	All Year	All Year	All Year
Arctic Class 6 4.	Aug. 15 to Sept. 15	Aug. 1 to Oct. 31	Jul. 15 to Nov. 30	Jul. 15 to Nov. 30	Aug. 1 to Oct. 15	Jul. 15 to Feb. 28	Jul. 1 to Mar. 31	Jul. 1 to Mar. 31
Arctic Class 4 5.	Aug. 15 to Sept. 15	Aug. 15 to Oct. 15	Jul. 15 to Oct. 31	Jul. 15 to Nov. 15	Aug. 15 to Sept. 30	Jul. 20 to Dec. 31	Jul. 15 to Jan. 15	Jul. 15 to Jan. 15
Arctic Class 3 6.	Aug. 20 to Sept. 15	Aug. 20 to Sept. 30	Jul. 25 to Oct. 15	Jul. 20 to Nov. 5	Aug. 20 to Sept. 25	Aug. 1 to Nov. 20	Jul. 20 to Dec. 15	Jul. 20 to Dec. 31
Arctic Class 2 7.	No Entry	No Entry	Aug. 15 to Sept. 30	Aug. 1. to Oct. 31	No Entry	Aug. 15 to Nov. 20	Aug. 1 to Nov. 20	Aug. 1 to Nov. 30
Arctic Class 1A 8.	No Entry	No Entry	Aug. 20 to Sept. 15	Aug. 20 to Sept. 30	No Entry	Aug. 25 to Oct. 31	Aug. 10 to Nov. 5	Aug. 10 to Nov. 20
Arctic Class 1 9.	No Entry	No Entry	No Entry	No Entry	No Entry	Aug. 25 to Sept. 30	Aug. 10 to Oct. 15	Aug. 10 to Oct. 31
Type A 10.	No Entry	No Entry	Aug. 20 to Sept. 10	Aug. 20 to Sept. 20	No Entry	Aug. 15 to Oct. 15	Aug. 1 to Oct. 25	Aug. 1 to Nov. 10
Type B 11.	No Entry	No Entry	Aug. 20 to Sept. 5	Aug. 20 to Sept. 15	No Entry	Aug. 25 to Sept. 30	Aug. 10 to Oct. 15	Aug. 10 to Oct. 31
Type C 12.	No Entry	No Entry	No Entry	No Entry	No Entry	Aug. 25 to Sept. 25	Aug. 10 to Oct. 10	Aug. 10 to Oct. 25
Type D 13.	No Entry	No Entry	No Entry	No Entry	No Entry	No Entry	Aug. 10 to Oct. 5	Aug. 15 to Oct. 20
Type E 14.	No Entry	No Entry	No Entry	No Entry	No Entry	No Entry	Aug. 10 to Sept. 30	Aug. 20 to Oct. 20

Source: *Sailing Directions, Arctic Canada*, Vol. III, at 17 (1981).

Column X Zone 9	Column XI Zone 10	Column XII Zone 11	Column XIII Zone 12	Column XIV Zone 13	Column XV Zone 14	Column XVI Zone 15	Column XVII Zone 16
All Year	All Year	All Year	All Year	All Year	All Year	All Year	All Year
All Year	All Year	All Year	All Year	All Year	All Year	All Year	All Year
All Year	All Year	All Year	All Year	All Year	All Year	All Year	All Year
All Year	All Year	Jul. 1 to Mar. 31	All Year	All Year	All Year	All Year	All Year
Jul. 10 to Mar. 31	Jul. 10 to Feb. 28	Jul. 5 to Jan. 15	June 1 to Jan. 31	June 1 to Feb. 15	June 15 to Feb. 15	June 15 to Mar. 15	June 1 to Feb 15
Jul. 20 to Jan. 20	Jul. 15 to Jan. 25	Jul. 5 to Dec. 15	June 10 to Dec. 31	June 10 to Dec. 31	June 20 to Jan. 10	June 20 to Jan 31	June 5 to Jan 10
Aug. 1 to Dec. 20	Jul. 25 to Dec. 20	Jul. 10 to Nov. 20	June 15 to Dec. 5	June 25 to Nov. 15	June 25 to Dec 10	June 25 to Dec 20	June 10 to Dec 10
Aug. 10 to Dec. 10	Aug. 1 to Dec. 10	Jul. 15 to Nov. 10	Jul. 1 to Nov. 10	Jul 15 to Oct. 31	Jul. 1 to Nov. 30	Jul 1 to Dec 10	June 20 to Nov. 30
Aug. 10 to Oct. 31	Aug. 1 to Oct. 31	Jul. 15 to Oct. 20	Jul. 1 to Oct. 31	Jul. 15 to Oct. 15	Jul 1 to Nov. 30	Jul 1 to Nov 30	June 20 to Nov 15
Aug. 1 to Nov. 20	Jul. 25 to Nov. 20	Jul. 10 to Oct. 31	June 15 to Nov. 10	June 25 to Oct. 22	June 25 to Nov. 30	June 25 to Dec. 5	June 20 to Nov. 20
Aug. 10 to Oct. 31	Aug. 1 to Oct. 31	Jul. 15 to Oct. 20	Jul. 1 to Oct. 25	Jul. 15 to Oct. 15	Jul. 1 to Nov. 30	Jul. 1 to Nov. 30	June 20 to Nov. 10
Aug. 10 to Oct. 25	Aug. 1 to Oct. 25	Jul. 15 to Oct. 15	Jul. 1 to Oct. 25	Jul. 15 to Oct. 10	Jul 1 to Nov. 25	Jul. 1 to Nov. 25	June 25 to Nov. 10
Aug. 15 to Oct. 20	Aug. 5 to Oct. 20	Jul. 15 to Oct. 10	Jul. 1 to Oct. 20	Jul 30 to Sept 30	Jul 10 to Nov 10	Jul 5 to Nov 10	Jul. 1 to Oct. 31
Aug. 20 to Oct. 15	Aug. 10 to Oct. 20	Jul. 15 to Sept. 30	Jul. 1 to Oct. 20	Aug. 15 to Sept 20	Jul. 20 to Oct 31	Jul 20 to Nov 5	Jul 1 to Oct 31

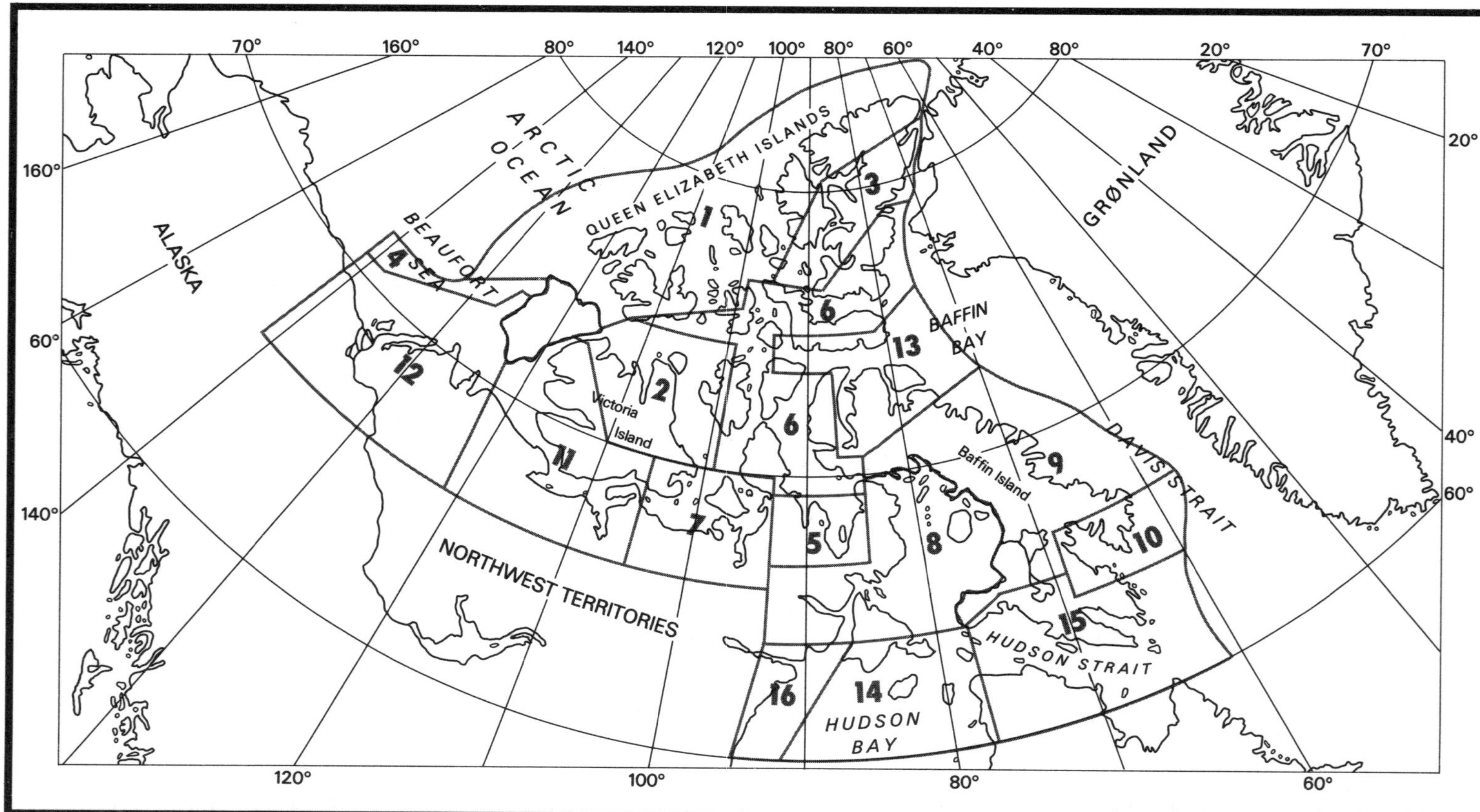

Fig. 17 : SHIPPING SAFETY CONTROL ZONES
Prepared for the author by the Canadian Hydrographic Service, Dept. of Fisheries and Oceans, Ottawa.
Source : S.O.R. / 72 - 303, Canada Gazette, Part II, Vol. 106, No. 16, P. 1468 (23 Aug. 1972)

Cooperation with Other Arctic States

Canada's cooperation with its Arctic neighbors, particularly with the United States, is desirable. Since Canada and the United States together front on three oceans, share four maritime boundary regions, and have joint defense agreements, cooperation is indeed indispensable. However, their commonality of interests in the Arctic is not complete, especially in relation to the transportation of hydrocarbons from the Beaufort Sea area. In order to satisfy the needs of the American eastern seaboard, the United States might wish to use the Northwest Passage free of any authority and control by Canada, especially since the United States has decided not to sign the 1982 Law of the Sea Convention, at least for the time being.

In addition, the United States has indicated that it might not be prepared to recognize parts of the convention as international law even when the convention is in force. It is somewhat uncertain whether the United States would readily accept the establishment of straight baselines by Canada around its archipelago, lines which would allow Canada to gain more control over the Northwest Passage. Indeed, there are seems to be a fundamental difference of opinion between the two countries as to whether or not the Northwest Passage is an international strait, with the consequent difference of opinion as to the rights of navigation therein.

It would seem to follow that it might be in Canada's best interests to intensify its cooperation with other Arctic states, particularly with Denmark and Norway, and possibly Iceland as well. An attempt at cooperation with the Soviet Union might also be advantageous and justified. Such efforts should not be adversely regarded by the United States, since none would affect the cooperative and joint arrangements existing between the two countries.

Cooperation with Denmark and Greenland would be absolutely essential in order to open up the Northwest Passage for shipping, and this cooperation has started already. As was brought out during the hearings by the National Energy Board of Canada on the application of the Arctic Pilot Project, the Greenlanders were very sensitive to the possibility of their marine environment being adversely affected by the transportation of hydrocarbons through the Davis Strait and Baffin Bay. Consequently, a Mine Environmental Cooperation Agreement was concluded between Canada and Denmark in August 1983. The agreement provides for cooperation in the identification, monitoring and review of vessel routing areas outside territorial waters with a view to protecting the marine environment.[435] Included in the agreement is an annex dealing with pollution incidents resulting from shipping activities.

A considerable degree of cooperation already exists with Norway through Canada's participation in NATO and its commitment to the protection of the northern flank. Having regard to Norway's experience in operating conventional submarines in northern waters and Canada's intention not to acquire nuclear submarines in the foreseeable future, Canada could perhaps obtain Norway's cooperation and assistance in this respect.

The possibility of cooperation between Canada and the Soviet Union in the Arctic should not be disregarded either. A "General Exchanges Agreement" has existed between the two countries since 1971, whereby they undertake to "facilitate the exchange of visits by scientists and scientific research workers and the exchange of scientific information."[436] With special reference to the Arctic, both governments have obligated themselves to "facilitate professional, technical and administrative contacts and exchanges in the fields of transport, communications, urban development, *development in the north* and in other regions where the environment presents similar problems of adaptation, and construction related to these fields."[437] Although rather little has been done in the implementation of the above agreement, certainly as it relates to the Arctic, additional efforts might prove fruitful. In particular, Canada might benefit from some of the expertise developed by the Soviet Union for year-round navigation in ice-covered waters. Cooperation might also be extended to participating in some of the scientific investigations being carried on in the Arctic Basin from drifting ice islands. The Soviet Union has been operating its twenty-sixth drifting ice station from which it has been collecting scientific data of various kinds, a number of which are useful to improve navigational facilities. The scientific and technological cooperation just envisaged presumes, of course, the existence of a sufficiently suitable political climate.

CONCLUSION

Although the policy implications of the commercial development and possible internationalization of the Northwest Passage have been spelled out in each of the preceding chapters, they may be summarized in a single statement for each of the three bases of concern:

Marine Environment. Considering the potential impacts of year-round shipping of oil and gas on the ecologically sensitive areas in and adjacent to the Northwest Passage, Canada should acquire and maintain both *de jure* and *de facto* control over commercial shipping through the passage, with a view to preventing major harm to, or irreversible disturbance of, the ecological balance of those areas.

Inuit. Considering the potential impacts of year-round shipping of oil and gas on the historic way of life of the Inuit, based on hunting and fishing in the Northwest Passage and adjacent areas, Canada should endeavor to settle outstanding Inuit claims to those areas with all possible expediency; it could then invoke such settlement in support of the validity of its sovereignty claim over the waters of its Arctic Archipelago, with a view to preventing the gradual disappearance of the historic way of life to which the Inuit hold and which Canada has a duty to protect.

National Security. Considering the strategic importance of the Arctic and the freedom of navigation which all ships would enjoy, including the submerged operation of submarines in the Northwest Passage, if it were under an international regime, Canada should develop an appropriate surveillance and protection capability in the area to insure its national security.

SUMMARY AND POLICY IMPLICATIONS FOR CANADA

Each of the chapters of this book has its own summary or conclusion, but it may be helpful to re-state in general terms the conclusion that has been reached on the main points that have been examined in this study of the Northwest Passage.

Description. Only two of the five basic routes of the Northwest Passage are potentially suitable for navigation by deep draft (20 meters) ships: Route 1, through the Prince of Wales Strait and Route 2, through the M'Clure Strait. Because the M'Clure Strait is usually clogged with multi-year old ice from the Beaufort Sea, Route 1 would be the preferred route in the event of shipping of hydrocarbons from the Beaufort Sea area.

Historical Development. All the bodies of water constituting the five basic routes of the Northwest Passage were discovered by British expeditions before the transfer of the Arctic islands to Canada in 1880. After the transfer, beginning in 1903, Canada dispatched regular expeditions and patrols which eventually navigated all of the routes of the Northwest Passage. Of the forty complete crossings of the passage in the whole of its history, twenty-seven were by Canadian ships. Of the thirteen foreign crossings, ten were American, one Norwegian, one Dutch and one Japanese. The last three were by small craft.

Future Development. It appears certain that the present intense exploration of the vast hydrocarbon resources of the Arctic will lead to eventual production and shipping through the Northwest Passage. The technology for both production and year-round shipping has been developed, but considerable uncertainty remains as to when these will begin. A realistic date for such beginning would seem to be around 1990.

Legal Status. The waters of the Northwest Passage are claimed by Canada to be "internal" on the basis of an historic title, but straight baselines around the Arctic Archipelago have not yet been established to confirm the status of those waters and delimit their precise geographical extent. Irrespective of the exact status of the waters, the Northwest Passage is not an international strait at the moment and only the right of suspendable innocent passage applies. If a sufficient degree of international shipping takes place, the Northwest Passage may become an international strait and the right of non-suspendable transit passage would apply. In that event, Canada would still be able to adopt and enforce special marine pollution prevention standards because the Northwest Passage is located in ice-covered areas virtually year-round.

Policy Implications. The internationalization of the Northwest Passage would have policy implications for the marine environment, the Inuit, and Canada's national security. For an adequate protection of the marine environment, Canada should exercise appropriate control over commercial shipping. Because of the likely serious impact on the traditional way of life of the Inuit, Canada should endeavor to settle their outstanding legal and off-shore claims expeditiously. It could then rely on such settlement for partial support of its claim to sovereignty over the waters. Considering the freedom of navigation for *all* ships which would result from an international regime, Canada should develop an appropriate monitoring and defense capability in the Arctic to guarantee its national security.

CHAPTER NOTES

NOTES TO CHAPTER 1

1. For a description of the ice regime for the eastern approaches, see *Sailing Directions, Arctic Canada* (Ottawa: Queen's Printer, 1982), Vol. 1, at 156-159 and *Beaufort Sea-Mackenzie Delta Environmental Impact Statement* (Calgary: Dome Petroleum, 1982), Vol. 3B, Northwest Passage Setting, at 1.1-1.21. This latter publication will be hereinafter referred to as *Beaufort EIS.*

2. R.D. Kassler, "Western Arctic Trafficability Tests", abstract in *Proceedings of the 33rd Alaska Science Conference* (1982), and typewritten text provided by the author.

3. For a diagram of these different types of ice zones, see *Beaufort EIS, supra* note 1, Vol. 3A, Beaufort-Delta Setting, at 1.2; and, for a general description of ice conditions in the Beaufort Sea, see *id.*, at 1.1-1.19.

4. From the writer's own observation, the polynya at the south end entrance of Amundsen Gulf had already extended to the full entrance of the gulf and to a very considerable distance into the Beaufort Sea, on 14 June 1982.

5. See "Submarine Pingos in the Beaufort Sea", 174 *Science*, 16-18 (1971).

6. For a description of the various routes of the Northwest Passage, see mainly the following: *Sailing Directions, Arctic Canada*, 1982, *supra* note 1, at 159-163 and (1981), Vol. III, at 87-222, and *Beaufort EIS*, *supra* note 1, Vol. 3B, at 1.4-1.3 and 1.49-1.59.

7. For a study of iceberg movement pattern in this area, see B.R. de Lange Boom et al., "Iceberg Motion in Lancaster Sound and Northwest Baffin Bay, Summer 1978", 35(1) *Arctic* 219-233 (1982). Analysis of 11 weeks of data indicates that icebergs entering Lancaster Sound follow the south shore of Devon Island to Cape Warrender and then move either southwestward or toward the center of Lancaster Sound.

8. *Sailing Directions, Arctic Canada* (Ottawa: Queen's Printer, 1981), Vol. III, at 198-199.

9. See G.P. Steele, *Seadragon, Northwest Under the Ice* (New York: E.P. Dutton, 1962), at 161-172.

10. See *Sailing Directions, Arctic Canada, supra* note 8, at 211.

11. M'Clintock Channel, separating Victoria Island from Prince of Wales Strait and running

from Larsen Sound to Viscount Melville Sound, was navigated in 1962 by the CCGS *John A. Macdonald*; see *ibid.*, at 186. Theoretically, it could be considered as a second variation to Route 3, but there are no advantages in distance or in prevailing ice conditions.

12. See *Sailing Directions, Arctic Canada, supra* note 8, at 164.

13. *Ibid.*, at 126.

14. For a description of navigational conditions in Simpson Strait, see *ibid.*, at 168-172.

15. See *Sailing Directions, Arctic Canada, supra* note 8, Vol. II, at 105.

16. See *Beaufort EIS, supra* note 1, Vol. 3B, at 1.59.

17. See *Sailing Directions, Arctic Canada, supra* note 15, Vol. II, at 76.

18. *Ibid.*, at 56.

19. *Ibid.*, at 90; this quotation is a passage taken from the *Report of Proceedings* submitted by Captain T.C. Pullen, Commanding Officer of HMCS *Labrador* in 1956.

20. See *Sailing Directions, Arctic Canada, supra* note 2, at 117.

NOTES TO CHAPTER 2

21. The main sources used for this chapter are: *Sailing Directions, Arctic Canada* (Ottawa: Queen's Printer, 1982), Vol. I; Andrew Taylor, *Geographical Discovery and Exploration of the Queen Elizabeth Islands* (Ottawa: Queen's Printer, 1964); and Alan Cooke and Clive Holland, *The Exploration of Northern Canada 500 to 1920*, a Chronology (Toronto: Arctic History Press, 1978).

22. See Taylor, *ibid.*, at 32.

23. *Ibid.*, at 82.

24. For an excellent recent study on this question, see W. Gillies Ross, "The Annual Catch of Greenland (Bowhead) Whales in Waters North of Canada 1719–1915: A Preliminary Compilation", 32 *Arctic* 91-121 (1979).

25. The Hudson Bay whale fishery was exploited from 1765 to 1915 by both British and American whalers, particularly by the latter, beginning in 1860; see *ibid.*, at 112-113.

26. The Beaufort Sea whale fishery, which extended into Amundsen Gulf, was exploited from 1889 to 1908 by American whalers; see *ibid.*, at 113-118.

27. For statistics of whaleships and whale catch from 1719 to 1911, see *ibid.*, at 100-106.

28. American whaling in the Davis Strait fishery took place in two periods: from 1729 to about 1775 and from 1846 to 1892; see *ibid.*, at 96-97.

29. See *Sailing Directions, Arctic Canada, supra* note 1, Vol. I, at 66.

30. *Ibid.*

NOTES TO CHAPTER 3

31. Since the transfer was effected by a simple Order-in-Council rather than by legislation, it is possible that Canada had doubts as to the sufficiency of the Order-in-Council to effect a proper transfer. Be that as it may, Great Britain enacted the Colonial Boundaries Act in 1895, which specified that where the boundaries of a colony have been altered by Order-in-Council or letters patent, such boundaries were deemed to have been the boundaries of the colony from the date of the alterations. If remedial legislation was necessary, the 1895 Act remedied any possible defect which the 1880 Order-in-Council might have contained. For a thorough discussion of this question, see Gordon W. Smith, *Canada's Arctic Archipelago: 100 Years of Canadian Jurisdiction* (Ottawa: Department of Indian and Northern Affairs, 1980), Publication No. QS-8276-000-BB-A1.

32. Taylor, *supra* note 21, at 111.

33. Gordon W. Smith, *An Historical and Legal Study of Sovereignty in the Canadian North and Related Problems of Maritime Law*, part A, Volume I, at 208, part of an ongoing study.

34. Cited by Taylor, *supra* note 21, at 116.

35. *Ibid.*, at 117.

36. *Ibid.*

37. See *Polar Record*, Vol. 4, No. 27, at 134 (1944).

38. H. Larsen, *The Northwest Passage* (Ottawa: Queen's Printer, 1948), at 2.

39. Andrew Collier, Commissioner of the Canadian Coast Guard, in Canada, Senate Standing Committee on Foreign Affairs, Subcommittee on National Defense, *Proceedings*, Issue No. 35, at 7 (23 November 1982).

40. *Ibid.*, at 26-27.

41. See Department of Transport, *Position Statement*, submitted to the Beaufort Sea Environmental Assessment Review Panel, 16 August 1982.

42. The writer is greatly indebted to Cyril Champ of the Canadian Hydrographic Service who provided the information contained in this section.

43. R.W. Timbrell, in *Proceedings, supra* note 38, Issue No. 18, at 12 (26 May 1981).

44. Harriet Critchley, *Proceedings, supra* note 38, Issue No. 32, at 23 (8 June 1982).

45. *Ibid.*, at 25.

46. *Ibid.*, at 9.

47. Information obtained by letter of the writer, dated 29 July 1983, from Col. I.E. Creelman, Deputy Chief of Staff Operations for Commander, Maritime Command, Halifax.

48. Department of Indian Affairs and Northern Development, *Annual Report*, 1981, at 115 (1982).

NOTES TO CHAPTER 4

49. Transport Canada, *Arctic Marine Transportation Forecast of Ship Movements: 1985, 1990, 1995*, revised by Norman Carrière, at 4-52 (1981).

50. *Infra*, Chapter 6.

51. See generally, "The Arctic", in *International Petroleum Encyclopedia, 1983* (Tulsa, Okla.: Penwall Publishing, 1983), 418 pp, at 4-29.

52. At the time of writing, the effect of financial difficulties at Dome Petroleum, one of the major operators in the Arctic, was unknown.

53. "Proven reserves" constitute oil and gas extractable under current price/cost relationships and state of technology. Data from W.C. Thomas and M.E. Thomas, "Public Policy and Petroleum Development: the Alaska Case", 35(3) *Arctic* 349-357, at 350 (1982).

54. *Ibid.*

55. F. Bregha, "Petroleum development in Northern Alaska", in *Marine Transportation and High Arctic Development: Policy Framework and Priorities, Symposium Proceedings* (Ottawa: CARC, 1979), 223-253, at 227.

56. Thomas and Thomas, *supra* note 53, at 355.

57. R. Mast, R. McMullin, K. Bird and W. Brosge, "Resource appraisal of undiscovered oil and gas resources in the William D. Douglas Arctic Wildlife Range", U.S. Dept. of the Interior, *U.S. Geological Survey Open File Report 80-916* (1980) cited in Thomas and Thomas, *supra* note 53; Bregha, *supra* note 55.

58. Thomas and Thomas, *supra* note 53, at 355.

59. See generally M. Conant, "The Call of the Arctic", 25 *Oceanus* 51-57 (1982/83) and "The Great Arctic Energy Rush", *Business Week* 52-56 (24 January 1983).

60. Conant, *supra* note 59, at 52.

61. G. Mull, *U.S. Geological Survey* (1977) cited in Bregha, *supra* note 7, at 9.

62. "The Arctic", *supra* note 51, at 13-14.

63. Canada, Department of External Affairs, *Communiqué No. 27* (28 April 1982).

64. Northern Pipeline Agency, *Annual Report* 1981–1982 (1983); "The Arctic" (1983), *supra* note 51, at 14.

65. *Maritime Services to Support Polar Resource Development* (Washington: National Academy Press, 1981), at 46.

66. 1980 estimate by Nova cited in Bregha, *Canadian Arctic Marine Energy Projects* (Ottawa: CARC, 1982), 52 pp., at 10.

67. 1980 estimate by Dome cited in Bregha (1982), *supra* note 66, at 10. It should be noted that this estimate includes stratigraphic traps.

68. 1978 Gulf estimate cited in Bregha (1982), *supra* note 66, at 9.

69. 1978 Dome estimate cited in Bregha (1982), *supra* note 66, at 9. It should be noted that this estimate is expressed at 100 BTU/cf.

70. Canada, National Energy Board, *Canadian Energy Supply and Demand 1980–2000*, at 143.

71. Canada, Department of Indian and Northern Affairs, *Communiqué No. 1-8232* (20 January 1983); "Beaufort Activity Moves Into High Gear", 34 *Oilweek* 20-29 (1983); "Canadian East Coast and Arctic Offshore", 18 *Ocean Industry* 27-31 (1983).

72. "Canadian East Coast and Arctic Offshore" (1983), *supra* note 71, at 30.

73. This optimistic projection was put forward by Dome Petroleum assuming that the federal government would be willing to delay collection of taxes and royalties until Dome's substantial capital costs are paid back. It should be noted that Dome Petroleum is consistently one of the most optimistic projectors of both resource potential and development time frames. "NEP Grants Spur Northern Exploration", (Toronto) *Globe and Mail*, at B13 (6 June 1983). See also "Recession Makes Canada Net Oil Importer", (Toronto) *Globe and Mail*, at B3 (6 June 1983).

74. Estimate by NOVA cited along with Dome estimate in table 10-13 of *Canadian Energy Supply and Demand 1980–200, supra* note 70.

75. This opinion has been expressed throughout the literature relating to development of these reserves.

76. *Beaufort Sea-Mackenzie Delta Environmental Impact Statement* (Calgary: Dome Petroleum, 1982), 7 vols., Vol. 2 (hereinafter referred to as *Beaufort EIS*).

77. Canada, Senate, Report of the Special Committee on the Northern Pipeline, *Marching to the Beat of the Same Drum: Transportation of Petroleum and Natural Gas North of 60°* (March 1983) (hereinafter referred to as "Senate Report").

78. *Ibid.*, at 31.

79. *Ibid.*, at 15.

80. *Beaufort EIS* (1982), *supra* note 76, Vol. 2 at 3.9; Senate Report (1983), *supra* note 77, at 16.

81. *Ibid.*, at 6.12-6.42.

82. *Ibid.*, at 6.13-6.16; "Expanded Export Market Revitalizes Polar Gas Project", 18 *Ocean Industry* 413-414 (1983).

83. *Annual Report* (1983), *supra* note 64.

84. "Polar GAs Proposes Mackenzie Pipeline", (Toronto) *Globe and Mail*, at B-1 (18 March 1983); Canada, National Energy Board, *Regulatory Agenda*, at 6 (1 March 1983).

85. *Fourteenth Annual Report 1981* (Calgary: Panarctic, 1982), at 2; *Panarctic in the Canadian Arctic Islands* (Notes distributed to Heads of Mission Arctic Tour in July 1982).

86. Senate Report, *supra* note 77, at 26-29; "Canadian East Coast and Arctic Offshore", *supra* note 71, at 31.

87. *Panarctic in the Canadian Arctic Islands, supra* note 85.

88. Bregha, *supra* note 66, at 35. It should be noted, in addition, that hearings before the National Energy Board were adjourned in August 1982 "until the sponsors of the project can come up with a definitive proposal for the export of LNG." *NEB News Release* (1 September 1982).

89. "Polar Gas Proposes Mackenzie Pipeline", *supra* note 84.

90. Bregha, *supra* note 66, at 40-42.

91. *Panarctic in the Canadian Arctic Islands, supra* note 85.

92. See generally R.F. Keith, A. Kerr and R. Vles, "Mining the North", 9 *Northern Perspectives* (Ottawa: CARC), 1-7 (1981).

93. See generally *Beaufort EIS* (1983), *supra* note 76, Vols. 2, 7; United States, Senate, Committee on Governmental Affairs, *Hearings on s. 1562, to provide comprehensive national policy dealing with national needs and objectives in the Arctic* (1982), particularly at 285-342.

94. *Beaufort EIS, supra* note 76, Vol. 2, at 4.19-4.25.

95. *Ibid.*, at 4.50.

96. *Ibid.*, at 4.25-4.27.

97. *Ibid.*, at 4.41-4.43.

98. *Ibid.*, at 4.19; "Beaufort Activity Moves Into High Gear", 34 *Oilweek* 20-29 (1983); "Canada Logs Progress in Beaufort Operations", *Oil and Gas Journal* 48-51 (3 January 1983).

99. *Beaufort EIS, supra* note 76, Vol. 2, at 4.19-4.25; "Beaufort Sea and Its New Drilling Innovations", 34 *Oilweek* 30-34 (1983); A. Marks, "The Evolution of Esso's Artificial Islands", 5 *APOA Review* 11-14 (1982/83).

100. *Beaufort EIS, supra* note 76, Vol. 2, at 4.43-4.47.

101. *Panarctic in the Canadian Arctic Islands* (1982), *supra* note 37; "Panarctic Techniques Succeed in Arctic Islands Region", *Oil and Gas Journal* 50 (3 January 1983).

102. For a number of reasons, native peoples' groups and environmental groups have asserted that development might have an unacceptable impact on the people and environment of the Arctic. These considerations are discussed in Chapter 10 of this book.

NOTES TO CHAPTER 5

103. See generally J. Pallister, "Petroleum Transportation by Pipeline", 5(3) *APOA Review* 15-21 (1982/83) and cited references.

104. See "Pipeline cost is reduced $10 billion", (Calgary) *Globe and Mail*, at B-22 (27 September 1983).

105. *Beaufort EIS, supra* note 76, Vol. 2; Pallister, *supra* note 103; "Polar Gas Proposes Mackenzie Pipeline", *supra* note 84.

106. *Beaufort EIS, supra* note 76, Vol. 2, at 6.1 to 6.2.

107. See *supra*, p. 64.

108. See generally *Beaufort EIS, supra* note 76, Vol. 2, at 6.16 to 6.42; J. Pallister, "Marine Transportation of Oil and Natural Gas", 6(1) *APOA Review* 17-23 (1982); Senate Report, *supra* note 29, at 35-44.

109. See generally *Arctic Pilot Project: Environmental Statement Shipping Component* (Calgary: Petro Canada, 1979); A. Marks, "A Technical Description of the Arctic Pilot Project", 5(1) *APOA Review* 11-14 (1982); F. Bregha, "Arctic Pilot Project: CARC's Memorandum to Cabinet", 10(3) *Northern Perspectives* (Ottawa: CARC) 1-12 (1982); Senate Report, *supra* note 77, at 42-44.

110. According to Marks, *supra* note 109, the tankers would be class 10. No other source examined by the author indicated any ships other than class 7 icebreakers.

111. Senate Report, *supra* note 77, at 28.

112. Bregha, *supra* note 66, at 42.

113. See generally U.S. Department of Commerce, MARAD, *Arctic Marine Commerce Study*, Vols. I-III (1973); Bregha, *supra* note 55.

114. U.S. Department of Commerce, MARAD, *Conceptual Design for a Nuclear-Powered Icebreaking Tanker Transportation System* (1978); see also *U.S. Arctic Oil and Gas National Petroleum Council* (Washington: National Petroleum Council, 1981).

115. *Statement of Seatrains Lines, Inc., Concerning Icebreaking Tankers*, 7 pp. (15 May 1978).

116. Statement of R.N. Tikko reproduced in 5(2) *Arctic Seas Bulletin* (Ottawa: CARC) (1980); see also Bregha, *supra* note 55.

117. *Ibid.*

118. See P.T. Veliotis, "A Submarine LNG Tanker Concept for the Arctic", paper presented at GASTECH 81 LNG/LPG Conference, 20-23 October 1981 (Hamburg, Germany); Senate Report, *supra* note 77, at 41.

119. *Sailing Directions, Arctic Canada* (Ottawa: Queen's Printer, 1981), Vol. III, at 198-199.

120. Pallister (1983), *supra* note 108, at 22.

121. "Semi-submersible Icebreaking Tanker", *Ocean Industry* 38-40 (October 1975).

122. Canada, Indian and Northern Affairs, *Lancaster Sound Region: 1980–2000*, Green Paper (Ottawa: DIAND, 1982), at 92.

123. Japanese Ministry of Transport Study, *Conceptual Design of Arctic Tanker* (October 1981).

124. See generally Canada, Department of Energy Mines and Resources, *National Energy Program: Update 1982.*

125. Canada, Indian and Northern Affairs, *Communiqué* 1-8237 (10 March 1983).

126. Canada, Indian and Northern Affairs, *Communiqué* 3-8205. *Notes for Remarks by the Honourable John C. Munro, Minister of Indian Affairs and Northern Development* (The Canadian Club, Edmonton, Alberta) (17 June 1982), at 8 and 10.

127. *Ibid.*, at 13-14.

128. Senate Report, *supra* note 77, at 4.

129. *Ibid.*

130. *Ibid.*, at 45-46.

131. See generally Transport Canada, *supra* note 49, at 53-85; Ch. 1 text, at p. 7.

132. See generally Bregha, *supra* note 66; Bregha, *supra* note 55; Transport Canada, *Forecasts of Marine Shipments of Arctic Oil and Gas*, 28 pp. (1979).

133. See previous discussion in this Chapter.

134. *Ibid.*

135. Transport Canada, *Position Statement to the Beaufort Sea Environmental Assessment Panel*, at 11 (1982).

136. See generally *Beaufort EIS, supra* note 76, Vol. 2, Ch. 5; *Arctic Pilot Project, supra* note 109, at 3.40-3.49, 7.1-7.2.

137. Transport Canada (1982), *supra* note 135, at 13-14 and Appendix 1.

138. *Ibid.*

139. *Ibid.*, Appendix 1 at 29.

140. *Ibid.*, text at 30-38.

141. *Beaufort EIS, supra* note 76, Vol. 2, at 5.7.

142. *Ibid.*, at 3.35.

143. Environment Canada, AES, *Ice Services in Canada*, 10 pp. (undated).

144. Environment Canada, AES, *Ice Atlas: Canadian Arctic Waterways*, 199 pp. (1981).

145. *Beaufort EIS, supra* note 76, Vol. 2, at 5.46-5.47; *Arctic Pilot Project, supra* note 109, at 3.42-3.43.

146. See generally *Beaufort EIS, supra* note 76, Vol. 2, at 5.46-5.47.

147. *Ibid.*; see generally A.L. Gray, L.E. Livingstone and R.K. Hawkins, "Testing Radar Systems in Polar Ice", 11(1) *Geos* 4-9 (1982); B. Bullock and M. Kirby, "Technology Transfer at Work", 11(1) *Geos* 4-6 (1982); W.F. Weeks, "Sea Ice: The Potential of Remote Sensing", 24 *Oceanus* 29-48 (1981).

148. Gray et al., *supra* note 147; Bullock and Kirby, *supra* note 147.

149. "REMSCAN: the Eyes and Ears of Arctic Tankers", 1(3) *Beaufort* 19-21, at 20 (1982).

150. Weeks, *supra* note 147, at 46-48.

151. See generally *Beaufort EIS, supra* note 48, Vol. 2, at 5.47-5.49; Transport Canada, *supra* note 135, at 42, 50-51 and Appendix 1, at 30-31.

152. Canada, Federal Environmental Assessment and Review Office, *Arctic Pilot Project (Northern Component), Report of the Environmental Assessment Panel*, at 93-108.

153. See "Beaufort Proponents Tackle EIS Deficiencies", 6(1) *APOA Review* 7-8 (1983).

154. See generally Transport Canada, Coast Guard, *Control of Pollution from Shipping in Water Under Canadian Jurisdiction* (1981).

155. Transport Canada, *supra* note 135, at 18-20, 25-26, 47-48.

156. *Beaufort EIS, supra* note 48, Vol. 6, Ch. 6.

157. Transport Canada, *supra* note 135, at 6-9.

158. *Ibid.*, at 8.

NOTES TO CHAPTER 6

159. Canada, *House of Commons Debate*, 15 May 1969, at 8720; emphasis added.

160. *Ibid.*

161. Canada, *Proceedings of Standing Committee on Indian Affairs and Northern Development*, No. 1, 16 December 1969, at 6.

162. 12 *Canadian Yearbook of International Law*, at 279 (1974); emphasis added.

163. Canada, *Proceedings of Standing Committee on External Affairs and National Defence*, No. 24, 22 May 1975, at 6; emphasis added.

164. Canada (External Affairs), *Statement and Speeches*, No. 80/24, 24 October 1980, at 2.

165. J.N. Moore, "The Regime of Straits and the Third United Nations Conference on the Law of the Sea", 74 *A.J.I.L.* 77-121, at 112 (1980).

166. For a review of those attempts, see D.P. O'Connell, *The International Law of the Sea* (Oxford: Clarendon Press, 1982), Vol. I, at 309-316.

167. Art. 36, UN Convention on the Law of the Sea, A/CONF.62/122, 7 October 1982.

168. R.R. Baxter, *The Law of International Waterways* (Cambridge, Mass.: Harvard University Press, 1964), at 4-5 and note 12.

169. *Ibid.*, at 7-8.

170. Ch. De Visscher, *Problèmes de confins en droit international public* (Paris: Pedome, 1969), at 141.

171. *Supra* note 167, Art. 35, para. a.

172. O'Connell, *supra* note 166, at 316 and 320.

173. For a similar view, see Moore, *supra* note 165, at 112; see also R.J. Grammig, "The Yoron Jima Submarine Incident of August 1980: A Soviet Violation of the Law of the Sea", 22 *Harvard International Law Journal* 331-353, at 346 (1981).

174. See, for instance, statement of Ambassador J.A. Beesley in Committee II, New York, 1 April 1976, 6-page text.

175. See statement of Ambassador Malik, 4 April 1973, in A/AC.138/S.C.II/S.R.69, at 5.

176. E. Bruel, *International Straits* (London: Sweet and Maxwell, 1947), Vol. 1, at 42-43.

177. *Ibid.*, at 43; emphasis added.

178. *Ibid.* On these qualifying expressions, see also O'Connell, *supra* note 166, at 301-306.

179. (1949) *I.C.J. Rep.*, at 29.

180. (1949) *I.C.J. Pleadings*, Vol. II, at 242.

181. *Supra* note 179.

182. *Supra* note 180, at 354.

183. *Supra* note 179, at 28.

184. *Ibid.*

185. *Ibid.*

186. Art. 17, *I.L.C. Yearbook*, Vol. II, at 258 (1956); emphasis added.

187. G.C. Fitzmaurice, "The Law and Procedure of the International Court of Justice; General Principles and Substantive Law", 27 *B.Y.I.L.* 1-41, at 28 (1950); emphasis added.

188. *Supra* note 179.

189. Baxter, *supra* note 168, at 3; emphasis added.

190. *Ibid.*, at 9.

191. D.P. O'Connell, *International Law* (London: Stevens, 1970), Vol. I, at 497; emphasis added.

192. O'Connell, *supra* note 166, at 308; emphasis added.

193. *Ibid.*, emphasis added.

194. See this writer's own account in "International Straits", 7 *Thesaurus Acroasium* 64-100, at 72-86 (1977).

195. See the United States' Draft Articles of 1971 in A/AC.138/S.C.II/L.4 and those of the Soviet Union of 1972 in A/AC.138/S.C.II/L.7.

196. See "Draft Articles on Navigation through the Territorial Sea, including Straits Used for International Navigation", introduced by the 8-member group in 1973, in A/AC.138/S.C.II/L.18.

197. See A/CONF.62/C.2/L.3.

198. *Supra* note 167, Art. 35, para. c.

199. *Ibid.*, Art. 36.

200. *Ibid.*

201. *Ibid.*

202. *Supra* note 167, Art. 38, para. 1 and Art. 45, para. 1(a).

203. *Ibid.*, Art. 45, para. 1(b).

NOTES TO CHAPTER 7

204. For a study of the legal status of the Arctic Ocean, see this writer's *Law of the Sea of the Arctic, with Special Reference to Canada* (Ottawa: University of Ottawa Press, 1973), at 174-179.

205. Canada, *House of Commons Debates*, 17 April 1970, at 6015.

206. Canada, Standing Senate Committee on External Affairs and National Defence, *Proceedings*, Issue No. 25, at 18 (29 April 1970).

207. See Table of Full Transits of the Northwest Passage (1903–1982) in Chapter 3 of this book.

208. R.R. Baxter, *The Law of International Waterways* (Cambridge, Mass.: Harvard University Press, 1964), at 3, note 5, where he quotes from the *Economy Light and Power Co.* v. *United States* (1923), 256 U.S. 113, 123, which applied the test of navigable capacity.

209. See in particular Jessup, *The Law of Territorial Waters and Maritime Jurisdiction* (New York: G.A. Jennings & Co., 1927), at 120 and Gidel, *Le Droit International Public de la Mer* (Paris: Recueil Sirey, 1934), Vol. III, at 195.

210. Art. 14.

211. Art. 17.

212. Art. 14, para. 4.

213. Art. 19, para. 2.

214. (1949) *I.C.J. Rep.*, at 30.

215. Art. 19, para. 2(2).

216. Art. 19, para. 1.

217. Art. 18, para. 2.

218. Art. 19, para. 1.

219. This is a controversial point. See D.P. O'Connell, *supra* note 166, at 273-274.

220. For an excellent review of the law on this question, including doctrinal history and state practice, see *ibid.*, at 274-298.

221. See dissenting opinion of Judge Krylov, (1949) *I.C.J. Rep.*, at 74.

222. See "Commentary" to Article 24, in *I.L.C. Yearbook*, Vol. II, at 276-277 (1956).

223. See Articles 14 to 17.

224. See Article 23.

225. See G. Tunkin, "The Geneva Conference on the Law of the Sea", 1 (London) *International Affairs* 47-52, at 49 (1958).

226. See, in particular: Jessup, "The UN Conference on the Law of the Sea", 59 *Colm. L.R.* 234-268, at 248 (1959); J.H.W. Verzijl, "The United Nations Conference on the Law of the Sea, Geneva, 1958", 6 *Netherlands Int'l L.R.* 1-42, at 34 (1959), and R.R. Baxter, *supra* note 208, at 167-168.

227. J.H.W. Verzijl, *International Law in Historical Perspective* (Leyden: Sijthoff, 1971), Vol. IV, at 188.

228. Art. 30.

229. Report of the Canadian Delegation, December 1982.

230. Art. 20.

231. Art. 21.

232. Art. 24, para. 1.

233. Art. 25.

234. Art. 21, para. 1(2).

235. Art. 211, para. 4.

236. Art. 211, para. 2.

237. Art. 19, para. 2(2).

238. Art. 234.

239. For a discussion of this conclusion, see this writer's study "La contribution du Canada au développement du droit international pour la protection du milieu marin: le cas spécial de l'Arctique", 11 *Etudes Internationales* 441-466 (1980).

NOTES TO CHAPTER 8

240. A. Pageot, *Canadian Arctic Policies – A Framework for Marine Development and Activities in the North*, at 10-15 of 17-page text distributed at Seminar on Arctic Marine Technology, Dalhousie University, 14 June 1983.

241. *Ibid.*, at 12.

242. *Ibid.*, at 14.

243. This approach is examined in a book entitled *The Waters of the Canadian Arctic Archipelago in International Law* to be published by the present author.

244. (1951) *I.C.J. Rep.* 4.

245. *Ibid.*, at 21.

246. Department of Transport, Position Statement, Appendix 1, at 22-23.

247. See W.E. Butler, *The Northeast Arctic Passage* (Alphen aan den Rijn: Sijthoff and Noordhoff, 1978).

248. *Ibid.*, at 95.

249. D.M. Johnston (ed.), *Arctic Ocean Issues in the 1980's*, Proceedings of Workshop, June 10-12, 1981 (1982).

250. Canada, *House of Commons Debates*, 24 October 1969, at 39.

251. Canada, *House of Commons Debates*, 16 April 1970, at 6028.

252. Art. 38, para. 2, UN Convention on the Law of the Sea, A/CONF.62/122, 7 October 1982.

253. See the 1971 Draft Articles of the United States in A/AC.138/S.C.II/L.4 and those of the Soviet Union of 1972 in A/AC.138/S.C.II/L.7.

254. *Ibid.*

255. Statement of 3 August 1971, by John R. Stevenson, reproduced in 65 *Department of State Bulletin*, at 261-266 (1971).

256. Henry A. Kissinger, *International Law, World Order and Human Progress*, text distributed at a meeting, 11 August 1975, at 7; text is reproduced in 73 *Department of State Bulletin* 353-362 (1975).

257. *Ibid.*

258. See John N. Moore, *supra* note 165, at 78, note 5 (1980). For a list of those involved on both sides of this debate, see *id.*, at 92, note 27.

259. See Art. 32 of the Vienna Convention.

260. See the present writer's lectures, *supra* note 194, at 85-86 and "The Northwest Passage in International Law", 17 *C.Y.I.L.* 99-133, at 122 (1979). For a similar interpretation, see also H.B. Robertson, Jr., "Passage Through International Straits: A Right Preserved in the Third United Nations Conference on the Law of the Sea", 20 *Virg. J. Int'l L.* 801-851, at 843-846; and D.P. O'Connell, *supra* note 166, at 333.

261. Art. 38, para. 1, UN Convention on the Law of the Sea, A/CONF.62/122, 7 October 1982.

262. *Ibid.*, Art. 42, para. 2.

263. *Ibid.*, Art. 39, para. 1; emphasis added to "normal modes".

264. D.P. O'Connell, *supra* note 166, at 333.

265. *Ibid.*

266. William T. Burke, "Submerged Passage Through Straits: Interpretation of the Proposed Law of the Sea Treaty Text", 52 *Wash. L. Rev.* 193-220, at 214 (1977).

267. Moore, *supra* note 165, at 89.

268. See Art. 45; this has been explained earlier in this chapter.

269. See Art. 21.

270. See the earlier discussion on the definition of transit passage in this chapter.

271. This possibility is envisaged by Article 43.

272. Art. 233.

273. Moore, *supra* note 165, at 112.

274. For a discussion of this, see this writer's study, *supra* note 239.

275. For the special measures adopted by the Soviet Union, see the Decree of the Council of Ministers, dated 16 September 1971, approving a law for the administration of the Northern Sea Route, reproduced (in English) in 9 *Int'l Legal Materials*, at 645 (1972).

NOTES TO CHAPTER 9

276. See generally *Beaufort Sea-Mackenzie Delta Environmental Impact Statement* (Calgary: Dome Petroleum, 1982), 7 Vols. (hereinafter referred to as *Beaufort EIS*), Vol. 3A, at 3.75-3.83, Vol. 3B, at 2.91-2.95; Indian and Northern Affairs Canada, "IBP Ecological Site Approved", *Communiqué* 1-8214 (30 July 1982).

277. *Ibid.*

278. *A Comprehensive Conservation Policy and Strategy for the Northwest Territories and Yukon – Draft Discussion Paper* (Ottawa: Northern Environment Directorate, DIAND, 1982), at 53-67.

279. *Ecological Sites in Northern Canada*, D.N. Nettleship and P.A. Smith, editors (Ottawa: Canadian Committee for the International Biological Program, 1975), at 3. The IBP, active from 1964 to 1974, was a cooperative program between 58 nations and the International Council of Scientific Unions. It should be noted that the following Ecological Sites adjacent to the Northwest Passage alternate routes were proposed by IBP, but were not mentioned in the *Beaufort EIS*: Islands of Dolphin and Union Strait (site 3-6), Perry River Sanctuary, Queen Maud Sound (site 4-8), Coats Island, Hudson Bay (site 6-3), Akpatok Island, Ungava Bay (site 6-6) and Digges Sound Region, Hudson Strait (site 6-7).

280. *Beaufort EIS, supra* note 276, Vol. 3A at 4.2-4.10, 4.21-4.62.

281. *Ibid.*, at 3.8-3.28; I. Stirling, "The Biological Importance of Polynyas in the Canadian Arctic", 33(2) *Arctic* 303-315 (1980).

282. *Ibid.*

283. See for example M. Bradstreet and W. Cross, "Trophic Relationships at High Arctic Ice Edges", 35(1) *Arctic* 1-12 (1982); P. McLaren, "Spring Migration and Habitat Use by Seabirds in Eastern Lancaster Sound and Western Baffin Bay", 35(1) *Arctic* 88-111 (1982).

284. *Beaufort EIS, supra* note 276, at 2.91-2.95; see *The Lancaster Sound Region: 1980–2000 (Green Paper)*, Indian and Northern Affairs, Canada (1982) (hereinafter referred to as *Lancaster Sound*); *Lancaster Sound: Issues and Responsibilities*, E.F. Roots, editor (Ottawa: Canadian Arctic Resources Committee, 1980) for summaries of the attributes of this region and the public debate surrounding its future use.

285. *Lancaster Sound, supra* note 284, at 47-51; *Beaufort EIS, supra* note 276, at 2.1-2.86.

286. *Lancaster Sound, supra* note 284, at 47.

287. *Ibid.*, at 53-60.

288. Bradstreet and Cross, *supra* note 283; *Beaufort EIS, supra* note 276, at 2.1-2.86.

289. See generally E.F. Roots, "Environmental Aspects of Arctic Marine Transportation and Development" in *Marine Transportation and High Arctic Development: Policy Framework and Priorities, Symposium Proceedings*, J.B. Wright, editor (Ottawa: Canadian Arctic Resources Committee, 1979), at 69-98.

290. See *Beaufort EIS, supra* note 276, Vol. 4, at 4.2-4.37.

291. *Ibid.* Impacts are evaluated in this industry submission on a scale, criticized in submissions to the Beaufort Sea Environmental Assessment Panel as being subjective (*infra* note 306), ranging from negligible, minor and moderate to major. Impacts on all birds and all mammals except ringed seals and narwhals are described as negligible or minor to moderate.

292. *Lancaster Sound: Issues and Responsibilities* (1980), *supra* note 284. CARC maintains that scientific knowledge of the complex arctic ecosystem is insufficient to predict ecological impacts with an acceptable degree of certainty.

293. *Beaufort EIS, supra* note 276, Vol. 4, at 4.1-4.3.

294. I. Stirling and W. Calvert, "Environmental Threats to Marine Mammals in the Canadian Arctic", 21 *Polar Record* 433-449 (1983).

295. *Beaufort EIS, supra* note 276, Vol. 4, at 4.3-4.5.

296. Federal Environmental Assessment Review Office, *Arctic Pilot Project (Northern Component), Report of the Environmental Assessment Panel* (1980), at 67.

297. *Lancaster Sound, supra* note 284.

298. *Beaufort EIS, supra* note 276, Vol. 4, at 4.5.

299. *Technical Review of the Environmental Impact Statement for the Beaufort Sea Hydrocarbon Production Proposal*, at 28 (1983).

300. *Beaufort EIS, supra* note 276, at 4.5.

301. *Ibid.*, at 4.5-4.33; see footnote 291.

302. *Ibid.*, at 4.8.

303. *Ibid.*, at 4.11-4.30.

304. *Ibid.*

305. See written 1983 submissions to the Beaufort Sea Environmental Assessment Panel by the following: Environment Canada (submission I-12) 30 pp., at 3-8; Inuit Tairisat of Canada (submission I-18) 18 pp., at 13; Department of Fisheries and Oceans (submission I-19) 59 pp., at 25-26; Department of Indian Affairs and Northern Development, Vol. I (submission I-20), 45 pp., at 26.

306. *Ibid.* On the latter point, see particularly submissions I-12, at 19-20; I-18, at 1-6; I-19, at 10-16; I-20, at 22; I-33, at 49-50. See also 1983 submission by Beaufort Sea Alliance (submission I-5) 21 pp., at 8.

307. *Beaufort EIS, supra* note 276, at 4.29.

308. *Ibid.*

309. *Supra* note 306.

310. See R. Lemberg, *A Critical Risk Analysis Evaluation of the Environmental Impact Assessment: Beaufort Sea Hydrocarbon Production Proposal* (Montreal: Lemberg Consultants (Canada, 1983).

311. *Beaufort EIS, supra* note 276, Vol. 6, at 2.2-2.4.

312. *Ibid.*, at 2.8.

313. Lemberg, *supra* note 310, at 2-12.

314. *Beaufort EIS, supra* note 276, Vol. 6, Ch. 3, 5, 6.

315. *Ibid.*, at 3.1.

316. *Ibid.*, at 3.2-3.7.

317. Chapter 4, p. 76.

318. *Beaufort EIS, supra* note 276, Vol. 6, Ch. 5.

319. *Oil and Dispersants in Canadian Seas – Research Appraisal and Recommendations*, J.B. Sprague, J.H. Vandermeulen and P.G. Wells, eds. (Ottawa: Environment Canada, Environmental Protection Service, 1982). Dr. Vandermeulen noted in conversation in 1983 that reservations about the use of dispersants have eased slightly since the writing of this report in the late 1970s.

320. *Beaufort EIS, supra* note 276, at 5.19-5.23.

321. These problems are acknowledged in the *Beaufort EIS, supra* note 276. For a detailed account of the administrative problems and delays encountered with the grounding in Foxe Basin of the *Edgar Jourdain* with approximately 100 tons of diesel fuel, see W. Finan, "The Hall Beach Incident", 9(4/5) *Northern Perspectives* 2-7 (1981).

322. *Beaufort EIS, supra* note 276, Vol. 6, at 4.8-4.9; E.M. Levy, "Oil Pollution and Seabirds: Atlantic Canada 1976–77 and Some Implications for Northern Environments", 11 *Marine Pollution Bulletin* 51-56 (1980); see generally *Beaufort EIS, supra* note 276, Vol. 6, Ch. 4 and references cited, especially *Oil and Dispersants, supra* note 319.

323. *Beaufort EIS, supra* note 276, Vol. 6, at 4.2-4.4; N. Snow, "Effects of Petroleum Hydrocarbons on Phytoplankton and Macrophytes", and P.G. Wells, "Zooplankton", in *Oil and Dispersants, supra* note 319, at 55-64 and 65-80, respectively.

324. *Beaufort EIS, supra* note 276, Vol. 6, at 4.-6-4.7; W.R. Penrose, "Impacts of Hydrocarbons and Dispersants on Fish", in *Oil and Dispersants, supra* note 319, at 81-86.

325. *Beaufort EIS, supra* note 276, Vol. 6, at 4.4-4.6; J.A. Percy, "Benthic and Intertidal Organisms", in *Oil and Dispersants, supra* note 319, at 87-104.

326. *Beaufort EIS, supra* note 276, Vol. 6, at 4.8-4.9; R. Brown, "Birds, Oil and the Canadian Environment", in *Oil and Dispersants, supra* note 319, at 105-112.

327. E.M. Levy, "Oil Pollution and Seabirds: Atlantic Canada 1976–77 and Some Implications for Northern Environments", 11 *Marine Pollution Bulletin* 51-56, at 56 (1980).

328. *Beaufort EIS, supra* note 276, Vol. 6, at 4.7-4.8; B.D. Smiley, "The Effects of Oil on Marine Mammals", in *Oil and Dispersants, supra* note 319, at 113-124.

329. These impacts are defined in *Beaufort EIS, supra* note 276, Vol. 4, at 1.4, as those likely to persist for more than five years after a disturbance.

330. See generally *Oil and Dispersants* (1982), *supra* note 319.

331. F.S. Chia, "Reproduction of Arctic Marine Invertebrates", 1 *Marine Pollution Bulletin* 78-79 (1970).

332. R.C. Clark, Jr. and J.S. Finley, "Effects of Oil Spills in Arctic and Subarctic Environments", and H.R. Sanborn, "Effects of Petroleum on Ecosystems", both in *Effects of Petroleum on Arctic and Subarctic Marine Environments and Organisms*, D.C. Malins, ed. (New York: Academic Press, 1977), Vol. II, at 337-357 and 411-476 respectively.

333. *Arctic Pilot Project (Northern Component), supra* note 296, at 64. Quantitative risk factors were not available to the author.

334. *Arctic Pilot Project Environmental Statement, Shipping Component* (Calgary: Petro-Canada et al., 1979), Chapter 4.

335. *Ibid.*, at 4-5. Other estimates of safe distances vary and have gone as high as over 100 miles.

336. The occurrence of these impacts would of course depend on the location, timing and type of accident.

337. See generally *Control of Pollution from Shipping in Waters Under Canadian Jurisdiction* (Ottawa: Transport Canada, Coast Guard, 1981).

338. R.S.C. 1970 (1st Supp.) c. 2, s. 11.

339. *Ibid.*, s. 12.

340. *Arctic Waters Pollution Prevention Regulation*, C.R.C. 1978 c. 353, s. 6.

341. R.S.C. 1970 (1st Supp.) c. 2, s. 3; R.S.C. 1970, c. S-9, s. 727(2) as amended by R.S.C. 1970 (2nd Supp.), c. 27, s. 3.

342. *Lancaster Sound: Issues and Responsibilities, supra* note 284, at 51.

343. *Control of Pollution, supra* note 337 and private discussions.

344. See Chapter 4.

345. Presented to the Standing Committee on Indian Affairs and Northern Development, 28 March 1972.

346. *An Energy Strategy for Canada: Policies for Self Reliance* (Ottawa: Supply and Service Canada, 1976).

347. Department of Mines and Resources (Ottawa: Supply and Services Canada, 1980).

348. See Chapter 4.

349. Released by the Northern Environment Directorate, October 1982.

NOTES TO CHAPTER 10

350. D. Mann, *The Socio-economic Impact of Non-renewable Resource Development on the Inuit of Northern Canada*, Vol. 8 (94 pp.) (Inuit Tapirisat of Canada Renewable Resources Project, University of Western Ontario and University of Waterloo, 1975); Indian and Northern Affairs Canada, *The Inuit* (Ottawa: DIAND, 1980).

351. Inuit Tapirisat of Canada, Baffin Region Inuit Association, Labrador Inuit Association, Brief to the Special Committee of the Senate of the Northern Pipeline (18 May 1982) reproduced in Canada, Senate Special Committee on the Northern Pipeline, *Proceedings*, Issue No. 26, at 26A: 3-19 (18 May 1982).

352. See M. Freeman, "Contemporary Inuit Exploitation of the Sea Ice Environment", Paper presented at the Sikumiut Workshop, McGill University, Montreal, 15 April 1982.

353. G. Wenzel, "Inuit and Polar Bears: Cultural Observations From a Hunt Near Resolute Bay, N.W.T.", 36(1) *Arctic* 90-94.

354. Mann, *supra* note 350.

355. Testimony of Simon Awa, President of Baffin Regional Inuit Association in *Proceedings, supra* note 351, at 26: 12-13.

356. See generally *Beaufort EIS, supra* note 276, Vol. 3B, at 2.86-2.91, Vol. 5, Ch. 12; C.W. Hobart, "Impacts of Industrial Development on Hunting and Trapping Among Canadian Inuit", in *Proceedings of the First International Symposium on Renewable Resources and the Economy of the North*, M. Freeman, ed. (Ottawa: Association of Canadian Universities for Northern Studies, 1981), at 202-218.

357. *Beaufort EIS, supra* note 276, Vol. 5, Chs. 1-5, 10-14; H. Meyers, "Traditional and Modern Sources of Income in the Lancaster Sound Region", 21 *Polar Record* 11-22 (1982).

358. Inuit Tapirisat of Canada, Brief to Special Committee, *supra* note 351, at 26A: 5.

359. Submission of Inuit Tapirisat of Canada to the Beaufort Sea Environmental Assessment Panel (February 1983).

360. *Beaufort EIS, supra* note 276, Vol. 5.

361. *Beaufort EIS, supra* note 276, Vol. 3B, at 2.86-2.91.

362. *Ibid.*, Vol. 3A, at 3.65-3.75.

363. *Ibid.*

364. Inuit Tapirisat of Canada, Brief to Special Committee, *supra* note 351, at 26A: 4-5.

365. See Chapter 9 regarding Canada's protective rights.

366. Inuit Tapirisat of Canada, Brief to Special Committee, *supra* note 351, at 26A: 7.

367. "Arctic Marine Transportation Issues", A report to the Canadian Arctic Resources Committee (Arctic Ocean Program), Ottawa (May 1983).

368. *Beaufort EIS, supra* note 276, Vol. 5, at 12.12.

369. *Ibid.*

370. Hobart, *supra* note 356.

371. *Beaufort EIS, supra* note 276, Vol. 5, at 12.14-12.15.

372. See generally P. Jull and N. Bankes, "Inuit Interests in the Arctic Offshore", a paper presented at the CARC Third National Workshop on People, Resources and the Environment North of 60° (1983); M. Denhez, "Aboriginal Rights and the Sovereignty of Countries", a paper prepared for the Inuit Tapirisat of Canada (1982), an edited version of which appears in 10(5) *Northern Perspectives* 2-8 (1982).

373. See, for example, the Inuit Tapirisat of Canada Brief to the Special Committee, *supra* note 351, at 26A: 9.

374. Jull and Bankes (1983) and Denhez (1982), *supra* note 372.

375. Denhez, *supra* note 372.

376. Jull and Bankes, *supra* note 372.

377. (1973) 4 W.W.R. 1-91, at 2.

378. *Ibid.*, at 15 and 74.

379. *Ibid.*, at 91.

380. *Hamlet of Baker Lake et al.* v. *Minister of Indian Affairs and Northern Development et al.* (1980) I.F.C. 518-582.

381. *Ibid.*, at 565, 566 and 568.

382. See map reproduced in 6(4) *Northern Perspectives* 7 (1978).

383. P. Jull and N. Bankes, *supra* note 372.

384. See *In All Fairness: A Native Claims Policy* (Ottawa: DIAND, 1981).

385. The agreement in principle does, however, recognize preferential Inuvialuit (western Inuit) rights to hunt and fish throughout the western Arctic.

386. See "Inuit and the Ice: Implications for Canadian Arctic Waters", 21 *Canadian Yearbook of International Law* (1983), by D. Pharand and D. Vanderzwagg.

387. P. Jull, "Nanavut", 10(2) *Northern Perspectives* 1-8 (1982); Jull and Bankes, *supra* note 372.

388. Quoted from P. Jull and N. Bankes, *supra* note 372.

389. Inuit Tapirisat of Canada, Brief to the Special Committee, *supra* note 353, at 26A: 9-10.

390. See Chapter 9 of this book.

NOTES TO CHAPTER 11

391. 12 *Documents on Canadian External Relations*, at 1546 (1946).

392. *Ibid.*, at 1549-1554.

393. *Ibid.*, at 1565-6.

394. 24 *Foreign Affairs* 638-647, at 681 (1946).

395. L.B. Pearson, "Canada's Northern Horizon", 31 *Foreign Affairs* 581-591, at 585-6 (1953).

396. The NORAD agreement has been periodically renewed, the latest renewal being for 5 years and dated 11 March 1981.

397. H. Critchley, "Canadian Security Policy in the Arctic: The Context for the Future", in *Marine Transportation and High Arctic Development: Policy Framework and Priorities* (Ottawa: CARC, 1979), at 181-209.

398. D.S. Macdonald, *White Paper on Defense*, at 18 (1971).

399. R.H. Falls, "Security in the North", in *Policies of Northern Development* (Kingston, Ontario: Group for International Politics, Department of Political Science, Queen's University, 1973), at 138.

400. W.R. Anderson, *Nautilus – 90°N* (Cleveland: World Publishing Co., 1959), at 224.

401. "Under Ice Cruise in the Arctic Basin: U.S.S. *Sargo*", 10(66) *Polar Record* 279 (1960).

402. L. Dulberger, "Sonar Hides Submarines Under Polar Ice", 34 *Electronics* 18-19, at 18 (1961).

403. J.T. Strong, "The Opening of the Arctic Ocean", 87 *U.S. Naval Proceedings* 58-65, at 62 (1961). For a detailed description of the passage through the islands of Barrow Strait, see J.P. Steele, *SEADRAGON Northwest Under the Ice* (New York: E.P. Dutton, 1962), at 165-173.

404. The sources used in compiling this list are A.S. McLaren, "The Development of Cargo Submarines for Polar Use", 21 *Polar Record* 369-381 (1983) and those cited within that source.

405. Canada, House of Commons, Standing Committee on External Affairs and National Defence, "Fifth Report to the House", in *Proceedings*, Issue No. 35, at 35-10 (24/25 March 1969).

406. *Supra* note 398, at 16.

407. *Ibid.*, at 18.

408. *Ibid.*

409. *Ibid.*

410. "The DND Roles, Objectives and Tasks", in *Canada's Maritime Defence: Report of the Sub-Committee on National Defence of the Standing Committee on Foreign Affairs* (Ottawa: Supply and Services Canada, 1983), at 101-107.

411. *Ibid.*, at 102.

412. *Ibid.*, at 104.

413. *DEFENCE 82* (Ottawa: Department of National Defence, 1983), at 18-19.

414. *Supra* note 410, at 28.

415. *Ibid.*

416. *Ibid.*, at 32.

417. *Canada's Maritime Defence, supra* note 410, at 35.

418. *DEFENCE 82, supra* note 413, at 28.

419. *Ibid.*, at 56.

420. *Canada's Maritime Defence, supra* note 410, at 33-38.

421. N. Tracy, *Canada's Foreign Policy Objectives and Canadian Security Arrangements in the North*, Extra-Mural Paper No. 8, Operational Research and Analysis Establishment (Ottawa: Department of National Defence, 1980), at 49.

422. *Ibid.*, at 50.

423. *Supra* note 410, at 33-34.

424. *Ibid.*, at 39.

425. *Ibid.*, at 51.

426. *Ibid.*

427. *Ibid.*

428. *Ibid.*, at 92.

429. *Ibid.*, at 52.

430. *Ibid.*, at 93.

431. The former possibility was suggested by General Jacques Dextraze, former Chief of Defence Staff and by Brigadier C.E. Beattie, Commanding Officer of the Northern Region, at an Arctic Bay military briefing. The latter possibility has been put forward in Tracy, *supra* note 421, at 80-94.

432. *Canada's Maritime Defence, supra* note 410, at 50.

433. See generally T. Armstrong, "Soviet Capabilities in Arctic Marine Transport", in *Marine Transportation and High Arctic Development: Policy Framework and Priorities* (Ottawa: CARC, 1979), at 210-222.

434. Canada, Standing Senate Committee on Foreign Affairs, Sub-Committee on National Defence, *Proceedings*, Issue No. 35, at 18 (23 November 1982).

435. See Canada, Department of External Affairs, *Communiqué No. 98* (26 August 1983).

436. Art. 2, General Exchanges Agreement Between the Government of Canada and the Government of the Union of Soviet Socialist Republics", *Canada Treaty Series*, No. 40 (1971).

437. *Ibid.*, Art. 4.

SELECTED BIBLIOGRAPHY

This bibliography is generally limited to the more recent sources and to publications not always found in most libraries. For a more complete bibliography on Arctic waters, see this writer's publication *The Law of the Sea of the Arctic with Special Reference to Canada* (Ottawa: University of Ottawa Press, 1973), 325-355.

The bibliography is divided into five parts, representing the main questions examined in the book.

I. DESCRIPTION AND HISTORICAL DEVELOPMENT OF THE NORTHWEST PASSAGE

A Century of Canada's Arctic Islands: 1880–1980, M. Zaslow, editor (Ottawa: Royal Society of Canada, 1981).

Appleton, T.A., *Usque ad Mare: A History of the Canadian Coast Guard and Marine Services* (Ottawa: Department of Transport, 1968).

Beaufort Sea-Mackenzie Delta Environmental Impact Statement (Calgary: Dome Petroleum, 1982), Vols. 1-3.

Canada, Department of Energy, Mines and Resources, Hydrographic Service, *Sailing Directions, Arctic Canada, 3rd Edition* (Ottawa: Queen's Printer, 1978–1982), 3 Vols.

Canada, Department of Indian Affairs and Northern Development, *Annual Report 1981* (Ottawa: DIAND, 1982).

Canada, Department of the Environment, AES, *Ice Atlas: Canadian Arctic Waterways* (Ottawa: DOE, 1981).

Canada, Department of Transport, *Position Statement*, submitted to (FEARO) Beaufort Sea Environmental Assessment Panel (August 1982).

Canada, Senate Standing Committee on Foreign Affairs, Subcommittee on National Defence, *Proceedings*, Issue Nos. 18 (26 May 1981); 32 (8 June 1982); 35 (23 November 1982).

Cooke, A. and C. Holland, *The Exploration of Northern Canada – 1500 to 1920, A Chronology* (Toronto: Arctic History Press, 1978).

Dunbar, M. and K.R. Greenaway, *Arctic Canada From the Air* (Ottawa: Queen's Printer, 1956).

de Lange Boom, B.R. et al., "Iceberg Motion in Lancaster Sound and Northwest Baffin Bay, Summer 1978", 35(1) *Arctic* 219-233 (1982).

Larsen, H., *The Northwest Passage* (Ottawa: Queen's Printer, 1948).

Ross, W.G., "The Annual Catch of Greenland (Bowhead) Whales in Waters North of Canada 1719–1915: A Preliminary Compilation", 32 *Arctic* 91-121 (1979).

Smith, G.W., *Canada's Arctic Archipelago: 100 Years of Canadian Jurisdiction* (Ottawa: DIAND, 1980).

Steele, G.P., *Seadragon Northwest Under the Ice* (New York: E.P. Dutton, 1962).

"Submarine Pingos in the Beaufort Sea", 174 *Science* 16-18 (1971).

Taylor, A., *Geographical Discovery and Exploration of the Queen Elizabeth Islands* (Canadian Department of Mines and Technical Surveys) (Ottawa: Queen's Printer, 1956).

II. FUTURE COMMERCIAL DEVELOPMENT OF THE NORTHWEST PASSAGE

Arctic Pilot Project: Environmental Statement Shipping Component (Calgary: Petro-Canada, 1979).

"Beaufort Activity Moves Into High Gear", 34 *Oilweek* 20-29 (1983).

"Beaufort Proponents Tackle EIS Deficiencies", 6(1) *APOA Review* 7-8 (1983).

"Beaufort Sea and Its New Drilling Innovations", 34 *Oilweek* 30-34 (1983).

Beaufort Sea-Mackenzie Delta Environmental Impact Statement (Calgary: Dome Petroleum, 1982), Vol. 2.

Bregha, F., "Arctic Pilot Project: CARC's Memorandum to Cabinet", 10(3) *Northern Perspectives* 1-12 (1982).

Bregha, F., *Canadian Arctic Marine Energy Projects* (Ottawa: CARC, 1982).

Bregha, F., "Petroleum Development in Northern Alaska" in *Marine Transportation and High Arctic Development: Policy Framework and Priorities, Symposium Proceedings* (Ottawa: CARC, 1979) at 223-253.

Bullock, B. and M. Kirby, "Technology Transfer at Work", 11(1) *Geos* 4-6 (1982).

Canada, Department of Energy, Mines and Resources, *National Energy Program*: Update 1982 (Ottawa: Supply and Services Canada, 1982).

Canada, Department of External Affairs, *Communiqué No. 67* (28 April 1982).

Canada, Department of Indian Affairs and Northern Development, *Communiqué* 3-8205 (17 June 1982); 1-8232 (20 January 1983).

Canada, Department of Indian Affairs and Northern Development, *Lancaster Sound Region: 1980–2000, Green Paper* (Ottawa: DIAND, 1982).

Canada, Department of the Environment, AES, *Ice Atlas: Canadian Arctic Waterways* (Ottawa: DOE, 1981).

Canada, Department of the Environment, AES, *Ice Services in Canada* (Ottawa: DOE, no date).

Canada, Department of Transport, "Arctic Marine Transportation Forecast of Ship Movements: 1985, 1990, 1995", Revised by Normand Carrière (1981).

Canada, Department of Transport, *Position Statement*, submitted to (FEARO) Beaufort Sea Environmental Assessment Panel (August 1982).

Canada, Department of Transport, *Ships Navigating in Ice: A Selected Bibliography* (1970–1980) (Ottawa: Supply and Services Canada, 1982).

Canada, Department of Transport, *Control of Pollution From Shipping in Water Under Canadian Jurisdiction* (Ottawa: Transport Canada, Coast Guard, 1981).

Canada, Federal Environmental Assessment and Review Office, *Arctic Pilot Project (Northern Component), Report of the Environmental Assessment Panel* (Ottawa: FEARO, 1980).

Canada, National Energy Board, *Canadian Energy Supply: 1980–2000* (Ottawa: Supply and Services Canada, 1981).

Canada, National Energy Board, *News Release* (1 September 1982).

Canada, Northern Pipeline Agency, *Annual Report 1981–1982* (1983).

Canada, Senate, Report of the Special Committee on the Northern Pipeline, *Marching to the Beat of the Same Drum: Transporation of Petroleum and Natural Gas North of 60°* (March 1983).

"Canada Logs Progression Beaufort Operations", *Oil and Gas Journal* 48-51 (3 January 1983).

"Canadian East Coast and Arctic Offshore", 18 *Ocean Industry* 27-31 (1983).

Gray, A.L. et al., "Testing Radar Systems in Polar Ice", 11(1) *Geos* 4-9 (1982).

Keith, R.F. et al., "Mining the North", 9 *Northern Perspectives* 1-7 (1981).
Marks, A., "A Technical Description of the Arctic Pilot Project", 5(1) *APOA Review* 11-14 (1982).
Marks, A., "The Evolution of Esso's Artificial Islands", 53 *APOA Review* 11-14 (1982/83).
Maritime Services to Support Polar Resource Development (Washington: National Academy Press, 1981).
National Petroleum Council, *United States Arctic Oil and Gas* (Washington: National Petroleum Council, 1981).
Pallister, J., "Marine Transportation of Oil and Natural Gas", 6(1) *APOA Review* 17-23 (1982).
Pallister, J., "Petroleum Transportation by Pipeline", 5(3) *APOA Review* 15-21 (1982/83).
"Panarctic Techniques Succeed in Arctic Islands Region", *Oil and Gas Journal* 50 (3 January 1983).
"REMSCAN: The Eyes and Ears of Arctic Tankers", 1(3) *Beaufort* 19-21 (1982).
"Semi-submersible Icebreaking Tanker", *Ocean Industry* 38-40 (October 1975).
"The Arctic" in *International Petroleum Encyclopedia, 1983* (Tulsa, Okla.: Penwall Publishing, 1983).
"The Great Arctic Energy Rush", *Business Week* 52-56 (24 January 1983).
Thomas, W.C. and M.E. Thomas, "Public Policy and Petroleum Development: The Alaska Case", 35(3) *Arctic* 349-357 (1982).
United States, Department of Commerce, Maritime Administration, *Conceptual Design For a Nuclear Powered Icebreaking Tanker Transportation System* (Washington, D.C.: MARAD, 1978).
United States, Department of the Interior, *Arctic Summary Report*, U.S. Geological Survey Open File Report 81-621 (1981).
United States, Senate, Committee on Governmental Affairs, Hearings on s. 1562, "To provide comprehensive national policy dealing with national needs and objectives in the Arctic" (1982).
Weeks, W.F., "Sea Ice: The Potential of Remote Sensing", 24 *Oceanus* 29-48 (1981).

III. THE LEGAL STATUS OF THE NORTHWEST PASSAGE

Arctic Ocean Issues in the 1980s, Proceedings of Workshop June 1981, D.M. Johnston, editor (Honolulu: Law of the Sea Institute, 1982).
Baxter, R.R., *The Law of International Waterways* (Cambridge, Mass.: Harvard University Press, 1964).
Bruel, E., *International Straits* (London: Sweet and Maxwell, 1947).
Burke, W.T., "Submerged Passage Through Straits: Interpretation of the Proposed Law of the Sea Treaty Text", 52 *Wash. L. R.* 193-220 (1977).
Butler, W.E., *The Northeast Arctic Passage* (Alphen aan den Rijn: Sijthoff and Noordhoff, 1978).
Canada, Department of Transport, *Position Statement*, submitted to (FEARO) Beaufort Sea Environmental Assessment Panel (August 1982).
Canada, Senate Standing Committee on Foreign Affairs and National Defence, *Proceedings*, Issue No. 25 (29 April 1970).
Corfu Channel Case (Merits), [1949] *I.C.J. Rep.*
Fisheries Case (United Kingdom v. *Norway),* [1951] *I.C.J. Rep.* 116.
Fitzmaurice, G.L., "The Law and Procedure of the International Court of Justice: General Principles and Substantive Law", 27 *B.Y.I.L.* 1-41 (1950).
Gidel, G., *Le Droit International Public de la Mer* (Paris: Recueil Sirey, 1932–1934), 3 Vols.
Grammig, R.F., "The Yoron Jima Submarine Incident of August 1980: A Soviet Violation of the Law of the Sea", 22 *Harv. Int'l L.J.* 331-353 (1981).

Jessup, P., *The Law of Territorial Waters and Maritime Jurisdiction* (New York: G.A. Jennings & Co., 1927).

Jessup, P., "The UN Conference on the Law of the Sea", *Colum. L. R.* 234-268 (1959).

Kissinger, H.A., "International Law, World Order and Human Progress", 73 *Dep't State Bull.* 353-362 (1975).

Koh, K.L., *Straits in International Navigation: Contemporary Issues* (London, Rome, New York: Oceana, 1982).

Maduro, M.F., "Passage Through International Straits: The Prospects Emerging from the Third United Nations Conference on the Law of the Sea", 12 *J. Mar. Law and Commerce* 65-95 (1980).

Moore, J.N., "The Regime of Straits and the Third Conference on the Law of the Sea", 74 *A.J.I.L.* 77-121 (1980).

O'Connell, D.P., *International Law* (London: Stevens, 1970).

O'Connell, D.P., *The International Law of the Sea* (Oxford: Clarendon Press, 1982), Vol. 1.

Pharand, D., "International Straits", 7 *Thesaurus Acroasium* 65-100 (1977).

Pharand, D., "La contribution du Canada au développement du droit international pour la protection du milieu marin: le cas spécial de l'Arctique", 11 *Etudes Internationales* 441-466 (1980).

Pharand, D., *Law of the Sea of the Arctic with Special Reference to Canada* (Ottawa: University of Ottawa Press, 1973).

Pharand, D., "The Northwest Passage in International Law", 17 *C.Y.I.L.* 99-133 (1979).

Reisman, W.M., "The Regime of Straits and National Security: An Appraisal of International Lawmaking", 74 *A.J.I.L.* 48-76 (1980).

Richardson, E., "Law of the Sea: Navigation and other Traditional National Security Considerations", 19 *San Diego Law Review* 553-576 (1982).

Robertson, H.B., Jr., "Passage Through International Straits: A Right Preserved in the Third United Nations Conference on the Law of the Sea", 20 *Virg. J. Int'l L.* 801-857 (1980).

Smith, B., "Innocent Passage as a Rule of Decision: Navigation vs. Environmental Protection", 21 *Columbia J. Transnational Law* 49-102 (1982).

Stevenson, J.R., "U.S. Draft Articles on Territorial Sea, Straits and Fisheries Submitted to U.N. Seabed Committee: Statement by Mr. Stevenson", 65 *Dep't State Bull.* 261-266 (1971).

Tunkin, G. "The Geneva Conference on the Law of the Sea", 1 (Moscow) *Int'l Aff.* 47-52 (1958).

Union of Soviet Socialist Republics, Statute of the Administration of the Northern Sea Route Attached to the Ministry of the Maritime Fleet (translation), 11 *International Legal Materials* 645-646 (1972).

United Nations, *Convention on the Law of the Sea*, A/CONF.62/122 (7 October 1982).

Verzijl, J.H.W., "The United Nations Conference on the Law of the Sea, 1958", 6 *Netherlands Int'l L. R.* 1-42 (1959).

De Visscher, Charles, *Problèmes de confins au droit international public* (Paris: Redome, 1969).

IV. POLICY IMPLICATIONS FOR THE MARINE ENVIRONMENT AND THE INUIT

Arctic Pilot Project Environmental Statement Shipping Component (Calgary: Petro-Canada, 1979).

Beaufort Sea-Mackenzie Delta Environmental Impact Statement (Calgary: Dome Petroleum, 1982), Vols. 3, 4, 6, 7.

Bradstreet, M. and W. Cross, "Trophic Relationships at High Arctic Ice Edges", 35(1) *Arctic* 1-12 (1982).

Brown, R., "Birds, Oil and the Canadian Environment", in *Oil and Dispersants* 105-112 (1982).

Calder et al. v. *Attorney General of British Columbia*, [1973] 4 W.W.R. 1-91 (S.C.C.).

Canada, Department of Energy Mines and Resources, *An Energy Strategy for Canada: Policies for Self Reliance* (Ottawa: Supply and Services Canada, 1976).

Canada, Department of Energy Mines and Resources, *The National Energy Program, 1980* (Ottawa: Supply and Services Canada, 1980).

Canada, Department of Energy Mines and Resources, *The National Energy Program: Update 1982* (Ottawa: Supply and Services Canada, 1982).

Canada, Department of Indian Affairs and Northern Development, *A Comprehensive Conservation Policy and Strategy for the Northwest Territories and Yukon – A Draft Discussion Paper* (Ottawa: Northern Environment Directorate, DIAND, 1982).

Canada, Department of Indian Affairs and Northern Development, "IBP Ecological Site Approved", *Communiqué* 1-8214 (30 July 1982).

Canada, Department of Indian Affairs and Northern Development, *In All Fairness: A Native Claims Policy* (Ottawa: DIAND, 1981).

Canada, Department of Indian Affairs and Northern Development, *The Inuit* (Ottawa: DIAND, 1980).

Canada, Department of Indian Affairs and Northern Development, *The Lancaster Sound Region: 1980–2000 (Green Paper)* (Ottawa: DIAND, 1982).

Canada, Department of Transport, *Control of Pollution from Shipping in Waters Under Canadian Jurisdiction* (Ottawa: Transport Canada, Coast Guard, 1981).

Canada, Federal Environmental Assessment and Review Office, *Arctic Pilot Project (Northern Component) Report of the Environmental Assessment Panel* (Ottawa: FEARO, 1980).

Canada, Federal Environmental Assessment and Review Office, *Submissions to Beaufort Sea Environmental Assessment Panel* by: Beaufort Sea Alliance (I-5); Environment Canada (I-12); Inuit Tapirisat of Canada (I-18); Department of Fisheries and Oceans (I-19); Department of Indian Affairs and Northern Development (I-20), Vol. I (1983).

Chia, F.S., "Reproduction of Arctic Marine Invertebrates", 1 *Marine Pollution Bull.* 78-79 (1970).

Clark, R.C., Jr. and J.S. Finley, "Effects of oil spills in Arctic and Subarctic Environments", in *Effects of Petroleum on Arctic and Subarctic Marine Environments and Organisms* (1977) at 337-357.

Denhez, M., "Impact of Inuit Rights on Arctic Waters", 10(5) *Northern Perspectives* 2-8 (1982).

Dunbar, M.J., *Marine Transportation and High Arctic Development: A Bibliography* (Ottawa: CARC, 1979).

Ecological Sites in Northern Canada, D.N. Nettleship and P.A. Smith, editors (Ottawa: Canadian Committee for the International Biological Programme, 1975).

Effects of Petroleum on Arctic and Subarctic Marine Environments and Organisms, D.C. Malins, editor (New York: Academic Press, 1977), 2 Vols.

Finan, W., "The Hall Beach Incident", 9(4/5) *Northern Perspectives* 2-7 (1981).

Haines, J.R. and R.M. Atlas, "In Situ Microbial Degradation of Prudhoe Bay Crude Oil in Beaufort Sea Sediments", 7(2) *Marine Environmental Research* 91-102 (1982).

Hamlet of Baker Lake et al. v. *Minister of Indian Affairs and Northern Development et al.* (1979), 107 D.L.R. (3d) 513-565 (Fed. Ct., Tr. Div.).

Hobart, C.W., "Impacts of Industrial Employment on Hunting and Trapping Among Canadian Inuit", in *Proceedings of the First International Symposium on Renewable Resources and the Economy of the North*, M. Freeman, editor (Ottawa: Association of Canadian Universities for Northern Studies, 1981) at 202-218.

Inuit Tapirisat of Canada, Baffin Region Inuit Association, Labrador Inuit Association, Brief to the Senate Special Committee on the Northern Pipeline, reproduced in Canada, Senate Special Committee on the Northern Pipeline, *Proceedings*, Issue No. 26 at 26A: 3-19 (18 May 1982).

Jull, P., "Nunavut", 10(2) *Northern Perspectives* 1-8 (1982).

Lancaster Sound: Issues and Responsibilities, E.F. Roots, editor (Ottawa: CARC, 1980).

Lemberg, R., *A Critical Risk Analysis of the Environmental Impact Assessment: Beaufort Sea Hydrocarbon Production Proposal* (Montreal: Lemberg Consultants [Canada], 1983).

Lester, G.S., *The Territorial Rights of the Inuit of the Canadian Northwest Territories: A Legal Argument*, Ph.D. Dissertation, York University (Toronto, Ontario) (1981), 2 Vols.

Levy, E.M., "Oil Pollution and Seabirds: Atlantic Canada 1976–77 and Some Implications for Northern Environments", 11 *Marine Pollution Bulletin* 51-56 (1980).

Mann, D., *The Socio-economic Impact of Non-renewable Resource Development on the Inuit of Northern Canada*, published by the University of Western Ontario and University of Waterloo for the Inuit Tapirisat of Canada (1975).

McLaren, P., "Spring Migration and Habitat Use by Seabirds in Eastern Lancaster Sound and Western Baffin Bay", 35(1) *Arctic* 88-111 (1982).

Meyers, H., "Traditional and Modern Sources of Income in the Lancaster Sound Region", 21 *Polar Record* 11-22 (1982).

Oil and Dispersants in Canadian Seas – Research Appraisal and Recommendations, J.B. Sprague, J.H. Vandermeulen and P.G. Wells, editors (Ottawa: Environment Canada, Environmental Protection Service, 1982).

Penrose, W.R., "Impacts of Hydrocarbons and Dispersants on Fish", in *Oil and Dispersants* (1982) at 81-86.

Percy, J.A., "Benthic and Intertidal Organisms", in *Oil and Dispersants* (1982) at 87-104.

Roots, E.F., "Environmental Aspects of Arctic Marine Transportation and Development", in *Marine Transportation and High Arctic Development: Policy Framework and Priorities, Symposium Proceedings*, J.B. Wright, editor (Ottawa: CARC, 1979), at 69-98.

Sanborn, H.R., "Effects of Petroleum on Ecosystems", in *Effects of Petroleum on Arctic and Subarctic Marine Environments and Organisms" (1977) at 411-476.*

Smiley, B.D., "The Effects of Oil on Marine Mammals", in Oil and Dispersants (1982) at 113-124.

Snow, N., "Effects of Petroleum Hydrocarbons on Phyloplankton and Macrophyles", in *Oil and Dispersants* (1982) at 55-64.

Stirling, I., "The Biological Importance of Polynyas in the Canadian Arctic", 33(2) *Arctic* 303-315 (1980).

Stirling, I. and W. Calvert, "Environmental Threats to Marine Mammals in the Canadian Arctic", 21 *Polar Record* 433-449 (1983).

Wells, P.G., "Zooplankton", in *Oil and Dispersants* (1982) at 65-80.

Wenzel, G., "Inuit and Polar Bears: Cultural Observations From a Hunt Near Resolute Bay, N.W.T.", 36(1) *Arctic* 90-94 (1983).

V. POLICY IMPLICATIONS FOR CANADA'S NATIONAL SECURITY

Anderson, W.R., *Nautilus – 90° North* (Cleveland: World Publishing Co., 1959).

Armstrong, T., "Soviet Capabilities in Arctic Marine Transport", in *Marine Transportation and High Arctic Development: Policy Framework and Priorities* (Ottawa: CARC, 1979) at 210-222.

Calvert, J., *Surface at the Pole* (London: Hutchison, 1961).

Canada, Department of National Defence, *DEFENCE 82* (Ottawa: DND, 1983).

Canada, Senate Standing Committee on Foreign Affairs, Sub-Committee on National Defence, *Canada's Maritime Defence: Report* (Ottawa: Supply and Services Canada, 1983).

Canada, Senate Standing Committee on Foreign Affairs, Sub-Committee on National Defence, *Proceedings*, Issue 35 (23 November 1982).

Critchley, H., "Canadian Security Policy in the Arctic: The Context for the Future", in *Marine Transportation and High Arctic Development: Policy Framework and Priorities* (Ottawa: CARC, 1979) at 181-209.

Dulberger, L., "Sonar Hides Submarines Under Polar Ice", 34 *Electronics* 18-19 (1961).

Falls, R.H., "Security in the North", in *Policies of Northern Development*, N. Orvik, editor (Kingston, Ontario: Group for International Policies, Department of Political Science, Queen's University, 1973).

Griffiths, F., *A Northern Foreign Policy*, Wellesley Papers 7/1979 (Toronto: Canadian Institute of International Affairs, 1979).

Lyon, W.K., *The Polar Submarine and Navigation of the Arctic: Research Report 88* (San Diego: U.S. Navy Electronics Laboratory, 1959).

Lyon, W.K., "The Submarine and the Arctic Ocean", 11(75) *Polar Record* 699-705 (1959).

McLaren, A.S., "Exploration Under the Arctic Ice", *Explorers Journal* 34-39 (March 1982).

McLaren, A.S., "The Development of Cargo Submarines for Polar use", 21 *Polar Record* 369-381 (1983).

McLaren, A.S., "Under the Ice in Submarines", 107 *U.S. Naval Proceedings* 105-109 (1981).

Pearson, L.B., "Canada Looks Down North", 24 *Foreign Affairs* 638-647 (1946).

Pearson, L.B., "Canada's Northern Horizon", 31 *Foreign Affairs* 581-591 (1953).

Steele, J.P., *SEADRAGON, Northwest Under the Ice* (New York: E.P. Dutton, 1962).

Strong, J.T., "The Opening of the Arctic Ocean", 87 *U.S. Naval Proceedings* 58-65 (1961).

The Arctic in Question, E.J. Dosman, editor (Toronto: Oxford University Press, 1976).

Tracy, N., *Canada's Foreign Policy Objectives and Canadian Security in the North*, ORAE Extra-Mural Paper No. 8 (Ottawa: Operational Research and Analysis Establishment, Department of National Defence, 1980).

"Under Ice Cruise in the Arctic Basin: U.S.S. *Sargo*", 10(66) *Polar Record* 279 (1960).

SUBJECT INDEX

Arctic clause, 107-109, 119-120
Arctic Pilot Project, 76

British expeditions, 22-37

Canadian Arctic Islands: resource potential, 64-67
Canadian Coast Guard, 54-55
Canadian expeditions, 38-58
Canadian Hydrographic Service, 55-56
Canadian naval activities, 56-57
Commercial development: environmental policy, 122-134; Inuit policy, 134-143
Cooperation with Arctic States, 157, 158

Definitions: Northwest Passage, 1; international strait, 89-95
Dempster lateral line, 73
Dome: icebreaking tanker proposal, 75-76; preferred route, 77

Eastern approaches, 2-4
Eastern Arctic Patrol, 43-44
Ecologically sensitive areas: Beaufort Sea, 122-126; Lancaster Sound, 124-125
Environmental impacts, 125-131
Environmental policy, 122-134

First sailing, 38-39
Forecasting: ice, 85; weather, 85
Functional criterion: international straits, 91-95; Northwest Passage, 101-102

General Dynamics, 79
Geographic criterion: international straits, 90-91; Northwest Passage, 99-101
Globtik tankers, 78-79

Ice: conditions generally, 2-20; forecasting, 85
Icebreaking capability, 84, 113, 153
Impacts of year-round shipping: appraisal of policy implications, 143; off-shore rights, 141-143; socio-economic impacts, 139-141
Innocent passage, 102-105
International straits: classification, 95-98; definition, 89-95; functional criterion, 91-95; geographic criterion, 90-91; legal status, 89-95; measures to deny international character, 111-114
Inuit culture, 134-136
Inuit economy, 136-139
Inuit policy and commercial development, 134-143

Law of the Sea Convention (1982), 89-90, 91-98, 102-109, 114-120
Legal status: international straits, 89-95; Northwest Passage, 99-109, 110-121

Mackenzie Delta/Beaufort Sea: resource potential, 62-64
Marine traffic: projections, 82-83; support systems, 83-87

National security of Canada, 144-159
Nunavut government, 142-143

Patrois of RCMP, 44-45
Pipeline systems: Alaska highway pipeline, 71; Beaufort Sea-Edmonton, 74; Dempster Lateral, 73; Polar Gas, 73
Polar Gas 'Y' Pipeline, 73
Pollution: prevention of, 86; right of protection, 107-109, 119-120
Protection of Canadian sovereignty, 111-113, 147-151, 151-158

Protection of coastal state: generally, 106-107, 118-119; in the Arctic, 107-109, 119-120

Resource development technology, 68-70
Resource potential: Alaska North Slope/ Beaufort Sea, 60-62; Mackenzie Delta/ Beaufort Sea, 62-64; Canadian Arctic Islands, 64-67
Right of passage: innocent, 102-105; transit, 114-118; warships, 104-105, 115-117
Routes, 6-21

Search and rescue, 85-86
Seatrain Lines, 78
Shipping accidents, 127-132
Shipping safety control zones, 154-155
Sovereignty of Canadian protection, 111-113, 147-151, 151-158
Straight baselines, 111-112
Strategic importance, 144-146
Submarine activities, 147-149
Support systems, 83-87
Surveillance of Northwest Passage, 151-153

Tanker accidents, 127-132
Tanker systems: Arctic Pilot Project, 76; Dome's, 75; General Dynamics, 79; Globtik, 78-79; Seatrain, 78; Trans-Canada Pipelines Project, 76; US Maritime Administration, 78
Territorial Sea Convention (1958), 91, 93, 102-107
Trans-Canada Pipelines Project, 76
Transit passage, 114-118
Transits of Northwest Passage: full, 50-52; partial, 53
Transportation mode, choice of, 80-81

US Maritime Administration, 78
User agreements, 113-114

Warship, passage of, 104-105, 115-117
Weather forecasting, 85
Western approaches, 4-5
Whalers, 37

NAME INDEX

Amundsen, Roald, 38-39
Anderson, W.R., 183
Armstrong, T., 185
Austin, Horatio T., 29
Austin, J., 181

Baffin, W., 23
Baker Lake Case, 141-142
Bankes, N., 182
Baxter, R.R., 90, 94, 102
Beattie, C.E., 185
Beesley, J.A., 100, 101
Belcher, Sir Edward, 33
Bering Strait, 4-5
Bernier, J.E., 41-43
Bradstreet, M., 177
Bregha, F., xxi, 165, 167, 168, 169
Broughton, William R., 25
Brown, R., 179
Bruel, E., 92
Bullock, B., 170
Burke, W.T., 117
Butler, W.E., 175
Button, T., 23
Bylot, R., 23

Calder Case, 141
Calvert, W., 178
Carrière, N., 165
Cashen, R., xxi
Champ, C., xxi
Chia, F.S., 180
Chrétien, Jean, 133
Clark, R.C., 180
Clarke, J.Y., 53
Clerke, Charles, 24
Collier, A., 164
Collinson, Sir Richard, 32-33
Conant, N., 165
Cook, James, 24
Cooke, A., 163
Corfu Channel Case, 90-95, 101, 103-104
Creelman, I.E., 165
Critchley, H., 145
Cross, W., 177

Davis, John, 23
DeHaven, Edwin J., 30
Denhez, M., 182
De Visscher, C., 90
Dextraze, J., 185
Dulberger, L., 183
Duncan, Charles, 25

Falls, R.H., 183
Finan, W., 179
Fisheries Case, 112
Fitzmaurice, G.L., 93
Forsyth, C.C., 30
Foxe, Luke, 24
Franklin, Sir John, 27-28, 28-37
Fraser, L., xxi
Freeman, M., 181
Frobisher, Martin, 22-23

Gibbons, W., 23
Gidel, G., 104
Goldwater, B., 116
Graham, G., xxi
Gray, A.L., 147

Hobart, C.W., 181, 182
Holland, C., 163
Hudson, Henry, 23

Inglefield, E.A., 31

Jessup, P., 173

Johnston, D.M., 175
Jourdain, E., 179
Joy, A.H., 44-45
Jull, P., 182-183

Kane, Dr. E.K., 35
Kassler, R.D., 4
Kellett, Henry, 34
Kennedy, William, 31
Kissinger, H.A., 115
Krylov, M., 104

Lacasse, J.-P., xxi
Landry, R., xxi
Larsen, H., 45
Legault, L.H., xx
Lemberg, R., 128, 178
Low, A.P., 39-41

Macdonald, D.S., 183
Mac Eachen, A., 88
MacGuigan, M., 89
MacPhee, S.B., xxi
Malins, D.C., 180
Mangone, G.J., xxi
Mann, D., 181
McLaren, A.S., 184
McLaren, P., 177
M'Clintock, Sir F. Leopold, 36
M'Clure, Robert, 31-32
Meyers, H., 181
Middleton, C., 24
Moor, William, 24
Moore, J.N., 89, 117
Mull, G., 165
Munk, Jens, 23
Munro, J., 169

O'Connell, D.P., 91, 117

Pageot, A., 175
Pallister, J., 168, 169
Parry, W.R., 25-26
Pearson, L.B., 145
Penny, William, 30
Penrose, W.R., 179
Percy, J.A., 179
Pullen, T.C., xxi, 52, 140, 163
Pullen, W.J.S., 34-35

Rae, Dr. John, 35
Roberts, A., xxi
Robertson, H.B., 176
Roots, E.F., 177
Ross, Sir James, 28-29
Ross, Sir John, 25, 27, 30
Ross, W.G., 163

Sharpe, M., 100
Smiley, B.D., 180
Smith, Francis, 24
Smith, G.W., xxi, 164
Snow, N., 179
Sprague, J.B., 179
Steele, G.P., 7
Stefansson, Vilhjalmur, 43
Stirling, I., 178
Strong, J.T., 183

Taylor, A., 163, 164
Taylor, George, 25
Thomas, M.E., 165
Thomas, W.C., 165
Timbrell, R.W., 56
Tracy, N., 151
Trudeau, P.E., 88, 113-114
Tunkin, G., 104

Vancouver, George, 25
Vandermeulen, J.J., 179
Vanderzwagg, D., 183
Veliotis, P.T., 118
Verma, S., xxi
Verzijl, L.H.W., 104

Wells, P.G., 179
Wenzel, G., 181

Young, Sir Allen, 36

GEOGRAPHICAL INDEX

Amundsen Gulf, 10-11

Baffin Bay, 2-4
Barrow Strait, 7-9
Beaufort Sea, 4-5, 60-64
Bellot Strait, 17-18
Bering Strait, 4-5

Chukchi Sea, 4-5
Coronation Gulf, 14-15

Davis Strait, 2-4
Dease Strait, 14
Dolphin and Union Strait, 15

Foxe Basin, 18-19
Foxe Channel, 18
Franklin Strait, 12-13
Fury and Hecla Strait, 19-20

Griffith Island, 7, 8
Gulf of Boothia, 20

Hayes Channel, 7, 8
Hudson Strait, 18

Intrepid Passage, 7, 8

James Ross Strait, 15

Kettle Passage, 7, 8

Labrador Sea, 2-4
Lancaster Sound, 13, 124-125
Lowther Island, 7, 8

M'Clure Strait, 11-12

Peel Sound, 12
Prince of Wales Strait, 10, 77
Prince Regent Inlet, 17
Princess Royal Islands, 8, 10

Queen Maud Gulf, 13-14

Rae Strait, 16
Rasmussen Basin, 16

Simpson Strait, 16-17
St. Roch Basin, 16

Victoria Strait, 13
Viscount Melville Sound, 9

Young Island, 7, 8

SHIP INDEX

Advance, 35
Aklavik, 44, 46
Archerfish, 149
Arctic, 41, 42, 43, 44
Arctic Shiko, 49, 51
Assistance, 29, 33
Atule, 148

Baffin, 47, 54
Beaver Mackenzie, 48, 51
Bluefish, 149
Boarfish, 148
Bramble, 46, 50
Breadalbane, 31

Camsell, 48, 51
Canmar Explorer II, 48, 51
Carp, 148
C.D. Howe, 54
Cormorant, 150

Dreadnought, 149

Enterprise, 31, 32, 34
Erebus, 27

Flying Fish, 149
Fox, 36
Fram, 41
Franklin, 48, 51
Fury, 26, 27

Gjoa, 15, 38, 41, 50
Gurnard, 149

Hawkbill, 149
Hecla, 26
Hudson, 47, 49, 51
Investigator, 11, 31, 32, 33, 34, 41

Isabella, 27

J.E. Bernier, 13, 48, 49, 51
J.E. Bernier II, 48
John A. Macdonald, 12, 13, 47, 48, 50, 51, 54, 102, 153, 163

Kigoriak, 48, 51
Kresnogvardeyets, 148

Labrador, 19, 21, 46, 50, 54, 101, 153, 163
Leninsky Komsomol, 148
Louis St-Laurent, 13, 48, 51, 54, 84, 153

Manhattan, 5, 9, 47, 48, 50, 51, 88, 101
Mermaid, 49, 51
Morgan Stanley, 49, 51

Nascopie, 44
Nautilus, 147, 148
Neptune, 39, 41
Northwind, 47, 50, 101
North Star, 33, 34, 35

Pandora II, 20, 36, 48, 49, 51
Pierre Radisson, 48, 51
Pintado, 149
Pioneer, 33
Polar Circle, 49, 51
Preserver, 57
Prince Albert, 31

Redfish, 148

Queenfish, 148

Resolute, 33

Sargo, 147, 148

Seadragon, 7, 46, 50, 101, 147, 148, 149, 183
Silversides, 149
Skate, 50, 101, 148
Skidegate, 48, 51
Sovereign, 149
Spar, 46, 50
Staten Island, 47, 51, 101
Storis, 14, 46, 50
St. Rock, 17, 45, 46, 50

Terror, 27
Theta, 20, 51
Trepang, 149

Victory, 27
Whale, 148
Williwaw, 48